# THE

## EVOLVING
## BARGAIN

# THE

# EVOLVING BARGAIN

## STRATEGIC IMPLICATIONS OF DEREGULATION AND PRIVATIZATION

# WILLIS EMMONS

HARVARD BUSINESS SCHOOL PRESS
*Boston, Massachusetts*

Library of Congress Cataloging-in-Publication Data

Emmons, Willis.
    The evolving bargain : strategic implications of deregulation and
    privatization / Willis Emmons.
        p. cm.
    Includes bibliographical references and index.
    ISBN 0-87584-901-6 (alk. paper)
    1. Deregulation.   2. Privatization.   3. Industrial policy.   I. Title.

    HD3850.E45 2000
    338.9—dc21                                               00-035061

*The paper used in this publication meets the requirements of the American
National Standard for Permanence of Paper for Publications and Documents
in Libraries and Archives Z39.48-1992.*

# Contents

# *Preface*

*The role of government* in the world's market economies has changed dramatically over the past two decades. Evidence abounds of a fundamental shift in government's role and the rise of a "new market economy." Beginning in the mid-1970s, reform legislation in the United States brought deregulation to a growing number of industries including securities brokerage, airlines, natural gas, petroleum, trucking, railroads, banking, cable television, telecommunications, and electricity. Privatization of state-owned enterprises (SOEs), perhaps most strongly associated with Great Britain under Margaret Thatcher, has become a worldwide phenomenon—by 1999 government revenues from SOE sales had reached almost $1 trillion, and they continue to rise. Now, some governments are stepping aside to allow private corporations to build and manage mass transit systems and prisons, and even to oversee social security programs.

Managers and investors have encountered a number of surprises in doing business in the new market economy. Over the past decade, my research, teaching, and consulting activities have given me the opportunity to speak with hundreds of senior executives active in sectors undergoing deregulation and privatization around the globe. I have also been fortunate to meet with a wide range of senior managers whose companies act as suppliers, financiers, and consultants to these industries or interact with them as customers. A common theme that has emerged from my discussions with these individuals is that traditional ways of thinking about opportunity and risk, market dynamics, strategy, and performance are inadequate for confronting the managerial challenges of the new market economy. Ironically, many executives have found that, in the wake of deregulation and privatization, government—and the political process—continues to play a critical role in shaping their ability to create and capture value.

Firms hoping to compete in newly liberated markets, for example, have often found it much more difficult to enter these markets than expected, or have entered them only to achieve poor financial results. Established firms frequently find that their increased freedom of action is offset by new or continuing government restrictions in such areas as pricing, product selection, service quality and availability, marketing, investment, and expansion into other lines of business. In addition, managers have found that privatization is often accompanied by the creation of new regulatory agencies.

Managers have also been confronted with ongoing changes in the rules of the game after governments have implemented programs of deregulation and privatization. For some sectors, such as the U.S. cable television industry, policy changes have been both continuous and dramatic since the initial reform program was put in place. In other sectors, such as the British power generation industry, the evolution of the relationship between the state and the market has been more gradual and more subtle. Nevertheless, each twist and turn in government policy may have profound implications for the performance of any participant in the sector, as affirmed by the experiences of executives operating in a wide range of countries and industries.

As I have watched firms respond to the new market economy, it has become clear to me that popular notions of deregulation and privatization can blindside managers to some of the most important challenges they face in this dynamic environment. By viewing these reforms as a shift from government intervention to the absence of government, executives may fail to see the fundamental truth that firms continue to be critically dependent on the state for defining and enforcing their rights. In effect, every firm is engaged in a bargain with the state that is ultimately a bargain with the broader society in which it operates. This bargain evolves over time, in ways that can be highly favorable or unfavorable to the firm.

It is easy to understand why managers would prefer to believe that deregulation and privatization remove the state and the political process as determinants of company performance. In the postreform arena, senior executives in established firms are anxious to focus on transforming their organizations into market-driven, efficient, and profitable enterprises.

Potential entrants face the challenge of building new organizations and establishing a sustainable presence in the liberated market. At the same time, investors in the reform sectors would prefer to concentrate on such factors as technology, market characteristics, and firm-specific competencies in assessing risk and return.

Yet the state continues to shape opportunities and outcomes following reform. Therefore, it is not only naïve but potentially dangerous for managers in the new market economy to motivate strategy design and implementation by asking themselves, "What do I do now that the government is out of the way?" In contrast, in this book I argue that senior executives and investors should incorporate the following questions into their assessment of the postreform environment:

+ How does government continue to shape my opportunities and risks?

+ How sustainable is my firm's current bargain?

+ How can I design and implement a strategy that leverages and shapes the evolving bargain to my greatest advantage?

*The Evolving Bargain* is designed to enable managers and investors to address these questions in the age of the new market economy. The book provides lessons from the experiences of firms that have faced the managerial challenges of deregulation and privatization in a variety of industry sectors and countries. Many of the examples included in the book have been drawn from the nearly 200 personal interviews I have conducted with senior executives in these companies.

In writing this book, I owe a debt of gratitude to scholars of regulation, deregulation, public ownership, and privatization who have analyzed these topics from the perspectives of economics, political science, history, law, and business administration.[1] I have also benefited significantly from insights provided by scholars of industrial organization and business strategy.[2]

What ultimately distinguishes *The Evolving Bargain* from other explorations of deregulation and privatization is that the book is managerial in focus and cross-national and cross-industry in coverage. Its emphasis on the dynamic relationship between firms and the state in the new market economy also sets it apart from most other works. It is my profound hope that in laying out a framework for tackling the complexity of deregulation and privatization, this book will energize managers in their quest to succeed in a rapidly changing global economy.

# Acknowledgments

*I would first* like to thank the nearly two hundred senior executives who generously agreed to be interviewed as part of the research effort underlying *The Evolving Bargain*. Although only a small number of these executives are cited by name in the book, each of the men and women interviewed has contributed in important ways to the development of the book's framework and real-world illustrations of the strategic implications of deregulation and privatization. I am also grateful to scores of managers who have provided additional insights to the book through their comments and questions in presentations of the work in progress.

I am indebted to the Division of Research at the Harvard Business School for its generous financial support. I am especially grateful to Dwight Crane, senior associate dean and director of research, for his unwavering support of the project. The division's resources were critical for funding the extensive international component of the research and for securing my outstanding research assistants, David Hsu and Martín Calles. I would also like to thank MBA candidates Edward Simnett and Jeffrey Bell, Baker Library business research analysts Hilah Geer and Chris Allen, and faculty assistants Eric Schwarz and Chris Albanese for their excellent assistance. Ann Walter, administrative director of the Division of Research, provided helpful advice throughout the project.

Many faculty colleagues at Harvard Business School provided valuable comments and suggestions on preliminary drafts of *The Evolving Bargain*. These individuals included James Austin, Joseph Badaracco,

Carliss Baldwin, Christopher Bartlett, Richard Caves, Rafael Di Tella, Alexander Dyck, William Fruhan, Regina Herzlinger, Linda Hill, Yasheng Huang, Rosabeth Moss Kanter, Robert Kennedy, Nancy Koehn, George Lodge, Thomas McCraw, Anita McGahan, David Moss, Forest Reinhardt, Richard Rosenbloom, Julio Rotemberg, Michael Rukstad, Bruce Scott, Debora Spar, Howard Stevenson, Richard Tedlow, Peter Tufano, Richard Vietor, Louis Wells, and Michael Yoshino. José Gómez-Ibáñez, John Meyer, and Raymond Vernon of Harvard's Kennedy School of Government, Adam Jaffe (Brandeis University), Ravi Ramamurti (Northeastern University), Marcelo Paladino (IAE), Philip Rosenzweig (IMD), Alice Hill, Steve Krognes, Francisco de Asís Martínez-Jérez, and Joel Singer also provided valuable feedback on draft materials. All errors of fact and interpretation in the final version, however, remain mine alone.

I would like to thank the editorial staff and board of Harvard Business School Press for their enthusiastic support of *The Evolving Bargain*. Director Carol Franco and acquisitions editor Nicola Sabin provided thoughtful guidance throughout the book's development. Amanda Gardner helped greatly in the final production stages.

My strongest appreciation is reserved for Barbara Feinberg and Jake Sullivan. Barbara's amazing editorial eye and intellectual creativity, combined with her extraordinary ability to motivate and encourage, was critical to bringing this book to completion. Jake Sullivan has remained a bedrock of support from beginning to end, never losing faith in me or in *The Evolving Bargain*.

# Introduction

*A casual glance* at the newspaper over the past decade might lead us to assume that everything heretofore state-owned or regulated is now for sale—from postal systems (the Netherlands) to social security systems (Chile) to stock exchanges (the United States). The titles of several recently published books reinforce this notion: *The Retreat of the State; Everything for Sale; Market Unbound; One World, Ready or Not.*[1] The idea is also captured by a cartoon published in *The New Yorker* magazine featuring a newscaster who announces: "And, in a move sure to attract the attention of regulators, the private sector made a bid to acquire the public sector."[2] This cartoon, perhaps unintentionally, cites a central truth within the large-scale move toward deregulation and privatization: *sure to attract the attention of regulators.* Firms operating in the new market economy do not find the state in full-fledged retreat. In fact, as *The Evolving Bargain* makes clear, new forms of regulation often accompany market reforms.

The economic, political, and social changes we have witnessed in the past decade have arrived so swiftly and carry such profound implications that many managers have difficulty making sense of the new landscape. Is there any connection among these changes? Are there common features in deregulation and privatization that span countries and industries across the globe? How can companies make strategic decisions and investments in light of these changes—and manage them successfully? Helping individuals answer these questions is the core purpose of this book.

1

## THE NEW MARKET ECONOMY

Two major trends characterize the new market economy: *deregulation* and *privatization*—terms that are sometimes lumped together under the word *liberalization*. Deregulation refers to an increasing reliance on markets, not governments, to guide economic activity. Specifically, markets, not governments, are allocating more resources—determining which participants can enter markets and which cannot. Privatization, for its part, refers to an increasing reliance on private firms, not government enterprises, for the provision of goods and services. That is, increasingly it is private firms that produce goods and services, whether directly or through outsourcing arrangements under government contracts.

The move toward deregulation and privatization is propelled by a series of broad (macro) factors that operate primarily at the country level, where many national economies have suffered poor performance. In some cases the political context has changed in consequence of or in response to economic conditions. But industry-level factors are also involved, for example when a particular industry or individual firm has exhibited poor financial or operating performance, inferior quality of goods and services, or lack of dynamism in terms of innovation.

### Deregulation

Deregulation is a broad concept that encompasses easing or eliminating government restrictions in three major areas: a firm's *freedom of entry* into a market, its *freedom of action* within a market, and its *profitability* (maximum or minimum) within the market. Thus any particular instance of deregulation has the potential to increase the number and types of participants in the market, the business strategies they employ, and the financial incentives (both the "carrots" of potential profits and the "sticks" of potential losses) they face in doing business.

The scope of industries, markets, and entire sectors affected by deregulation is vast and growing rapidly. We are all familiar with the usual suspects—the telecommunications, energy, and transportation sectors; but added to these are seemingly untouchable social realms such as health care and education, which have opened up areas for more forms of participation and, in some cases, competition. Other sectors, such as financial services, have been experiencing deregulation in fits and starts for over thirty years in the United States, culminating most recently in a major legislative reform of the Depression-era Glass-Steagall Act.

Deregulation, however, has produced a number of paradoxes. First is the persistence of regulation in the wake of deregulation. The United States, for instance, has experienced an enormous amount of regulatory change in the telecommunications sector since the early 1980s, impacting local telephone, long-distance, wireless, cable television, and a variety of other communications services. Overall there has been a significant opening up of markets in the sector. Despite this, as a regulatory agency the Federal Communications Commission (FCC) has seen annual increases in its budget, staff, and number of rules issued. In fact, the FCC is probably mentioned more frequently in the press today than when the telecommunications industry was "regulated."

A second paradox concerns the notion of free markets in a deregulated environment. In many instances, the freedom of new firms to enter the market and the freedom of customers to choose among competing producers is advanced through mandatory access requirements imposed on established firms, or incumbents, controlling some type of critical infrastructure or other scarce resource. One model many countries employ in the power sector, for example, is that which requires owners of transmission and distribution networks to make their infrastructure available to any third party, including competitors. This happens in telecommunications as well, where the company heretofore controlling local telephone service must often, as part of deregulation, make access to its interconnections available to potential competitors. It happens with respect to airports regarding gate access for competitor airlines; in ground transportation, with access to roads; and even in areas like health care and financial services. This situation suggests that freedom is often in the eye of the beholder when the specifics of deregulation are examined.

A third paradox concerns the impact of deregulation on industry structure. In theory, deregulation presumes greater competition—more firms competing within an industry in a particular geographic market. For example, when the U.S. airline industry was deregulated in the late 1970s, it was expected that many new airlines would spring up and provide significant competition over the long run, reducing the relative size and power of incumbent air carriers. Yet by the 1990s, business in the U.S. airline industry was equally as concentrated in the hands of a small number of players as it was at the time of deregulation. Companies like American Airlines and United Airlines have greater market share than they had at the time of deregulation, and nearly all the new airlines that then entered either failed or were acquired by incumbents. These trends are not unique either to the airline industry or to the United States. The frenzy of merger and acquisition activity in national and international telecommunications markets in the 1990s is another example of eventual industry consolidation following deregulation.

The final paradox is that, while certain forms of regulation and government oversight of markets have been scaled back under deregulation, private enterprises are engaging more actively in litigation to settle disputes in deregulated sectors, while governments (and governmental entities such as the European Union) are pursuing increased antitrust action in these markets. Of course, the judicial system is itself a critical government institution. Thus, as litigation substitutes for more direct forms of regulation, the notion of deregulation leading to "less government" becomes quite murky in practice.

## Privatization

Privatization takes one of two principal forms. The first is simply the sale or transfer of state-owned enterprises (SOEs) to private sector entities. The second is a contracting out to a private company of services that were originally performed by a government entity. In some instances, the private contractor/concessionaire owns the assets associated with providing the services; in other cases, it operates assets owned by the government. The second form of privatization can also be viewed as a variation of deregulation, since it involves removing restrictions that previously blocked private enterprises from participating in certain sectors of economic activity.

The magnitude of the first form of privatization is striking, as seen in figure I-1 and figure I-2. When added up, the year-to-year revenues from privatization total nearly $1 trillion since the late 1980s. At the beginning of the period, the number was about $10 billion, while a decade later, annual revenues approached $150 billion. The rate of increase is only one important fact. Another concerns the types of businesses involved. Although a wide variety of sectors are represented, most involve capital-intensive industries characterized by long payback periods on investment. The infrastructure sector, which includes telecommunications, energy, transportation, and water businesses, has accounted for a large and growing share of privatization revenues.

One thing that these numbers don't convey, however, is that not all privatized companies are actually sold. With "voucher privatization," for instance, the government simply distributes shares to the population, as has happened in Russia and many eastern European countries. In addition, in many cases governments are not actually selling an entire company, only part of it, which at least in the short term reduces the magnitude of government revenues associated with privatization. As of 1999, for instance, the government of Germany still retained a majority shareholding in Deutsche Telekom, even though it had "privatized" the firm some three years prior. Moreover, privatization typically leads to a substantial increase in capital investment in the privatized business. Thus

Figure I-1    INTERNATIONAL PRIVATIZATION REVENUES, 1986–1999
(annual totals)

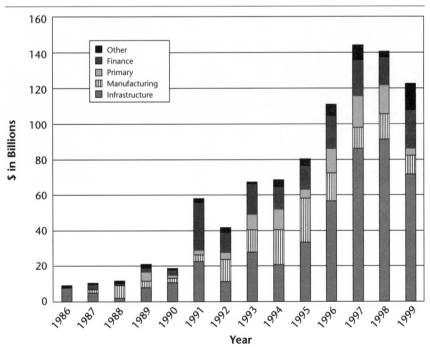

*Source: Adapted from Securities Data Corporation database statistics.*

the financial impact of privatization tends to reach far beyond the amount that the state takes in directly at any point in time.

As in the case of deregulation, there are a number of paradoxes associated with privatization. The first is the proliferation of new regulatory bodies following reform. The United Kingdom provides a good example. When the national telephone company, British Telecom, was privatized, the British government created OFTEL, the Office of Telecommunications. When the gas company, British Gas, was privatized, Ofgas—the Office of Gas Supply—was formed. When the electric utility sector was privatized, OFFER—the Office of Electricity Regulation—was put into place. When British Rail was privatized, not one but two new regulatory bodies were created: the Office of the Rail Regulator (ORR) and the Office of Passenger Rail Franchising (OPRAF).

A second paradox is that many instances of government policy described as privatization actually involve an ongoing government share-

Figure I-2    INTERNATIONAL PRIVATIZATION REVENUES, 1986–1999
(cumulative totals)

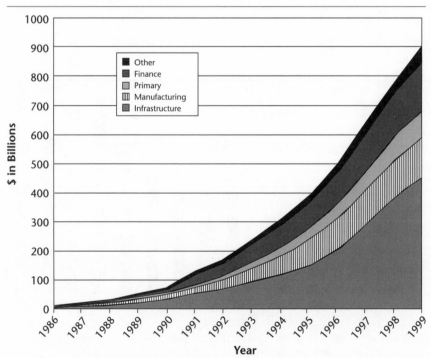

*Source: Adapted from Securities Data Corporation database statistics.*

holding in the affected company. In Malaysia, for example, for virtually every company that has been "privatized," government institutions continue to hold a majority of the shares in these firms. More typical are minority government shareholdings following privatizations. Retaining even a single share, including a so-called special share, golden share, or treasury share, often provides governments with important decision-making powers, such as the right to block mergers and acquisitions and/or set prices for certain goods and services provided by the firm.

A third paradox of privatization, and one that applies as well to deregulation, relates to the growing role of international institutions in the lead-up to and implementation of reforms. These bodies include the International Monetary Fund (IMF), the World Trade Organization (WTO), the European Union (EU), the North American Free Trade Association (NAFTA), and so on. So, while certain local or national regulatory bodies may not have as great an impact in determining the structure and shape of an industry following privatization, these international institutions are becoming increasingly powerful in determining the opportunities and risks for companies emerging from various forms of privatization and deregulation. And, as suggested by the media coverage of the December 1999 meeting of the WTO in Seattle, these international bodies will take on growing relevance in the new market economy.

## The Emergence of Neoregulation

In the new market economy, a growing number of firms in sectors not traditionally associated with extensive government controls now face greater government scrutiny and restrictions. Take for example the case of Microsoft, a company that historically faced little pressure from government regulators but in the 1990s was pursued with extraordinary vigor by U.S. antitrust authorities. A critical driver of this change has been an increasing perception among the public—both individual consumers and corporate clients—that Microsoft's operating system has become a type of basic infrastructure. Hence, Microsoft now confronts the type of scrutiny traditionally faced by companies with near monopoly control of access to essential facilities like rail systems, telecommunications networks, and electricity transmission systems.

We're also seeing an increasing role of government in the U.S. health maintenance organization (HMO) sector. HMOs have come under growing customer and supplier pressure and, in turn, government scrutiny, because of the perception that they control access to critical medical services that are not being provided or are being granted only sparingly. In response, federal and state legislators are looking to adopt various "patient bills of rights" for the sector. In 1999 California went so far as to pass a law for setting minimum nurse-to-patient staffing ratios throughout all hospital departments in the state.

Additional examples of such neoregulation abound, including restrictions on fees charged by operators of automatic teller machines (ATMs) and constraints imposed on firms utilizing technologies associated with genetic engineering. Although the specific drivers of neoregulation vary from case to case, the broader implication is that the new market economy remains a complex environment for conducting business—not only due to dramatic changes in technology and demand but also as a result of the evolving role of the state.

Designed to help make sense of the paradoxes inherent in deregulation and privatization, and the associated rise of neoregulation, this book offers strategic guidance to managers as they navigate through opportunity and risk in the new market economy. The text provides a wide range of industry and company examples drawn from research conducted primarily in countries outside the former Communist bloc, although its relevance extends broadly to any market undergoing liberalization.

The first three chapters develop the conceptual framework of the book. Chapter 1 lays out the critical ideas and basic argument; chapter 2 focuses on the dynamics of deregulation; and chapter 3 examines the dynamics of privatization. The next four chapters assess the challenges that firms face under reform bargains. These include the transformational challenges confronting established market incumbents (chapters 4 and 5), the challenges of competitive entry (chapter 6), and the challenges associated with private concessions or contracting with government institutions (chapter 7). The final chapters present a cautionary tale describing a collapse of a reform bargain (chapter 8) and a summary of strategic lessons for participants in the new market economy (chapter 9).

# 1 ✦ *The Evolving Bargain*

*Business enterprises* do not operate in a vacuum. When they produce goods and services, interact with suppliers and customers, conduct research and development, and, more generally, compete and cooperate with other firms, they are engaged in an evolving relationship—a bargain—with government institutions (the state) and with society at large. This bargain—the *enterprise bargain*—defines the firm's rights and obligations as well as the enforcement mechanisms associated with them. As shown in figure 1-1, the terms of the bargain are symmetrical: the rights of the enterprise imply obligations on the part of the state to uphold these rights, while the obligations of the firm correspond to rights enjoyed by the state and the broader society. It is useful to think of firms participating in more than one industry or political jurisdiction as being engaged in multiple enterprise bargains, each with a distinct set of rights, obligations, and enforcement mechanisms.

## THE ENTERPRISE BARGAIN

The terms of the enterprise bargain are defined through constitutions, laws of incorporation, general commercial code, bankruptcy law, tax statutes, trade law, antitrust laws, common law precedent, and community tradition.[1] For example, in a market economy, firms enjoy the right to acquire and use various forms of property in a wide range of applications.[2] A corresponding right is state protection of a firm's property from encroachment by other parties. General obligations typically include paying taxes, complying with various labor policies, and respecting the property of other firms and individuals.

9

Formal enforcement of the enterprise bargain typically resides with a judicial system and other government institutions charged with interpreting the firm's rights and obligations, resolving disputes, and applying penalties where appropriate. Occasionally, private institutions such as boards of arbitration will play a role in enforcement. Informal mechanisms may also come into play. For example, an enterprise or a state that does not fulfill its obligations may suffer damage to its reputation and, in turn, realize losses in current performance and future opportunities. Criminal elements and corrupt government officials may also play an informal role in the enforcement process.

The terms of a firm's enterprise bargain may be modified or supplemented in important ways depending on the particular industry or industries in which it operates. Pharmaceutical companies typically are obligated to conduct extensive safety testing before obtaining the right to sell a new drug. Historically, local telephone companies have been required to offer basic telephone service to residential customers at a reg-

Figure 1-1   THE ENTERPRISE BARGAIN

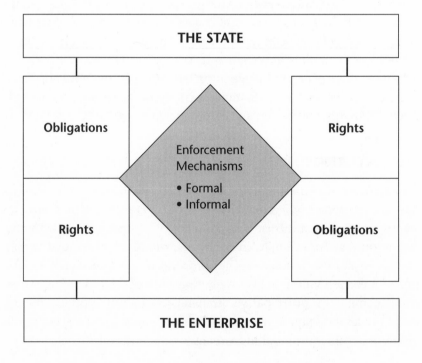

ulated price. Industry-specific regulatory agencies may play an important role in the enforcement of the firm's bargain.

The enterprise bargain also may contain firm-specific elements. A firm controlling an important piece of infrastructure, such as an electricity transmission network or a gas pipeline system, may be obligated to provide other companies access to its monopoly or near monopoly "gateway" to customers or suppliers. Some firms enjoy rights to special subsidies or other entitlements in the terms of their bargain. In the United States in the early 1990s, Alabama agreed to provide tax breaks and a range of infrastructure services—valued at $200 million—to Mercedes-Benz, which agreed to build a manufacturing plant with annual production capacity of 60,000 vehicles, employing 1,500 people.[3]

The Mercedes-Benz example provides a vivid illustration of the intuition behind the use of the word *bargain* to describe relationships between the state and firms. Fundamentally, bargains represent quid pro quos in which each party expects to obtain certain benefits while giving something in return. Over time, a mutual dependence evolves between the firm and the state.

Of course, the terms of some bargains are more attractive to firms than others. Assessing the attractiveness of a specific bargain may be difficult, especially if a firm's rights and obligations are not clearly defined or if there are significant uncertainties associated with the timing and effectiveness of enforcement. New or significantly modified bargains pose particular challenges in this respect.

## Interrelated Bargains

The commercial opportunities and risks a firm faces are shaped not only by its bargain with the state, but also by interrelated bargains between the state and other parties. In particular, the attractiveness of the firm's rights and obligations is influenced by the state's bargains with the firm's actual and potential competitors, suppliers, customers, and other parties affected by activity in the market in which the firm operates. Other affected parties include firms and noncommercial organizations whose well-being is influenced by activity in the primary market. These parties would include companies that provide substitute or complementary products and advocacy organizations such as environmental protection groups, trade associations, and community organizations.

The firm's enterprise bargain is enhanced, for instance, when the state limits potential competitors' entry into the market and when it subsidizes consumers for purchases of the market's goods and services. Alternatively, if competitors are able to secure bargains with more expansive rights and fewer obligations than those contained in the firm's own enterprise bargain, the value of the firm's bargain will be correspondingly lower. The web of interrelated bargains spanning the enterprise and other relevant participants is depicted graphically in figure 1-2. As this "chandelier" diagram suggests, the dynamics of business relationships within a market are influenced by the terms of bargains between each affected party and the state. The terms and, hence, the implementation of these interrelated bargains are shaped by political dynamics which, as in the case of market dynamics, evolve over time in response to external forces as well as strategic choices made by the firm and affected parties. For enterprises that participate in more than one product market or geographic market, and are thus engaged in multiple enterprise bargains, the web of interrelated bargains extends beyond that depicted in figure 1-2,

### Figure 1-2    WEB OF INTERRELATED BARGAINS

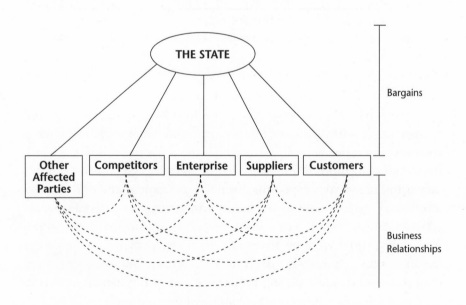

introducing additional complexity into the firm's assessment of opportunity and risk and its design of business strategy.

## Differences across Bargains

A number of factors contribute to differences in the terms and implementation of enterprise bargains. Some of these differences can be
explained by cross-national distinctions in social, political, and economic contexts. These distinctions affect the nature of each state's objectives regarding economic growth and distribution, national sovereignty,
and other noneconomic goals, as well as the institutions through which
government policies are determined and implemented. Corporate tax
rates differ sharply across countries, for example, as do judicial institutions and procedures. The extent of the state's willingness to allow private or foreign-owned firms to operate within the nation's borders affects
the ability of particular types of enterprises to participate in certain markets as well as the terms of that participation.

Differences at the industry level, in the nature of the product and the
economics of the production technology, for example, also have important implications with respect to the terms of bargains. Rights and obligations tend to be more restrictive for firms seeking to participate in markets in which the products are perceived to affect the basic health and
welfare of buyers and other parties—including goods and services viewed
as integral to national security and cultural identity. In these markets,
the state often limits the type and number of firms eligible to enter into
an enterprise bargain, while also placing greater limits on the business
strategies of firms permitted to participate in the industry. Of course, the
extent to which any particular product is perceived to affect basic health
and welfare varies across countries and over time.

Bargains in industries in which the basic production technology
involves large specialized investments with long payback periods also
tend to exhibit differences with respect to bargains in other sectors.
Specialized investments involve assets that are difficult if not impossible to redeploy in other geographic or product markets—for example,
physical infrastructure and specialized manufacturing facilities.[4] Given
the inflexibility of these investments, combined with uncertainties
regarding future trends in market and political dynamics, firms in these
sectors tend to be less willing to participate in enterprise bargains that

do not contain special terms. Such special terms might include guarantees with respect to minimum rates of return or underlying determinants of profitability—for example, prices charged to consumers or terms of access to critical production inputs. Other variations include exclusive rights to provide the relevant good or service in the market for a specific period of time.

From the state's perspective, industries involving sizable long-term investments raise concerns regarding market power and control, particularly when the relevant sector involves goods or services perceived as critical to basic welfare. Since the underlying economics of these industries may support only a small number of firms or a single producer, the state may be unwilling to engage in a bargain that does not include limits on the firm's profitability, restrictions on its pricing behavior, or obligations with respect to buyer access.[5] The enterprise bargain also may include restrictions on the firm's right to expand into other product markets so as to constrain its ability to leverage its market power into upstream, downstream, or other sectors. Alternatively, some states simply limit entry into such markets to government-owned enterprises.

In addition to distinct characteristics of countries or industries, particular features of firms may contribute to differences across bargains. Firms controlling a particularly valuable technology or other resources, such as capital and management experience, may be able to secure more attractive bargains with the state relative to other enterprises. Locally owned firms often enjoy superior rights or fewer obligations in their enterprise bargains as compared with those of comparable foreign-owned firms. The terms applicable to incumbents versus entrants may differ as well depending on the balance of the state's objectives relating to protection of established businesses versus promotion of competition.

## Evolution of Bargains

Enterprise bargains and their interrelated bargains evolve over time. In the case of newly established bargains, the associated rights, obligations, and enforcement mechanisms (both formal and informal) are tested and clarified as firms and other affected parties interact in the marketplace and in the political arena. In the early years of the U.S. cable television industry, for example, the rights and obligations of cable television operators, and the respective roles of the U.S. Federal Communications Commission and municipal governments in enforcing these terms, were defined more precisely through a series of court decisions extending over several years. Even when bargains have been in place for some time, their terms often continue to be tested and clarified in response to market and political dynamics.

Evolution may also occur in the form of changes in the terms of an enterprise bargain or interrelated bargains. General changes in the corporate tax rate, for example, tend to affect all bargains involving private, for-profit enterprises. Other changes might affect the enterprise bargains of firms in certain industries or specific firms within a single industry. In any case, the evolution of any part of a firm's web of interrelated bargains may have an important effect on the attractiveness of its particular enterprise bargain.

Changes in the terms of bargains are driven by various factors. Changes in general terms, such as tax rates, tend to emerge from broad shifts in the nation's economic, political, and social context. Although these shifts may also contribute to changes in industry- or firm-specific terms, market and political dynamics at the sectoral level tend to play important roles in driving these changes. For example, unprofitable firms in an industry often exert pressure on the state to alter the terms of their enterprise bargains (e.g., extending their right to subsidies) or the terms of certain interrelated bargains (e.g., barring the right of entry of foreign producers into the market).

Despite pressures to change the terms of bargains over time, however, various constraints may limit their adoption. Enforcement mechanisms associated with an enterprise bargain, for instance, might effectively shield the firm or the state from attempts to eliminate certain rights or add obligations. Yet in other instances, the pressures for change are so powerful, and the constraints so weak, that a particular bargain or entire web of bargains is significantly reconfigured or "re-formed"—hence the concept of the reform bargain.

## THE REFORM BARGAIN

A reform bargain represents a significant disjuncture in the evolution of the terms of an enterprise bargain and/or its web of interrelated bargains. Changes associated with deregulation and privatization are characteristic of *liberalizing* reform bargains. In contrast, changes involving more extensive regulatory constraints and nationalization—such as those adopted in many countries during and after the Great Depression—constitute *restrictive* reform bargains. This book focuses primarily on the dynamics and strategic implications of liberalizing reform bargains. (Throughout the text, the term *reform bargain* will refer to the liberalizing variety unless noted otherwise.)

Reform bargains entail fundamental changes in the terms of entry into particular markets and restrictions on actions and profitability within them. In many cases, reform bargains include changes in the ownership and/or the organizational structure of enterprises. In some instances, the reform bargain adopted for these markets will include the structural breakup of some or all incumbent firms. In addition, the terms of the reform bargain may incorporate restrictions on future mergers, acquisitions, or internal growth strategies that would substantially increase horizontal integration, vertical integration, or joint provision of multiple goods and services. As an alternative to restructuring, some reform bargains require incumbents that are vertically integrated or engaged in joint production to offer access to certain goods and services to entrants on a stand-alone basis ("unbundled")—particularly goods or services that involve the use of a gateway asset such as a transportation, local telecommunications, or utility distribution network.

Many variations of the reform bargain exist in practice. The precise changes in rules of entry and market involvement, as well as the ownership and structure of individual enterprises, differ across industries and countries, as does the timing and sequencing of these changes. So although *deregulation* and *privatization* are useful generalizations for describing reform bargains, they tend to oversimplify a process that leads to significant changes in a web of interrelated bargains without eliminating the state as a critical determinant of opportunity and risk.

The forces driving reform bargains may emerge from trends at the national, industry, and/or firm-specific level. Crises often serve as a catalyst. Sharp increases in government budget deficits, foreign debt, and inflation, as well as balance-of-payments crises and declines in economic growth may all provide motivation for reform bargains, on the assumption that bargains as currently structured are failing to promote acceptable macroeconomic performance. Dramatic political changes, which may or may not be related to changes in economic performance, may also play a key role in driving reforms, as the rise of Margaret Thatcher in the United Kingdom and Carlos Menem in Argentina attest.

At the industry or firm level, poor or rapidly deteriorating operating or financial performance often provide the impetus for the adoption of a reform bargain. Alternatively, a particular enterprise's expansion and exploitation of market power, if viewed as economically abusive or politically threatening, may serve as a driver of reform.

In developing the terms of a particular reform bargain, the state often must balance multiple objectives and work within serious constraints. At a macro level, the state may seek to improve, for example, government finances, the nation's balance of payments, and the overall climate for foreign investment. At the industry level, the state's goals may include increasing output, employment, efficiency, and technological sophistication, while lowering prices. Internal constraints might be social, economic, or political in nature, including, for example, public distrust of foreigners, scarcity of domestic capital, or weak government institutions for monitoring and enforcing bargains. External constraints might include competition from other states to secure attractive enterprise bargains and pressures from international institutions such as the International Monetary Fund and World Bank. The terms of the reform bargain inevitably involve trade-offs and compromises.

Once put into place, a reform bargain has important implications for market dynamics and political dynamics in sectors affected by the reforms. These dynamics in turn lead to the evolution of the reform bargain over time.

## Reform Bargains and Market Dynamics

Reform bargains shape market dynamics along two dimensions: market power and incentives. Changes in the terms of bargains relating to entry into and actions within the market, as well as those imposed on the size and structure of individual enterprises, affect the market power of both new and established participants in the market. Changes in market power, in turn, correspond to changes in negotiating leverage among these participants. Reforms that facilitate market entry tend to reduce the market power of incumbent producers, although reforms that grant producers greater freedom of action tend to increase their market power relative to suppliers and buyers.

The nature of a firm's ownership, as well as the treatment of profits and losses under the terms of its bargain, affect the firm's incentive to create and capture economic value. Reform bargains that shift ownership from public to private or ease restrictions on the firm's profits and losses tend to strengthen the firm's incentives to increase efficiency, to innovate, and to exploit and expand its existing market power.

The changes in market power and incentives associated with reform bargains typically generate a number of common market outcomes over a short-to-medium-term time frame. These outcomes include:

*higher levels of industry output*, since reform bargains typically increase the freedom of firms to participate in the industry, expand the range of strategic choices available to producers, and/or enhance firms' incentives to invest in productive assets;

*greater variance and instability in prices*, since reform bargains tend to increase producers' ability and incentives to vary price across buyer segments and over time;

*greater variety in features and quality of goods and services in the market*, since the reforms typically increase the ability and incentive of established firms to differentiate their products, while increasing the freedom of firms with alternative product features to enter the market.

Although there are occasional exceptions to these general outcomes, they provide a base on which to build expectations regarding market dynamics following reforms.

Despite common trends in postreform market outcomes, significant differences in market dynamics appear due to differences in the underlying characteristics of supply and demand in the market, the specific design of the reform bargain, and the strategic responses of new and established market participants. Four generic patterns of market dynamics emerge in the short to medium term following the adoption of a liberalizing reform bargain, including the competitive free-for-all, incumbent-on-top, black hole, and pie-sharing scenarios.

The *competitive free-for-all* is characterized by vigorous rivalry among producers of goods and services, which may include both established firms and entrants. This pattern emerges under two alternative sets of conditions. In the first case, the reform bargain opens the way to increased competition by eliminating restrictions on the right to enter the market. In this instance, the threat of entry is not undermined significantly by (1) structural barriers, such as large economies of scale and scope relative to the size of the market, excess capacity, high switching costs for buyers and suppliers, or patents; or (2) indirect barriers, such as government-enforced health, safety, environmental, or other product standards.

Alternatively, a competitive free-for-all may emerge even when structural barriers to entry are present in a market. If an incumbent controls gateway infrastructure critical for providing final goods and services—for example, a telecommunications or power transmission network—a reform bargain that obligates the firm to provide entrants access to the facility on favorable terms may enable vigorous competition to take root. Similarly, reform bargains designed to reduce switching costs or other more subtle barriers to entry may lead to a competitive free-for-all where underlying conditions are otherwise unfavorable.

Under either set of conditions, it is assumed that within the terms of the reform bargain, incumbents and entrants have strong incentives to create and capture value—in other words, to maximize profits—but are unable to collude to reduce the intensity of competition. The initial market dynamics that followed deregulation of the U.S. airline industry, the Argentine power generation industry, and the German telecommunications industry all exhibited strong features of the competitive free-for-all.

Under the *incumbent-on-top* scenario, the established producer(s) in the market continues to dominate following the reform bargain and is highly profitable. This dynamic typically results when the reforms involve privatizing the industry incumbent(s) in a sector characterized by major structural or indirect barriers to entry that are *not* counteracted through terms of the reform bargain. Even if competition arrives, it tends to be a minor inconvenience at best to the incumbent. Also, where there are two or more incumbents, these firms are able to collude, at least tacitly, to prevent a competitive free-for-all. In this context, not only do incumbents have a strong incentive to create value, they succeed in capturing a large share of that value. Examples of the incumbent-on-top pattern include the market dynamics that followed reform bargains in the British power generation industry and rail infrastructure sector and in the New Zealand telecommunications industry.

The *black hole* pattern describes a market dynamic in which the primary producers in the sector turn out to be very unprofitable under the reform bargain. In this scenario, firms experience much higher costs and/or lower revenues than anticipated at the time of reforms. Sometimes the poor results can be attributed to bad luck, such as unfavorable supply- and demand-side shocks, or bad forecasting. Yet ambiguities in the terms of the reform bargain and weak enforcement of critical rights and obligations often play an important role as well. For example, minimum revenue and profit guarantees may be watered down or ignored, or additional obligations may be imposed unilaterally on the enterprise by the state. Firms that make large investments in specialized assets with long payback periods are particularly vulnerable to an unfavorable evolution of the reform bargain after sinking the capital. In fact, the concept of "the obsolescing bargain" has a long history in the context of infrastructure investments by foreign corporations.[6] Examples of the black hole pattern include market dynamics following reform bargains associated with Mexican toll road concessions, U.S. school management contracting, and certain Argentine water sector privatizations.

The fourth pattern, the *pie-sharing* scenario, describes situations in which short-to-medium-term market dynamics lead to a relatively balanced sharing of economic value across market participants, although perhaps at the expense of some potential value creation. In these cases, the terms of the reform bargain contain rights and obligations that shape the distribution of value according to various fairness criteria. For example, industry producers may be prohibited from laying off workers in the initial years following the adoption of the reform bargain and may be required to offer specific services to consumers at regulated prices. Reform bargains structured to leave some or all of the shares of a state-owned firm in the hands of government institutions or affected parties (for example, employee unions) distribute economic gains more broadly.

An effect of the reform bargain's restrictions on profitability and ownership tends to be a tempering of the incentive to capture value, and as a consequence, to create value. Thus, although the "pie" created under these reform bargains tends to be more evenly distributed, it also tends to be smaller. Examples of pie-sharing patterns of market dynamics include Malaysian privatizations, New Zealand corporatizations, and French reform bargains in the air transport sector.

The four generic patterns of market dynamics provide useful archetypes for thinking about the short-to-medium-term implications of reform bargains under various conditions. In reality, the market dynamics associated with any particular reform bargain may draw on elements from more than one of these scenarios, resulting in a hybrid pattern. It is also important to emphasize that these patterns are subject to significant changes over the long term as trends in supply and demand, strategic behavior in the marketplace, political dynamics, and the reform bargain itself continue to evolve.

## Reform Bargains and Political Dynamics

Interactions between government officials, firms, noncommercial organizations, and individuals in the political arena shape the creation, enforcement, evolution, and reform of bargains with the state. Lobbying, contributing to political campaigns, political advertising, and even bribery are among the political strategies that firms have historically used to influence political dynamics and outcomes. At the same time, firms' actions in markets—their commercial strategies—shape political dynamics through their real and perceived effects on the welfare of individuals, noncommercial organizations, and other firms.[7]

A number of factors influence political dynamics following the adoption of a reform bargain, including changes in government institutions, political access and participation, quality and quantity of information, market dynamics, and expectations. The terms of a reform bargain often entail the establishment of new government institutions and/or changes in the powers or enforcement jurisdiction of existing institutions. These changes introduce uncertainty into subsequent political dynamics and reduce the relevance of firms' prior experience with specific regulatory institutions.

Reform bargains often occur in conjunction with broader changes in political access and participation in a nation. In other words, economic liberalization often occurs in close proximity to political liberalization, although the timing and sequencing differ from case to case. If citizens obtain stronger voting rights and improved access to various government institutions, including the judicial system, the character of the political dynamics tends to change significantly. In particular, consumers, workers, and lower income individuals typically play a greater role than before in shaping political outcomes.

Improvements in information often occur in conjunction with reform bargains. The sale of state-owned enterprises typically leads to greater disclosure and transparency of operating and financial data, particularly when firms are sold through public share offerings and subsequently listed on stock exchanges. Some nations, such as New Zealand, have adopted extensive information disclosure requirements for commercial enterprises as part of a broad liberalization agenda. Greater media freedoms accompany political liberalization in many countries, improving flows of information and facilitating the organization of diffuse groups for political action. Regardless of the impetus in any given case, improvements in information relating to the actions and performance of firms and, in many cases, government officials, serve to heighten their accountability within the political arena.

Market dynamics following the adoption of the reform bargain typically play an important role in shaping political dynamics. As participants adjust their commercial strategies in response to the reforms, changes occur in output, employment, prices, quality, profitability, capital investment, and other market indicators. Changes in value creation and value distribution reveal short-term winners and losers. In this context, "loser" is an ambiguous concept, since even some market participants and other affected parties who are better off in absolute terms following the reform bargain may see themselves as losers if their gains are smaller than others' or if outcomes fall below their previous expectations. In any case, losers may be motivated to enter the political arena to encourage an evolution in the terms of the reform bargain that is favorable to their interests. Changes in political access and participation, as well as improved access to information and media channels, may enhance the effectiveness of losers' efforts to modify the bargain.

Ultimately, the actions of firms within the market often play as important a role in the evolution of the reform bargain as their actions in the political arena. In either case, it is reasonable to expect that the bargain will continue to evolve in significant ways over time.

## Strategic Implications of Reform Bargains

Reform bargains present three types of managerial challenges. The first is the challenge of transforming established enterprises that emerge from the reform bargain with a host of problems and opportunities. In many cases, these firms are poorly suited for the demands of the new market economy. Strategic challenges exist at a broad level with respect to governance, leadership, and corporate strategy. These incumbents also face enormous challenges in designing and implementing operating strategies in the areas of human resources management, technology and production, procurement, sales and marketing, and finance and control. Finally, these companies confront the challenge of maintaining and adapting a government and public relations strategy—i.e. a political strategy—that is tailored to the new context of the reform bargain and its evolution over time.

The second major type of strategic challenge involves entry into postreform markets. As previously closed markets are thrown open to competition, opportunities to profit in the new market economy appear vast. Yet many of these opportunities are fraught with significant commercial and political risks. Competing against prereform incumbents is typically much more difficult than it would appear at the outset. Many incumbents retain important physical and intangible assets and often adjust more quickly to the postreform market dynamics than expected. Entry in the form of bidding for concessions or contracts also presents considerable challenges. In areas where products and services are closely connected to social welfare and where performance is difficult to measure, managing both expectations and political dynamics is often an even greater challenge than managing the commercial aspects of these businesses.

A final challenge is of critical importance to firms operating in sectors that traditionally have had less restrictive bargains with the state and may, by virtue of recent waves of privatization and deregulation, believe that liberalization is here to stay. Microsoft's battles with antitrust authorities beginning in the late 1990s, growing consumer and political opposition to genetic engineering, and increasing concerns over private control of information online suggest that even the computer, biotechnology, and Internet sectors are not immune from the forces of the evolving bargain. The ultimate challenge for firms in these situations is to retain their cultures of growth and innovation while developing strategies that will enable them to ride the wave of the evolving bargain without being swept out in its backwash.

# 2 ✦ *Dynamics of Deregulation*

*Robert L. Crandall*, the legendary chairman of American Airlines, announced his retirement in April 1998 after a twenty-five-year career at American. Crandall joined the carrier at a time when many of the basic strategic decisions in the U.S. airline industry were subject to government approval. In 1978, however, the government's role in the airline sector changed dramatically with the passage of the Airline Deregulation Act, a classic liberalizing reform bargain. Little did Crandall know that airline deregulation would be followed by liberalization in a wide range of industries in the United States and abroad. But it also would have been hard for Crandall to predict that the state would continue to play such an important role in shaping opportunity and risk in the airline industry in the decades following deregulation.

The U.S. airline sector offers an extraordinary example of the evolution of an enterprise bargain over time. The fortunes of individual airlines have risen and fallen, with the Crandall era representing just the latest in a series of strategic adjustments to reform bargains in the sector. To understand the causes and effects of deregulation in general, and the implications for American in particular, we look now at the industry's first enterprise bargains, established just prior to the 1920s. From there, we view the ways in which airlines' strategies to create and capture value have both shaped and been shaped by market dynamics, political dynamics, and the evolving bargain, culminating with the virtual rebirth of American Airlines under Bob Crandall.

## ESTABLISHING THE BARGAIN:
## THE AIRLINE INDUSTRY IN THE AIRMAIL ERA

The origins of the U.S. airline industry extend back to the efforts of adventurers like the Wright Brothers, who made their first flights at Kitty Hawk, North Carolina, in 1903.[1] In the years leading up to the First World War, air travel was viewed more as sport or entertainment than as a form of transportation. During the war (1914–1918), the U.S. government recognized the military potential of airplanes, but adapted them for combat and reconnaissance rather than for transporting troops and materiel.

Commercial demand for air transport services first arose from the U.S. Post Office—a state-owned enterprise with roots in the U.S. Constitution.[2] To initiate airmail service, the post office received an appropriation of $100,000 from the U.S. Congress in 1918 to subsidize start-up costs in excess of revenues anticipated from the sale of airmail stamps. By granting these subsidies, the government hoped that the expansion of airmail service would strengthen the nation's communications infrastructure, promoting commerce within and among the states. Initially, the post office contracted with the U.S. Army to deliver airmail, but soon provided the service with its own planes and pilots. Annual airmail subsidies had reached $2.75 million by 1925.

The terms of the U.S. Post Office's enterprise bargain adversely affected the business opportunities of the U.S. railroads, privately owned enterprises whose commercial activities included mail transport services. Railroad companies protested in the political arena that competition from a subsidized government enterprise was unfair. The U.S. Congress, increasingly dominated by laissez-faire-minded Republicans after the war, responded with the Air Mail Act of 1925. This legislation shifted airmail transport to private enterprises, which would contract with the U.S. Post Office to deliver mail on particular routes. An important government objective in the design of this liberalizing reform bargain was to make airmail service self-supporting.

Under the terms of the Air Mail Act, the post office granted four-year contracts through an unusual competitive bidding system. Carriers bid for the right to a specific percentage of airmail revenues generated on the relevant route, up to a maximum of 80 percent.[3] In response to carriers' concerns that the terms of these contacts exposed them to the risk of future declines in the price of airmail service, Congress amended the act in 1926 to compensate air carriers on a fixed-rate-per-pound basis.

Competition for airmail contracts was weak: most routes received only one bid. The post office did not even put the nation's one transcontinental route up for bid, since private operators appeared unable or unwilling to maintain the associated navigational infrastructure, including radio facilities, emergency landing fields, and lighting structures. Clearly, the terms of the airmail contracts were not very attractive to private carriers during this era. Nevertheless, the Air Mail Act gave birth to forerunners of some of today's major airlines. Colonial Airlines, a predecessor of American Airlines, was awarded the airmail contract to serve the Boston–New York route.[4]

In 1926 Congress took a more comprehensive approach to the nation's air transport sector with the passage of the Air Commerce Act of 1926. This legislation declared federal government sovereignty over U.S. airspace and placed responsibility for promotional activities (such as the establishment of airports and navigational infrastructure) and regulatory activities (such as licensing of air carriers and establishment of air traffic rules) with the secretary of commerce. Only carriers owned by U.S. citizens were eligible to receive licenses. Although air carriers were permitted to provide passenger air transport services in addition to airmail services, the general public's interest in air travel remained negligible until Charles Lindbergh made his dramatic transatlantic flight to Paris in 1927.[5]

The post office continued to contract additional airmail routes during the mid-1920s—including, eventually, transcontinental routes. But carrier profitability was weak, and airmail volumes grew only modestly. These disappointing outcomes generated pressures on Congress to amend the Air Mail Act in 1928, reducing airmail prices by 50 percent. Airmail volume doubled within a month, and carrier profitability soared with dramatic increases in capacity utilization. Yet government subsidies increased substantially, since the post office suffered losses on airmail business as revenues per pound fell while transport costs per pound remained fixed under the terms of existing airmail contracts.

During the late 1920s, the U.S. airline sector experienced rapid consolidation, as firms aimed to take advantage of scale and scope economies within and across the air transport and aircraft manufacturing industries. Three large holding companies (the Big Three) came to dominate the sector, and by 1930 held twenty-one of the nation's twenty-five airmail contracts. The largest, United Aircraft and Transport Corporation, secured controlling interests in a number of air transport companies as well as in the manufacturers Boeing, Northrup, Sikorsky, and Pratt & Whitney.

## Forces for Change

Walter F. Brown, appointed postmaster general by President Herbert Hoover in March 1929, approved of the evolving market dynamics in the airline sector. Brown favored the development of a highly integrated national air transport network, which he hoped to shape and control. In 1930 he convinced Congress to pass the Watres Act, which granted the postmaster general considerable discretionary authority in setting the terms of airmail contracts and extending and consolidating the nation's multiple and fragmented airmail routes. Brown promptly revised the compensation system for airmail transport, establishing a complex formula that varied payment by weight of mail load, size of contracted aircraft space, passenger capacity of the aircraft, technical sophistication of the equipment, and severity of flying conditions along the route. He revised this formula three times over a two-year period in consultation with airline industry executives.

Congress refused to include in the Watres Act a provision, proposed by Brown, allowing the postmaster general to award airmail contracts without competitive bidding. But Brown secretly invited representatives of the Big Three to Washington to negotiate routes and payments behind closed doors. As a result the Big Three obtained 90 percent of the nation's airmail business. A small number of holding-company shareholders reaped the lion's share of profits derived from these lucrative contracts, which by 1933 had increased the post office's annual airmail subsidy requirements to over $13 million.[6]

Postmaster General James Farley, appointed as Brown's successor in 1933 by Democratic president Franklin D. Roosevelt, uncovered evidence of Brown's questionable dealings with the Big Three. This evidence, combined with political pressure from airline operators locked out of airmail contracts under Brown, prompted a major congressional investigation, which substantiated accusations of fraudulent and collusive acts.[7] Despite considerable progress in the development of the nation's air transport network under Brown's tenure, the general public was outraged by the Big Three's ability to profit handsomely at taxpayer expense through a conspiracy with a government official. In an era characterized by a growing distrust of private enterprise—the Great Depression—the scandal triggered political pressure for major reforms in the airline sector.

In early 1934 Postmaster General Farley used his discretionary authority under the Watres Act to void all of the nation's airmail contracts. For a short time, the U.S. Army took over the job of airmail delivery—with somewhat chaotic results, including sixty-six accidents and twelve deaths.[8] Meanwhile, Congress passed the Air Mail Act of 1934, restrictive legislation that effectively dictated the airline industry's restructuring prior to the rebidding of airmail contracts. Under the act, it became illegal for any carrier to receive airmail contracts if it held ownership control of other carriers or aircraft manufacturers through shareholdings, interlocking board memberships, or other devices. In addition, the act barred mergers and acquisitions among airmail carriers that competed on any routes. American Airlines was created at this time as a stand-alone carrier out of the dismantling of Aviation Corporation, one of the former Big Three.

Despite the success of the Air Mail Act in breaking up the Big Three airline holding companies, the terms of the legislation led to unexpected behavior on the part of airmail carriers. The heavy restrictions on merger and acquisition activity encouraged carriers to pursue network growth through strategic underbidding for new routes. Bids came in near $0 per mile per cubic foot in some cases, since bidders assumed that they would be able to renegotiate contract terms at a later date once they had established operations along the route, including passenger service. In fact, this strategy was savvy, since the government proved unwilling to risk additional service disruption by allowing these firms to go bankrupt.

As carriers' financial losses mounted under the market dynamics following the 1934 act, Congress came under pressure to make additional changes. To balance the twin objectives of stable growth in the sector and prevention of abuses of market power, Congress passed the Civil Aeronautics Act of 1938. This act created an elaborate regulatory system under which the Civil Aeronautics Board (CAB) controlled entry, exit, price, company financial structure, and merger activity in the airline industry during the subsequent four decades. Due to constitutional restrictions on the powers of the federal government, the CAB's jurisdiction extended only to airlines providing interstate service. Yet in practical terms, few airlines provided exclusively intrastate service, and even in these cases, state-specific airline sector policy typically mirrored federal policy.[9]

## THE FIRST REFORM BARGAIN: REGULATED COMPETITION

Entry restrictions played a major role in the terms of enterprise bargains under the Civil Aeronautics Act of 1938. Any airline that wished to serve a particular route (a city-pair market) was required to obtain advance approval from the CAB.[10] In making its decisions, the board was required to reject applications inconsistent with the "public interest," including entry likely to result in "excessive competition." These terms proved highly favorable to incumbent airlines already serving routes at the time of the act's passage. Between 1938 and 1978, the CAB refused to grant rights for any new airline to serve noncommuter ("trunk") airline markets. In addition, the board was cautious in granting approval for industry incumbents seeking to expand their networks to include routes already serviced by a carrier. The industry structure did not remain entirely static, however, since the CAB approved the expansion of incumbent airlines into previously unserved markets and even into established markets when demand growth was substantial on the particular route. Carriers were also permitted to increase the frequency of flights along any route they served.

Under the terms of the reform bargain, airlines were free to propose fares for serving particular routes. All proposals were subject to review by the CAB, which was required to consider the public interest in its decisions, including "the need of each air carrier for revenue sufficient to enable such air carrier, under honest, economical, and efficient management, to provide adequate and efficient air carrier service."[11] These terms served to prevent price wars such as those that destabilized the industry in the mid-1930s. As a result of entry and price controls, competition in the industry centered on service quality, including frequency of flights, aircraft type, and in-flight amenities. Yet the real price of air transportation declined over time due to productivity improvements alongside rapid growth in demand.[12]

The terms of this restrictive legislation evolved only in minor respects from 1938 to 1978. The 1944 Chicago Convention on International Civil Aviation established a framework in which the U.S. government negotiated bilateral agreements with other nations regarding the rights and obligations of U.S. carriers in any particular foreign country, and of foreign carriers—virtually all state-owned enterprises—in the United States. These agreements were highly restrictive, with each nation limiting the routes, prices, and frequency of flights that foreign carriers could offer. All governments prohibited foreign carriers from providing service between cities in the domestic market. Also, the U.S. government barred foreigners from holding ownership control (voting rights) above 25 percent in any U.S. air carrier. Although these restrictions arguably enhanced national sovereignty and security, they clearly served to protect domestic air carriers from external competition.

An additional example of the reform bargain's evolution included the passage of the Federal Aviation Act in 1958. The act strengthened safety regulation in the industry and shifted responsibility for enforcement in this area from the CAB to the newly created Federal Aviation Administration (FAA).

Market dynamics in the airline industry through the 1950s and 1960s were characterized by relative stability in prices, passenger growth, and carrier profitability. Although the industry was subject to the destabilizing effects of business cycles in the U.S. macroeconomy, the CAB's strong influence over prices and capacity tended to reduce performance peaks and troughs over these cycles. Interestingly, some differences in profitability emerged across carriers, with medium-sized airlines generally faring best. These carriers tended to be large enough to achieve scale-related efficiencies, but small enough to be favored by the CAB when vying with larger carriers for permission to serve additional routes.[13]

The relative stability of market dynamics in the air transport sector, as well as in the U.S. political economy, led in turn to a political dynamic characterized by broad support for the status quo with respect to bargains in the sector through the late 1960s. Established carriers earned solid returns, airline employees received attractive salaries and benefits, and the flying public enjoyed safe, dependable, and comfortable service, with stable prices that declined moderately over time. In this environment, pressures for change were minimal.

## Forces for Change

During the early 1970s, air carriers encountered a series of problems that threatened the relative financial stability experienced over the previous decades. Most airlines made significant investments in the late 1960s in new aircraft equipped with the latest jet technology. But after taking on these sizable commitments, the U.S. economy began to experience stagflation—increases in inflation and unemployment—and a recession. This combination of factors harmed the industry's operating efficiency and financial performance through simultaneous increases in capacity and unit costs and declines in demand. As profitability fell, the carriers requested and received CAB approval to raise fares. But higher fares prompted additional decreases in demand, declines in profitability, and additional requests for price increases. The OPEC oil crisis of 1973–1974, which generated sharp increases in the price of jet fuel and further slowed the U.S. economy, prompted carriers to request price increases yet again. As this vicious cycle continued, some consumer advocates, low-cost regional airlines, and politicians—under the leadership of Senator Edward Kennedy—began to call for changes in airline regulation. Congressional hearings initiated by Kennedy in 1974 revealed that fares on routes within California and Texas, where market entry was relatively unrestricted, were up to 50 percent lower than interstate fares for routes of comparable length.[14] Questions were also raised in the hearings regarding the relationship that had developed over the years between established interstate carriers and the CAB, which had apparently contributed to higher costs and higher prices. The hearings, widely reported in the national press, helped build political support for deregulation in the air transport sector.[15]

The established interstate airlines vigorously opposed changes in the terms of entry and price-setting in the air transport market. They warned that chaos would result if airlines were free to offer and withdraw service at will. The carriers also argued that in the absence of price controls, the high fixed-cost nature of the air transport business would lead to cut-throat competition, causing the same type of financial distress that had preceded the adoption of the CAB model of regulation in the first place. In addition, opponents of deregulation questioned whether policy changes would endanger safety and perhaps even national security as the government loosened its control over the air transport sector. Airline employees and their unions strongly supported the carriers' position, fearing that deregulation would lead to downward pressure on salaries and benefits while also threatening job security.

In the end, the carriers and their employees were unable to sustain the political support needed to offset the considerable pressures for reform. In 1977 President Jimmy Carter appointed Alfred Kahn, a Cornell University economics professor and strong supporter of airline deregulation, as CAB chairman. Under Kahn, the CAB made dramatic changes in its traditional regulatory approach by approving numerous fare discount proposals and relaxing entry barriers on many routes.[16] The U.S. Congress extended and formalized these changes by passing the Airline Deregulation Act of October 1978, which not only reduced the powers of the CAB but eliminated the agency altogether by 1985. Safety regulation continued unchanged under the FAA, and jet service to a number of small cities was maintained through the late 1980s with government subsidies paid to carriers.

## THE SECOND REFORM BARGAIN: DEREGULATION

The reforms contained in the Airline Deregulation Act were wide-reaching. Entry deregulation dramatically reduced the market power of industry incumbents, since there were few structural barriers to entering their markets in the late 1970s. Potential entrants could lease planes and airport gate space with relative ease, and a weak labor market facilitated staffing. At the same time, the elimination of CAB rate controls effectively ended regulatory support of "reasonable profitability" protections for incumbents. Although deregulation did provide carriers greater freedom of action within the market, it was unclear whether such freedom would be of benefit to incumbents facing entrants with a more favorable cost structure.

Bob Crandall, who had come to American Airlines in 1973 as vice president of finance after a six-year stint at TWA, described 1979 as "one of the most difficult and tumultuous years in our history."[17] In addition to fierce competition from traditional airlines and new entrants, American confronted a second oil crisis, punishingly high interest rates, and a sharp recession. Confronted with these market dynamics, American posted a $121 million operating loss for the six months ending June 1980, just as Crandall was named the firm's president.

In the face of the tremendous pressures of deregulation, Crandall developed a range of actions for lowering costs and enhancing revenues. In the short run, he eliminated loss-making routes, grounded aircraft with poor fuel efficiency, and laid off a number of employees. Yet, in the longer term, Crandall implemented a number of strategies designed to increase barriers to entry and enhance American's competitive position vis-à-vis established carriers. This program included initiatives to increase scale and scope economies in aircraft deployment (the hub-and-spoke system),[18] reduce labor costs (the two-tier wage system), build customer loyalty (frequent flier programs), maximize revenue by customer type (yield management pricing), and establish a preference at travel agencies for American's flights (SABRE computer reservation system).[19] These strategies helped American accelerate its growth in passenger traffic and return to solid profitability by the mid-1980s (see table 2-1). Other major carriers adopted many elements of American's strategy, and by the late 1980s most of the newcomers and smaller traditional interstate airlines had disappeared through merger, acquisition, or liquidation.

Table 2-1  AMERICAN AIRLINES FINANCIAL AND OPERATING STATISTICS, 1977–1987
(in millions of U.S. dollars, unless otherwise noted)

| | 1977 | 1978 | 1979 | 1980 | 1981 | 1982 | 1983 | 1984 | 1985 | 1986 | 1987 |
|---|---|---|---|---|---|---|---|---|---|---|---|
| *Financial Performance* | | | | | | | | | | | |
| Total Revenue | 2,278 | 2,736 | 3,253 | 3,821 | 4,109 | 4,177 | 4,763 | 5,354 | 6,131 | 6,018 | 7,198 |
| Net Income | 82 | 134 | 87 | –76 | 47 | –20 | 228 | 234 | 346 | 279 | 198 |
| Capital Expenditures | 295 | 314 | 484 | 423 | 543 | 407 | 519 | 576 | 1,202 | 1,643 | 1,181 |
| Market Capitalization | 304 | 380 | 291 | 258 | 316 | 922 | 1,748 | 1,750 | 2,428 | 3,150 | 2,073 |
| Common Shareholder Equity | 697 | 722 | 786 | 695 | 731 | 836 | 1,300 | 1,513 | 2,181 | 2,485 | 2,681 |
| Return on Sales (%) | 3.6 | 4.9 | 2.7 | –4.0 | 0.4 | –0.5 | 4.8 | 4.4 | 5.6 | 4.6 | 2.8 |
| Return on Assets (%) | 3.5 | 4.4 | 2.4 | –5.0 | 0.1 | –0.8 | 4.4 | 4.0 | 5.2 | 3.7 | 2.3 |
| Return on Equity (%) | 10.2 | 16.2 | 9.8 | –18.9 | 2.0 | –2.1 | 14.9 | 13.2 | 15.2 | 11.1 | 7.0 |
| *Operating Performance* | | | | | | | | | | | |
| Total Revenue Passenger Miles (millions) | 24,634 | 29,407 | 33,400 | 28,200 | 27,798 | 30,900 | 34,100 | 36,702 | 44,135 | 48,788 | 56,794 |
| Load Factor (%) | 58.9 | 63.7 | 67.4 | 59.7 | 61.4 | 63.3 | 65.5 | 62.6 | 64.6 | 65.0 | 64.1 |
| U.S. Market Share (based on RPM's) | 12.7% | 13.0% | 12.7% | 11.1% | 11.2% | 11.9% | 12.1% | 12.0% | 13.1% | 13.3% | 14.0% |
| Employees (thousands) | 37.3 | 38.1 | 41.0 | 43.0 | 41.6 | 41.5 | 42.5 | 46.9 | 52.1 | 54.3 | 65.1 |

Source: AMR Corporation Annual Reports

Note: Financial data based on consolidated results of AMR Corporation, American Airlines's parent corporation.

Was government a passive observer of the airline industry following deregulation? No: government policy continued to shape opportunities and risks in the sector in important ways, despite the CAB phaseout. One prominent form of government involvement was in the area of anticompetitive behavior. Government policy also played a significant role in the areas of safety,[20] bankruptcy, labor policy, airports and the air traffic control system, and international air transport.

## Antitrust Policy

U.S. antitrust laws restrict firms from (1) monopolizing or attempting to monopolize a market and (2) restraining competition or attempting to restrain competition.[21] Antitrust policy[22] took on renewed relevance for the U.S. air transport sector after the CAB ceased to restrict airline entry and pricing. In general, rights and responsibilities relating to antitrust policies tend to remain unimportant under the terms of restrictive bargains, including those involving monopoly SOEs. But following the adoption of a liberalizing reform bargain, these latent terms often take on critical importance, given the increasing reliance on the presence or threat of competition to provide an effective curb on the market power of the incumbent(s).

Antitrust issues took on particular relevance for American Airlines in the early 1980s. In a telephone conversation between Bob Crandall and Braniff Airline CEO Howard Putnam in February 1982, Crandall said the following:

> *I think it's dumb as hell for Christ's sake, all right, to sit here and pound the [expletive] out of each other and neither of us making a [expletive] dime. . . . I have a suggestion for you. Raise your [expletive] fares 20%. I'll raise mine the next morning. . . . You'll make more money, and I will too.*[23]

Putnam, who taped the conversation, passed along the recording to the U.S. Department of Justice (DOJ), which in turn charged Crandall and American with attempted restraint of competition. In a 1985 out-of-court settlement, Crandall—without admitting guilt—agreed to keep detailed logs of his telephone conversations with other airline industry executives over a two-year period.

American also faced government scrutiny with respect to its computer reservation system (CRS). Smaller airlines and new entrants complained to the Department of Transportation (DOT) about the dominance of systems owned by American (SABRE) and United (Apollo), which accounted for 78 percent of all flight bookings in 1982.[24] This dominance allegedly harmed the competitiveness of other airlines, since the CRS owner's available flights appeared at the top of the agents' computer screens and tended to be selected first. In response, the DOT, in 1984, mandated that CRS screens show all available flights on a particular route in an unbiased manner.

Antitrust issues arose as well in the many mergers and acquisitions occurring in the airline industry in the 1980s. Under the terms of the Airline Deregulation Act, the DOT could block a proposed combination if it determined that the new entity would possess excessive market power at one or more airports. The 1986 merger of Northwest Airlines and Republic Airlines, for example, received extensive scrutiny due to the high market share the combined entity would hold in Minneapolis and Detroit. Yet ultimately, the DOT did not block this or any other proposed airline merger or acquisition in the two decades following deregulation.

In 1990 consumer groups filed a class action suit accusing major airlines, including American, of fixing prices by means of codes posted in computerized fare data. The airlines eventually agreed to a $458 million settlement including discount coupons for affected passengers, court costs, and attorneys' fees.[25] The DOJ pursued criminal litigation against the carriers for allegedly fixing prices in the equivalent of an "electronic smoke-filled room." The carriers eventually agreed to discontinue the practices, without admitting or denying the government's accusations.[26]

With the arrival of the Clinton administration, the Department of Transportation became more aggressive in pursuing alleged anticompetitive behavior in the airline industry. In 1993, for instance, DOT secretary Federico Pena accused Northwest Airlines of engaging in predatory actions designed to thwart new entrant Reno Air. In response, Northwest rescinded some of its pricing and scheduling changes.[27] Government jawboning, however, appeared to have only limited impact on the aggressive behavior of the major carriers. In response to growing consumer complaints of high and volatile airfares, the DOT in 1998 proposed strict guidelines defining "unfair exclusionary practices" in the airline industry. American and other major airlines vehemently opposed the proposed standards, claiming that they would unfairly restrict a carrier's ability to respond to competition.[28]

## Bankruptcy Policy

Government policy in the area of bankruptcy law also proved to be of importance to airline industry dynamics following deregulation. Through creative use of Chapter 11 of the bankruptcy statutes, Texas Air CEO Frank Lorenzo was able to break and renegotiate contracts signed between its Continental Airlines subsidiary, labor unions, and other suppliers, while continuing to operate the airline as a going concern from 1983 to 1985. In effect, Continental made sharp reductions in operating costs, under court protection, and emerged from bankruptcy with a dramatically improved competitive position—much to the chagrin of Crandall and his counterparts at the other major airlines.

## Labor Policy

Lorenzo, however, was not as successful a few years later when he attempted to repeat his strategy at Eastern Airlines, acquired by Texas Air in 1986. When Eastern's machinists threatened to strike in 1989, Lorenzo and federal mediators appealed to President George Bush to intervene and delay the action—a presidential prerogative contained in the terms of the Railway Labor Act, aimed at protecting the nation's transportation system from substantial disruption.[29] Bush declined. The striking machinists, supported by pilots and flight attendants who refused to cross picket lines, effectively grounded the airline. Eastern filed for Chapter 11 bankruptcy, and Lorenzo managed to put 30 percent of the airline's previous flights back in the air by summer with replacement workers.[30] The carrier's labor strife was never resolved, however, and ultimately Eastern Airlines was liquidated.

Interestingly, Bob Crandall's efforts to secure presidential intervention in a labor dispute several years later met with greater success. In February 1997, President Bill Clinton halted an impending strike by American Airlines pilots and by May, a settlement was reached without a disruption of service.

## Airports and Air Traffic Control

Airline industry dynamics following deregulation were also influenced by continued government ownership of two critical resources: the air traffic control system and airports. President Ronald Reagan's dismissal of striking air traffic controllers in 1981 created capacity bottlenecks in the U.S. air traffic control system, which tended to work to the disadvantage of airline entrants. Even in the late 1990s, the system continued to be constrained owing to years of underinvestment in technology.[31]

Airports, typically owned by specialized public authorities or local municipalities, also suffered in some cases from capacity constraints.

Potential entrants often complained that dominant carriers at individual airports were able to use long-term leasing arrangements or historical relationships with airport owners to control access to landing and takeoff slots, particularly at peak times of the day. The expansion of existing airports or the construction of new airports typically involved extensive review by local, state, federal, and/or other governmental bodies.

Airport access was also affected by a number of other constraints. For example, federal law limited the number of takeoff and landing slots available at certain airports for flight routes longer than 250 miles, so as to ensure adequate availability of capacity for "regional needs."[32] A variation of this policy prohibited aircraft with more than fifty-five seats from offering service through Love Field, an airport near Dallas that had the potential to serve as a competitive alternative to the Dallas–Fort Worth Airport, American Airlines' largest hub.[33]

Proposals to privatize the nation's air traffic control system and individual airports arose from time to time, but did not seem to enjoy strong enough public support to generate substantial ownership changes. Efforts to ease access to airport takeoff and landing slots achieved only limited success in the years following deregulation. Beginning in 1985, the DOT permitted the buying and selling of takeoff and landing rights at the nation's most capacity–constrained airports: New York's LaGuardia and JFK, Chicago's O'Hare, and Washington's Ronald Reagan National Airport. Airlines controlling slots, however, have been very reluctant to sell access to likely competitive entrants.[34] As a way of enhancing access, during 1997–1998 the DOT increased the number of slots by thirty at LaGuardia and fifty-three at O'Hare, awarding these rights to smaller, mostly new carriers.[35] As in the case of existing slots, these takeoff and landing rights were granted free of charge by the government.

## International Air Transport

Issues involving U.S. carriers in foreign markets and foreign carriers in the U.S. market continued to be highly influenced by government policy in the postderegulation era, although the terms of many bilateral agreements became less restrictive over time. Beginning with the Netherlands in 1992, the U.S. government negotiated a number of bilateral "open skies" treaties that permitted U.S. carriers to set routes and fares between cities in the United States and the foreign country with few restrictions, while granting reciprocal rights to the foreign country's carriers.[36] These governmental agreements were often reached in conjunction with the formation of alliances between carriers of the respective nations. In 1992 Northwest Airlines and the Dutch carrier KLM were granted permission by the U.S. and Dutch governments to coordinate their scheduling, ticketing, and baggage handling so as to enable passengers to travel seamlessly across and within the separate airline networks. A similar agreement was reached between United Airlines and Lufthansa in 1996.

Despite the move toward open skies treaties, U.S. carriers continued to face obstacles in serving foreign markets. American Airlines, for example, planned to enter the British market in 1990 by acquiring TWA's long-standing London routes (and associated landing and takeoff slots at Heathrow Airport) for $445 million. The British government, however, disputed TWA's right to sell access to Heathrow slots.[37] American's deal was eventually approved in 1991 as part of broader negotiations between the British and U.S. governments that also involved United Airlines' purchase of PanAm's Heathrow slots and the use by British Airways (BA) of "code-sharing" to list its flights under the name and flight number of its U.S. partner airline USAir.[38]

Changes in European Union policy increasingly affected the terms under which foreign carriers could participate in the airline markets of EU member nations.[39] In 1996 Bob Crandall and British Airway's chairman Robert Ayling sought to establish an alliance between the carriers to provide wide-ranging service integration. The proposed alliance initially was opposed by EU competition commissioner Karel Van Miert, who was concerned about the alliance's potential to dominate routes between London and the United States. In July 1998 Van Miert agreed to the deal on the condition that the carriers give up 267 London takeoff and landing slots with no compensation.[40] The U.K.'s competition agency, the Office of Fair Trading, subsequently recommended to the British minister for trade and industry that the carriers be allowed to sell the slots, which had an estimated market value of $800 million.[41] Britain's transport minister, however, supported Van Miert's position, arguing that the airport slots were ultimately the property of "the community" and not the airlines.[42] Meanwhile, the U.S. DOT insisted that it would approve the alliance only if the British government agreed to sign a comprehensive open skies agreement with the United States. Thus the proposed deal remained in limbo before being abandoned in 1999 by BA and American, frustrated with their inability to take advantage of the theoretical freedoms of a "deregulated" environment.

Table 2-2 AMERICAN AIRLINES FINANCIAL AND OPERATING STATISTICS, 1988–1998
(in millions of U.S. dollars, unless otherwise noted)

| | 1988 | 1989 | 1990 | 1991 | 1992 | 1993 | 1994 | 1995 | 1996 | 1997 | 1998 |
|---|---|---|---|---|---|---|---|---|---|---|---|
| *Financial Performance* | | | | | | | | | | | |
| Total Revenue | 8,824 | 10,480 | 11,720 | 12,887 | 14,396 | 15,701 | 16,137 | 16,910 | 17,753 | 18,570 | 19,205 |
| Net Income | 477 | 455 | −40 | −240 | −935 | −110 | 228 | 167 | 1,016 | 985 | 1,314 |
| Capital Expenditures | 1,186 | 2,395 | 2,901 | 3,536 | 3,299 | 2,080 | 1,114 | 928 | 547 | 1,390 | 2,661 |
| Market Capitalization | 3,153 | 3,608 | 3,014 | 4,794 | 5,090 | 5,079 | 4,042 | 5,673 | 8,019 | 11,128 | 10,034 |
| Common Shareholder Equity | 3,148 | 3,766 | 3,727 | 3,794 | 3,349 | 3,195 | 3,302 | 3,642 | 5,668 | 6,216 | 6,698 |
| Return on Sales (%) | 5.4 | 4.3 | −0.3 | −1.9 | −3.3 | −0.6 | 1.4 | 1.2 | 6.2 | 5.3 | 6.8 |
| Return on Assets (%) | 4.8 | 4.1 | −0.3 | −1.5 | −2.5 | −0.8 | 0.9 | 1.0 | 5.4 | 4.7 | 6.1 |
| Return on Equity (%) | 14.5 | 12.1 | −1.1 | −6.3 | −14.2 | −2.2 | 6.7 | 5.3 | 19.5 | 15.8 | 20.2 |
| *Operating Performance* | | | | | | | | | | | |
| Total Revenue Passenger Miles (millions) | 64,753 | 73,481 | 76,878 | 81,586 | 97,110 | 97,062 | 98,736 | 102,669 | 104,521 | 106,936 | 108,955 |
| Load Factor (%) | 63.5 | 63.8 | 62.3 | 61.7 | 63.7 | 60.4 | 64.8 | 66.2 | 68.5 | 69.5 | 70.2 |
| U.S. Market Share (based on RPM's) | 15.3% | 17.0% | 16.8% | 18.2% | 20.3% | 19.8% | 19.0% | 19.0% | 18.1% | 17.7% | 17.6% |
| Employees (thousands) | 77.1 | 89.0 | 102.8 | 116.3 | 119.3 | 118.9 | 109.8 | 110.0 | 111.3 | 113.9 | 103.4 |

Source: AMR Corporation Annual Reports

Note: Financial data based on consolidated results of AMR Corporation, American Airlines's parent corporation.

## AMERICAN AIRLINES LOOKS TO THE FUTURE

As Crandall prepared to step down from his posts as president, CEO, and chairman of American Airlines in 1998, he could well have marveled at the financial performance of the U.S. airline industry, which had just completed its third consecutive year of record profits.[43] American Airline's own performance had improved significantly during the 1990s, as the firm's load factor (capacity utilization) rose to 70 percent and its return on equity climbed above 20 percent (see Table 2-2). Despite the pressures of the competitive free-for-all, incumbents such as American had been able to prevail and prosper against repeated entry, in large part by redefining the business of air transportation to their advantage. In fact, by the late 1990s, the share of total passenger traffic accounted for by the nation's top four airlines—65 percent—equaled the proportion held by the top four at the time of deregulation.[44]

Yet a number of uncertainties loomed. It was difficult to predict whether vigorous U.S. economic growth, which had fueled strong demand for air transport during the mid-1990s, could be sustained. The competitive environment could be affected significantly by the DOT's proposed new rules on competitive behavior and by changes in the regulation of foreign entry on the part of the U.S. and foreign governments. Similarly, emerging policy in the area of airport landing and takeoff slots in the United States and abroad could have important implications for industry dynamics. One "wild card" was growing consumer dissatisfaction with the high volatility and wide variation in airline fares, which potentially could lead to broad-based pressure for government action to curb perceived industry abuses. Ultimately, American's enterprise bargain would continue to evolve as do the bargains of all firms operating in deregulated markets, even years after the initial adoption of reforms.

# 3 ✦ *Dynamics of Privatization*

*The story of Argentina's* telecommunications sector includes two reform bargains, each of which took place under the administration of a powerful and colorful president. The most recent reform involved the privatization of ENTel, the monopoly government-owned telephone company, from 1990 to 1992 under President Carlos Menem. During these years the enterprise was split into two parts and sold to private investors, including both Argentine and foreign shareholders. Decades earlier, in 1946, a reform bargain of quite the opposite character took place under President Juan Perón—namely, the nationalization of the private foreign-owned telephone company that had provided most of Argentina's telephone service since the late 1800s. This "flip-flopping" of ownership over the course of the twentieth century characterized the evolution of many large capital-intensive economic sectors, not only in Argentina but in many other nations. Thus the ENTel story illustrates a number of general insights into the dynamics of privatization.

At the time of ENTel's privatization, the performance of Argentina's telephone system was abysmal. The nation's telephone density was 11 telephone lines per 100 inhabitants,[1] as compared with about 45 lines per person in the OECD countries.[2] Only 50 percent of local calls and 25 percent of international calls were connected successfully. During 1989 alone, ENTel received more than 14 million complaints, including requests for repairs, over its 3 million installed lines. ENTel's financial condition was equally grim: the firm ran after-tax losses of 66 percent of revenues on average during the 1980s.[3]

Given the state of Argentina's telecommunications system in the 1980s, it may seem strange that ENTel itself emerged as a result of a reform process, initiated in the 1940s, to improve the performance of the telecommunications sector in particular and the Argentine economy in general. To understand the evolution and implications of the enterprise bargain in this sector, we turn to the industry's beginnings in the late nineteenth century.

## ESTABLISHING THE BARGAIN: THE ORIGINS OF ARGENTINE TELECOMMUNICATIONS

Several entrepreneurial enterprises introduced the citizens of Buenos Aires to the marvels of the new technology of telephony in the early 1880s. Most of these firms were financed by foreign investors, including the European-backed Unión Telefónica del Río de Plata (UTRP). In the industry's early years, enterprise bargains between telephone companies and the Argentine state (including federal, provincial, and local governments) included few obligations on the part of the firms.[4] Also, besides basic property rights protection—enforced by relatively stable government institutions—the companies enjoyed no special entitlements such as subsidies or monopoly guarantees. Argentina willingly agreed to bargains on attractive terms for UTRP and other foreign telephone companies since these firms were expected to provide capital, technology, and expertise to fuel growth in an intriguing new industry.

The outcome of these fairly nonrestrictive "laissez-faire" bargains,[5] however, was not the vigorous competition normally associated with free markets. UTRP itself was established as a merger of several telephone companies that had competed fiercely in the Buenos Aires market in the early years of telephony. Over time, through internal growth and acquisitions, UTRP came to dominate the industry. The last major merger took place in 1929, when the American multinational International Telephone and Telegraph (ITT) gained control of the combined system, which held a virtual monopoly on telephone service in Argentina's most populous provinces. The company's national market share settled at about 90 percent, with the balance accounted for by small firms serving mostly rural provinces, which were not interconnected with the larger UTRP system.[6] In the 1930s UTRP took increasing advantage of its market power by raising fees on a range of services and promptly disconnecting customers that refused to pay.

UTRP's dominance could be explained in large part by the economic characteristics of traditional (wire-based) telephone technology. Given the high fixed costs of wiring and interconnecting individual customers, it is typically much cheaper to build and operate a single integrated telephone network than multiple overlapping networks created through duplication of fixed investments.[7] These characteristics also describe a number of other industries, including electricity, natural gas, and water distribution,[8] cable television distribution, postal service, and railroads and subways. When overlapping systems develop independently in these natural monopoly sectors, it is not surprising to see industry consolidation occur—if permitted by the state—as a strategy for achieving cost reductions.[9] Mergers and acquisitions may also improve operating efficiency in industries with significant economies of scale or scope that fall short of being natural monopolies. Airlines, for instance, can obtain substantial cost benefits from high-volume hub-and-spoke systems.

Consolidation in these sectors also tends to be driven by revenue considerations. Competition among firms in high-fixed-cost industries can lead to brutal price wars in periods of overcapacity, as rivals strive to capture any margin over variable costs. The more difficult it is for firms to rid themselves of fixed costs—for example, in the case of highly specialized assets or long-term contracts—the more intense and lengthy the price wars are likely to be. As we saw in chapter 1, this "sunk cost" problem is especially prevalent in infrastructure industries, where many of the assets—wires, pipes, and rails—are highly immobile once installed and tend to have long economic life-spans.

## Outcomes of the Enterprise Bargain

From UTRP's perspective, the terms of its enterprise bargain were quite favorable. The firm's freedoms in the area of mergers and acquisitions, pricing, service quality, and system expansion provided reasonable assurance that it would be able to achieve profitability commensurate with the risks associated with long-term sunk cost investments in telephone system assets. These risks were related both to economic factors—for example, shifts in input costs and demand—and political factors, such as the imposition of price controls, changes in tax policy, and expropriation.

From the perspective of the Argentine state, its relationship with UTRP had important implications for the creation and distribution of economic value. UTRP's consolidation of most of Argentina's telephone system into a single network allowed it to achieve operating efficiency through the realization of scale and scope economies, and its private ownership status gave it the incentive to do so. Viewed broadly, UTRP's success at delivering desirable services to the Argentine population, while achieving substantial cost efficiencies, made a valuable contribution to the national economy. Yet, insofar as UTRP took advantage of its considerable market power, it was able to capture much of this added value for itself in the form of profits. It is not clear whether the absence of significant competition led UTRP to be less innovative over time.

Beyond its economic consequences, the relationship between UTRP and the Argentine state had implications along noneconomic dimensions. Foreign ownership of the nation's telecommunications infrastructure potentially threatened the state's ability to protect national sovereignty and maintain internal social and political order. Yet during the early part of the twentieth century, Argentina, a nation largely settled by European immigrants and at peace with its neighbors, did not appear particularly concerned about the security implications of private and foreign ownership in the telecommunications or other sectors of the economy. However, questions of security took on growing relevance for UTRP over time, as the nation's telephone system became an increasingly important means for integrating the diverse parts of the country and for connecting Argentina to the outside world.

Issues of fairness also took on greater relevance and came to be seen as integral to personal communications and commerce.[10] The absence of any telephone service whatsoever in some areas—particularly in remote and poorer communities—generated resentment, despite the fact that providing such service would not have been financially attractive using strict return-on-investment criteria. Similarly, the lack of interconnection between UTRP's telephone system and the smaller systems serving less populous provinces could be seen as unfair since it denied customers of the smaller systems telephone access to large Argentine cities, particularly Buenos Aires. UTRP's acceleration of customer disconnects in the early 1930s was also regarded by many as unfair, although as a private corporation, UTRP probably saw little reason to maintain service to nonpaying customers. Finally, the fact that UTRP was owned by a wealthy foreign corporation tended to exacerbate perceptions of inequity.

## Evolution of the Bargain

The growth of UTRP's monopoly reach and its blunt exercise of market power in the 1930s alienated actual and potential telephone users. Since these users included private citizens, businesses, and government entities, they represented a potential broad-based coalition of interests capable of pressuring the state to revise the terms of UTRP's bargain to their advantage. As telephone usage became more widespread and less regarded as a luxury service, the number of affected parties, and their sensitivity to outcomes in the sector, increased steadily.

Within this context, the Argentine government unilaterally modified the basic terms of its bargain with the nation's telephone companies. In 1935 the government required these enterprises to provide connections across individual telephone systems. A year later, Argentine president Agustín Justo issued an executive decree declaring telecommunications services to be "national" in character, which authorized the federal government to own or license firms in the industry, regulate service prices, and specify investment policy for service providers. The decree included a provision that gave the state the right to acquire the assets of any telephone operating company "with fair compensation."

Although the decree appeared to constitute a reform bargain, the effect of the changes was negligible in the short term. The state did not establish mechanisms for the implementation and enforcement of specific pricing and investment obligations. Furthermore, the federal government did not take advantage of its right to establish or acquire operating companies in the sector. The government, however, did declare some of UTRP's pricing and disconnection policies to be in violation of the decree. The firm ignored the government's finding until ordered by Argentina's Supreme Court to end these practices in 1939.[11] Despite this result, the failure of a weak central government to allay fundamental concerns over sectoral outcomes paved the way for a more dramatic reform in the 1940s.

## THE FIRST REFORM BARGAIN: NATIONALIZATION

During the early 1940s, Argentina experienced three military coups. Out of this instability emerged Juan Perón, a charismatic colonel elected president in 1946 on a populist platform with strong union support. Perón's nationalist rhetoric and faith in the ability of central government to lead economic and social development was representative of the era. The apparent failure of market capitalism during the Great Depression and the ostensible successes of Soviet central planning exerted a powerful influence on postwar economic policy around the world.[12] Moreover, the principles of national self-determination emerged with broad international legitimacy at the end of the Second World War.

In light of these trends, it is not surprising that Perón nationalized a number of private foreign enterprises in important infrastructure sectors early in his administration.[13] Nationalization, however, was not carried out through confiscation of assets but by means of acquisitions funded with nearly $1.7 billion in foreign exchange reserves that the nation had accumulated as a major raw materials exporter during the war. Argentina's strategy bore a striking resemblance to Britain's nationalization program, launched by Labour Party prime minister Clement Atlee in 1945.[14]

Soon after his election, Perón described the Argentine telecommunications sector as the nation's "central nervous system," declaring it essential for both economic development and defense. The reform bargain adopted for the sector included several components. First, the Argentine government agreed to pay ITT $95 million for UTRP's assets.[15] Second, the government contracted with ITT to manage operations of the nationalized firm during a period of transition, including the provision of training of Argentine managers.[16] Third, the Argentine government agreed to an ongoing supply arrangement between ITT's telecommunications equipment manufacturing subsidiary and the new state-owned enterprise.

From Perón's perspective, the nationalization of UTRP seemed to offer many benefits with few, if any, drawbacks. Placing all actions of the enterprise under the direct control of the state would presumably enhance the government's ability to address concerns related to security and fairness. In addition, the shift to public ownership boded well for distribution of economic value, since the telephone monopoly would no longer be motivated to charge monopoly prices to maximize profits. Given the transitional consulting/training arrangement with ITT, it seemed reasonable to assume that the enterprise would maintain its traditionally strong record with respect to operating efficiency. Finally, Perón presumably saw nationalization as a means of enhancing his own power and prestige and increasing his future chances for reelection—in other words, as a source of personal benefit.

The terms of the reform bargain were also favorable from ITT's perspective. This result may appear surprising at first glance given the rising public dissatisfaction with the firm's actions in the period leading up to nationalization. Furthermore, it would seem that UTRP's bargaining power vis-à-vis the state would have eroded over time as the firm sank more and more capital into the business during the first half of the 1900s—much of it into immobile assets—in effect, leaving itself vulnerable to extortion by the government.[17]

Yet UTRP enjoyed certain advantages in its prereform bargain with the state. The terms of the bargain included the right to "fair compensation" for any assets purchased by the state—a right subject to enforcement by Argentina's judiciary, whose historic record was strong in this regard. Informal enforcement mechanisms played a role as well. Although foreign-owned UTRP had few natural allies in Argentina, ITT's status as a major U.S.-based multinational raised the strong possibility of some form of U.S. government retaliation if the terms of the nationalization were seen as unfair to the firm's owner.[18] Finally, Argentina risked a loss in reputation as a desirable locale for foreign or even domestic private investment if it imposed a reform bargain perceived as abusive. While none of these factors guaranteed that UTRP would not be compelled to accept confiscatory changes in its bargain, they increased the probability that such action would impose substantial costs on Argentina. In the end, the terms of the arrangement reached between Argentina and ITT appeared to be mutually acceptable.[19]

In summary, the forces for change in UTRP's bargain with the Argentine state were initially spurred by outcomes in the telecommunications market that generated societal pressure for reforms. Yet, the ultimate timing, design, and implementation of the reform bargain was driven by broader contextual developments, including the election of Perón, international trends in political economy, and the availability of Argentina's foreign currency windfall.

## Outcomes of Nationalization

The nationalized UTRP became, in effect, the state-owned enterprise ENTel.[20] The federal government quickly took control of the firm's investment and pricing decisions. The Perón administration's strong commitment to national infrastructure development resulted in ENTel's making significant capital investments during the late 1940s and early 1950s.

These investments included the acquisition of many small telephone cooperatives, which expanded the geographic scope and improved the degree of integration of ENTel's network.[21] Telephone service prices were set with an eye to encouraging system usage while still ensuring profitable operations. Overall, the reform bargain appeared to address prior concerns related to security, fairness, and the creation and distribution of economic value in the sector, while leaving basic operating decisions mostly in the hands of qualified managers.

Short-term performance was impressive. By the mid-1950s, ENTel was one of the largest telecommunications carriers in the world, ranking among the top ten in number of lines installed and number of calls placed. In 1957 Argentina accounted for 43 percent of all telephones installed in South America although it contained only 15 percent of the region's population.[22] ENTel's operations were reasonably efficient and profitable. These outcomes, however, were not sustained over time.

ENTel's subsequent decline was linked to a number of factors. The design and implementation of the firm's strategy was hobbled by the multiple objectives of the firm's new owner, the federal government—a typical problem for state-owned enterprises. Control over individual aspects of ENTel's activities was held by the Ministry of Public Works (network growth and service offerings), the Ministry of Economy (budgeting and pricing), the Ministry of Labor (salaries and employment practices), and the Secretariat of Industry (procurement practices). Over time, this fragmentation created increasingly serious conflicts between the commercial interests of the enterprise and the social and political priorities of the various government bodies.

Perhaps if ENTel had been led by a strong chief executive, it might have been able to broker a common vision. Yet in reality, the firm suffered from extremely unstable leadership. The Argentine president appointed ENTel's chief executive and senior managers, and frequent changes in the government led to high turnover in ENTel's executive corps. From the late 1950s to the late 1980s, Argentina was led by fifteen presidents who, in turn, named twenty-eight different chief executives to head ENTel.[23] Not surprisingly, government ministers changed frequently as well during this period. This lack of continuity contrasted dramatically with the ten years of Perón's presidency from 1946 to 1955.

One change in the terms of ENTel's bargain in the 1960s had particularly important implications for outcomes in the telecommunications sector. National procurement legislation, adopted under President Arturo

Illia (1963–1966), required state enterprises to purchase all materials and services from domestic sources, with few exceptions.[24] This legislation spawned a number of joint ventures between Argentine partners and foreign telecommunications equipment manufacturers including Siemens, Alcatel, Telettra, NEC, and Equitel.[25] These "local" suppliers secured contracts with ENTel often at prices well above international levels[26] and became entrenched defenders of public ownership in the sector.

Argentina's telecommunications unions, which represented 98 percent of ENTel's workforce, also became staunch supporters of the status quo. The unions, in close coordination with the minister of labor, effectively acquired decision-making power for hiring, promotion, and terms of employment. Over time, the firm's employment rose to almost 50,000—disproportionately high by international industry standards. Workers enjoyed a thirty-five-hour work week and numbers of phantom employees padded the payroll. Illegal acts, such as inventory theft and black market installation of telephone lines, went unpunished.

ENTel's decline during the 1960s and 1970s paralleled the political, social, and economic deterioration of the Argentine nation, which was riven by military coups, terrorist and antiterrorist brutality, and widespread corruption. As Argentina's economy stagnated and inflation reached triple digits, ENTel's capital expenditures were cut back dramatically and the firm's technical sophistication, reliability, and efficiency eroded steadily over time. By the early 1980s, the average wait for a new telephone line was fourteen years—unless the customer was willing to make large "under the table" payments to renegade ENTel employees.[27]

Despite optimism over ENTel's prospects at the time of nationalization, the long-term outcomes associated with the first reform bargain were grim. First and foremost, Argentine society as a whole suffered from the anemic creation of economic value in the telecommunications sector due to ENTel's gross inefficiency, underinvestment, and lack of innovation. Furthermore, the distribution of value was skewed heavily toward workers, suppliers, and government officials and away from customers[28] and the loss-making enterprise.[29] In fact, the capture of value through corrupt and illegal practices was itself a primary drag on the overall creation of value. Although ENTel was wholly owned by the Argentine government, national security was threatened, arguably, by the network's poor condition. ENTel's bargain also failed to provide satisfying outcomes in the area of fairness, as access remained poor in the rural areas and quality of service became increasingly unstable.

In spite of the large and growing costs to Argentina of ENTel's bargain—in terms of foregone economic and noneconomic benefits—reform was difficult to achieve. Those who benefited from the status quo were highly organized and politically influential. In contrast, the likely beneficiaries of reform—primarily taxpayers and consumers—were largely fragmented. Ultimately, as was the case for the first reform bargain, the second reform bargain was accomplished only when the force of macro factors—in the form of a severe economic crisis—came to bear on the situation.

## THE SECOND REFORM BARGAIN: PRIVATIZATION

Following its humiliating defeat in the 1982 Falklands War,[30] Argentina's military government agreed to return the nation to civilian rule, resulting in the 1983 election of Raúl Alfonsín. The president's goals were ambitious: stabilize the nation's economic and political situation, introduce new social welfare safety net policies, and rationalize the role of the state in the Argentine economy. The condition of Argentina's telecommunications sector made it a natural target for reform.

In 1987 the government proposed a partial privatization plan in which the Spanish telephone company, Telefónica de España, would pay $250 million for a 40 percent ownership share of ENTel and $500 million for a twenty-five-year lease to operate the firm with monopoly rights throughout Argentina.[31] The plan, however, faced strong opposition from unions and local telecommunications equipment suppliers. Ultimately, the deal was blocked by the opposition Peronist Party, which had won a majority of seats in the Argentine Senate in the 1987 parliamentary elections.[32]

Although the Alfonsín government failed in its privatization effort, in 1988 it initiated a competitive bidding process for the provision of cellular telephone service in Buenos Aires. The victorious private consortium included BellSouth, Motorola, Citibank, and several Argentine companies. The government also eased purchase restrictions on ENTel, allowing the company to procure a higher percentage of its equipment from foreign vendors. Yet ENTel's financial condition continued to erode, as the firm's price increases were held below inflation and as the burden of taxes and foreign debt service rose steadily over the decade.

The Argentine economy as a whole also faltered during the Alfonsín administration. By 1989 the nation had fallen into a deep recession, foreign debt had risen to $65 billion, the federal deficit exceeded 18 percent of GDP, and inflation raged at an annual rate of 3,000 percent. Although a century earlier Argentina was one of the most prosperous nations in the world, at the close of the 1980s its GDP per capita had sunk to $2,520.[33] In May 1989 Peronist Party candidate Carlos Menem, a populist provincial governor, easily defeated the incumbent party's presidential candidate in national elections.[34]

The election of Carlos Menem, along with strong Peronist majorities in both houses of Congress, did not bode well for an ENTel reform bargain, given the Peronist Party's strong affiliation with unions and its traditional adherence to a state-led development strategy. Nevertheless, Menem defied prior expectations, moving aggressively to reform Argentina's crisis-bound economy. In August 1989 Congress granted Menem the right to issue executive decrees redefining the government's role in a number of areas. Soon afterward, Menem amended the National Telecommunications Law, eliminating the exclusive right of the state to provide telecommunications services. He then declared that ENTel would be privatized.

In a sense, Menem became as much a representative of a new era in international thought on the role of the state versus markets as Perón had been a purveyor of the old. Although a trailblazer within Argentina, Menem drew heavily on principles espoused by earlier reformers in the United States, Chile,[35] Great Britain, and other nations. The widespread failure of state ownership and highly restrictive bargains in the 1970s and 1980s had even led to dramatic political and economic reforms in the Soviet Union and eastern Europe by the end of the 1980s.[36]

To broaden the scope of reform, Menem appointed María Julia Alsogaray—a congressional representative from Argentina's small free-market party, the Unión de Centro Democrático—to oversee the privatization process. Also, Menem appointed major union leaders to the positions of minister of labor and secretary of communications. In January 1990 Menem defined the basic terms of reform through an executive decree entitled "Document on the Terms and Conditions for Privatization of Telecommunications Services."

Under this decree, ENTel's assets and employees were to be divided into four companies. One would provide basic local and domestic long-distance service to Argentina's northern provinces and a second would serve the southern provinces.[37] These two companies would own two additional firms through joint ventures: Telintar, which would assume

ENTel's international long-distance assets, and Startel, which would incorporate ENTel's value-added telecommunications services such as mobile telephony and data transmission. Initially, a 60 percent share of the northern and southern companies would be sold through competitive bidding, and a 10 percent share transferred to the telecommunications union on behalf of ENTel's employees. At a later date, the government would sell its remaining 30 percent stake though a public share offering. Bidders were required to offer a minimum of $100 million in cash for the northern company ($114 million for the southern company), with the remainder of each bid to be paid in the form of outstanding Argentine government foreign currency debt.[38]

As in the case of the first reform bargain forty years earlier, the forces for change included important sectoral factors. Although domestic telephone prices were low by international standards, consumer satisfaction with ENTel was extremely low due to poor service on existing lines and the difficulty of securing installation of new lines. In fact, some large business users had begun to develop their own proprietary telephone assets to secure more reliable, higher-quality service. Many rural provinces continued to be vastly underserved. Taxpayers faced the growing burden of ENTel's financial losses, which continued to mount in the face of price controls, corruption, and the bypassing of ENTel's network by means of cellular service and proprietary networks.

As for macro factors, Argentina's government deficit and foreign debt burden placed increasing pressure on the state to raise revenues and cut expenses. Internationally, state ownership had come under increasing attack as an inferior approach to national development. Finally, Menem's strong electoral mandate provided him with the power to implement the reform bargain, even in the face of entrenched interests.

## Terms of the Reform Bargain

Despite the numerous problems associated with state ownership of Argentina's telephone system, the liberalizing reform bargain adopted under Menem's leadership was not simply a return to the laissez-faire bargain UTRP enjoyed earlier in the century—a largely unrestricted private monopoly. In fact, the terms of the reform bargain were considerably more complex than those associated with either UTRP or ENTel. This complexity was rooted in a desire to avoid, or at least minimize, the unfavorable outcomes each of these earlier bargains had generated. In addition, some of the complexity could be attributed to a desire to smooth the transition to the reform bargain given the expected losses that entrenched interests would incur in the process. Ultimately, the reform bargain's terms represented a delicate balancing of affected parties' interests, including those of consumers of telecommunications services, taxpayers, workers, suppliers, potential bidders (foreign and domestic), and government officials.

The notion of balance was incorporated into terms affecting the ownership structure of the new telecommunications companies. The government required that each consortium include a major foreign telecommunications company and adopted bidding specifications that encouraged the participation of large foreign financial institutions and local business groups. Also, as noted above, 10 percent of the enterprises' shares remained under the control of ENTel's unions. Hence, the reform bargain's terms were designed to encourage the inflow of foreign capital, technology, and expertise, while at the same time enabling domestic interests to participate in the direction and financial benefits of the privatized firms. No consortium would be permitted to acquire both the northern and the southern companies, even if it offered the highest bid for each.

The division of ENTel's primary infrastructure into two separate companies reflected the desire to prevent the concentration of market power and political power into a single entity. It was also designed to promote direct and indirect competition[39] in the Argentine telecommunications sector over time, which would presumably spur greater efficiency, innovation, and lower prices. Under the terms of the reform bargain, however, each of the privatized companies was entitled to a seven-year monopoly on basic domestic service in its region and on Teleintar's international services.[40] Presumably, the initial monopoly would encourage bidders to pay more for ENTel's assets—a major benefit for the ailing government treasury. These terms were also seen as encouraging the winners to invest aggressively in the expansion and improvement of infrastructure so as to be well positioned for competition at the end of the monopoly period.

The Argentine government, however, was anxious to avoid the potential for monopoly pricing and low investment in remote and rural areas that had characterized the UTRP era. Thus, under the reform bargain, the companies' monopoly rights were contingent on the achievement of annual targets on a number of quantitative performance indicators, including new lines installed, call completion rate, line failure rate, repair time, and installation delay time.[41] If the firms substantially exceeded these target obligations they would be eligible for an extension of their monopoly rights for an additional three years. As for pricing, the companies were allowed to increase rates initially to levels that the government projected would support a 16 percent return on investment.[42] To encourage the local network to develop more rapidly, the firms were required to maintain a pricing structure that cross-subsidized domestic service with international revenues and residential service with business service revenues.[43] During the monopoly period, the companies would be permitted to increase prices at the rate of inflation, with adjustments to reflect the impact of exchange rate changes on costs.[44]

Interpretation and enforcement of this complex set of rights and obligations was delegated to a new regulatory body, the Comisíon Nacional de Telecomunicaciones, to be established by President Menem later in 1990. For all affected parties, the lack of clarity regarding this key institution created considerable uncertainty about the reform bargain's future evolution. Ultimately, it appears that they relied heavily on their faith in President Menem to ensure balanced outcomes in the sector.

In the highly uncertain context surrounding privatization, only three consortia submitted bids for ENTel's successor companies. The winning bidder for the southern company was a consortium that included Spain's dominant telephone company Telefónica de España (33 percent),[45] Citibank (57 percent), and the Argentine conglomerate Techint (10 percent).[46] Although the same consortium also submitted the highest bid for the southern company, the government awarded the firm to a second consortium including state-owned France Telecom (30 percent), the Italian telecommunications equipment manufacturer STET (30 percent), Morgan Bank (10 percent), and the Argentine conglomerate Pérez Companc (30 percent).[47] Ironically, the core members of the winning consortia were full or partial state-owned enterprises. Yet the strong government backing of these firms—a fact that presumably could be leveraged should future disputes arise in the bargain with the Argentine state—appears to have given them the confidence to participate in a bidding process shunned by many other potential participants.

Following the submission of bids, Argentine telecommunications workers went on strike in an effort to thwart privatization. President Menem reacted immediately, calling out the army to operate the telephone system and firing hundreds of workers. The strike ended soon thereafter, reconfirming the president's commitment to the reform bargain and his ability to ensure its implementation.

Before the sales were completed, the reform bargains were modified. The northern company's buyers argued that given the high rate of inflation that prevailed during the bidding process, the initial price increases for telecommunications services were inadequate for achieving a reasonable rate of return. After tense negotiations, the government agreed to an average price increase for both companies of 28 percent over levels initially specified. In exchange, the government required the firms to reduce their prices by 2 percent per year in real terms in the future to reflect anticipated gains in productivity. The first stage of the privatization became official in November 1990, when the winning bidders transferred cash and sovereign debt to the Argentine government. The new southern company became known as Telefónica de Argentina, and the northern as Telecom Argentina.

The bidders' ability to secure key changes in reform bargain terms during the bidding process itself reflected the state's relatively weak bargaining position at the time. The nation was just beginning to emerge from the chaos of hyperinflation, and Menem's broad reform program was still largely untested. Given the small number of bidders that showed any interest in privatization, Argentina did not want to risk the collapse of a deal that would serve as an important precedent for future privatizations.

## Outcomes of Privatization

During the remainder of the 1990s, Telefónica de Argentina and Telecom Argentina took a wide range of actions designed to transform the performance of the former ENTel through a significant restructuring of operations and a substantial increase in capital expenditures. Both firms achieved dramatic improvements in operating efficiency, measured in telephone lines per employee, while more than doubling the number of lines in service within five years of privatization (see tables 3-1 and 3-2.)

Also, as these firms reduced costs, their profitability increased significantly, since real prices declined only slightly during the monopoly period, in accordance with the terms of the reform bargain.[48]

Over time, public dissatisfaction with the high price of telephone services in Argentina, among the highest rates in the world, in combination with the strong profitability of the privatized firms, generated political pressure to revise the terms of the reform bargain. However, Telefónica and Telecom proved remarkably successful at avoiding an unfavorable evolution of the bargain due to several factors. First, the companies widely exceeded the minimum targets included in the reform bargain with respect to line installation and quality improvements. This helped generate goodwill and, more importantly, kept the firms free of any accusations of violating the bargain's terms.

Second, the precedent value of the ENTel privatization for future Argentine privatizations, as well as inflows of foreign investment in general, served as a strong informal mechanism for assuring enforcement of the terms of the bargain relating to pricing and the length of market exclusivity. The negative implications of the Argentine state reneging on its end of the bargain with Telefónica and Telecom could have been severe from the perspective of the government's fiscal position, the balance of payments, overall economic growth, and perhaps ultimately the stability of the Menem administration.

A third factor was the indirect participation of the Spanish, French, and Italian governments in the ownership of the privatized telephone companies through their stakes in the parent corporations. Any attempt of the Argentine government to violate its obligations with respect to the bargain could have led to a diplomatic crisis in addition to an economic one. A fourth factor was the important minority ownership stake held in the privatized firms by the Argentine conglomerates Techint and Pérez Companc. These firms held a visible and influential position in the Argentine political economy in general and in the privatized sectors in particular. They proved to be valuable allies in Telefónica's and Telecom's efforts to shape the political dynamics of the reform bargain over time.

Thus the pattern of market dynamics that emerged, and was sustained, through the 1990s in the case of the Argentine telecommunications privatization closely matched the incumbent-on-top scenario. Although there was some pie-sharing due to the allocation of shareholdings to

Table 3-1  TELECOM ARGENTINA FINANCIAL AND OPERATING STATISTICS, 1991–1998

(fiscal years ending in September; data in millions of Argentine pesos, unless otherwise indicated)

| | 1991 | 1992 | 1993 | 1994 | 1995 | 1996 | 1997 | 1998 | 1999 |
|---|---|---|---|---|---|---|---|---|---|
| **Financial Performance** | | | | | | | | | |
| Revenues | 882 | 1,214 | 1,616 | 1,959 | 1,980 | 1,983 | 2,585 | 3,174 | 3,183 |
| Operating Profit | 113 | 204 | 307 | 457 | 458 | 491 | 685 | 817 | 746 |
| Net Income | 55 | 152 | 2,123 | 287 | 307 | 260 | 307 | 374 | 358 |
| Assets | 2,130 | 2,311 | 2,831 | 3,569 | 4,428 | 4,984 | 5,793 | 6,192 | 7,141 |
| Common Shareholder Equity | 1,744 | 1,794 | 1,887 | 2,003 | 2,264 | 2,456 | 2,575 | 2,693 | 2,771 |
| Capital Expenditures | 131 | 659 | 1,090 | 1,177 | 873 | 936 | 803 | 939 | 1,197 |
| Return on Sales (%) | 6.3 | 12.5 | 13.2 | 14.7 | 15.5 | 13.1 | 11.9 | 11.8 | 11.2 |
| Return on Assets (%) | 2.6 | 6.6 | 7.5 | 8.0 | 6.9 | 5.2 | 7.6 | 8.6 | 8.3 |
| Return on Equity (%) | 3.2 | 8.5 | 11.3 | 14.3 | 13.6 | 10.6 | 12.4 | 14.5 | 13.3 |
| **Operating Performance** | | | | | | | | | |
| Total Lines Installed | 1,606,861 | 1,998,872 | 2,301,061 | 2,624,389 | 2,859,310 | 2,939,902 | 3,092,463 | 3,354,866 | 3,577,807 |
| Total Lines in Service | 1,428,623 | 1,691,114 | 1,910,078 | 2,291,028 | 2,594,659 | 2,824,395 | 3,086,069 | 3,349,307 | 3,422,596 |
| Employees | 17,179 | 17,041 | 15,638 | 14,453 | 13,762 | 12,956 | 13,397 | 13,490 | 14,040 |
| Lines/Employee | 83 | 99 | 122 | 159 | 189 | 218 | 277 | 331 | 369 |
| Lines in Service/100 Inhabitants | 11.8 | 10.7 | 11.8 | 14.0 | 16.0 | 17.1 | 17.7 | 18.8 | 19.1 |
| % Digital of Network | 12.0 | 32.4 | 54.4 | 72.2 | 85.6 | 95.6 | 100.0 | 100.0 | 100.0 |
| Public Telephones Installed | 11,048 | 15,814 | 20,524 | 25,173 | 28,494 | 32,583 | 46,039 | 57,932 | 71,407 |

Source: Telecom Argentina Annual Reports

Table 3-2  TELEFÓNICA DE ARGENTINA FINANCIAL AND OPERATING STATISTICS, 1991–1999
(fiscal years ending in September; data in millions of Argentine pesos, unless otherwise indicated)

| | 1991 | 1992 | 1993 | 1994 | 1995 | 1996 | 1997 | 1998 | 1999 |
|---|---|---|---|---|---|---|---|---|---|
| *Financial Performance* | | | | | | | | | |
| Revenues | 1,161 | 1,602 | 2,172 | 2,611 | 2,732 | 2,752 | 2,996 | 3,435 | 3,400 |
| Operating Profit | 219 | 371 | 558 | 660 | 716 | 742 | 906 | 918 | 922 |
| Net Income | 122 | 224 | 333 | 420 | 458 | 385 | 474 | 511 | 456 |
| Assets | 2,976 | 3,097 | 3,530 | 4,763 | 5,373 | 5,804 | 6,324 | 6,548 | 7,011 |
| Common Shareholder Equity | 2,440 | 2,472 | 2,602 | 3,133 | 3,350 | 3,492 | 3,717 | 3,184 | 3,340 |
| Capital Expenditures | 213 | 619 | 943 | 733 | 706 | 800 | 495 | 686 | 610 |
| Return on Sales (%) | 10.5 | 14.0 | 15.3 | 18.2 | 16.8 | 14.0 | 15.8 | 14.9 | 13.4 |
| Return on Assets (%) | 4.1 | 7.2 | 9.4 | 10.5 | 10.3 | 7.8 | 8.9 | 9.3 | 8.7 |
| Return on Equity (%) | 5.0 | 9.1 | 12.8 | 14.6 | 15.7 | 11.5 | 13.6 | 13.7 | 14.3 |
| *Operating Performance* | | | | | | | | | |
| Total Lines Installed | 2,023,078 | 2,257,771 | 2,666,527 | 3,013,448 | 3,562,123 | 3,911,965 | 4,118,185 | 4,232,756 | 4,384,041 |
| Total Lines in Service | 1,782,355 | 2,008,447 | 2,213,317 | 2,595,929 | 3,027,815 | 3,325,000 | 3,766,017 | 3,973,798 | 3,934,178 |
| Employees | 18,107 | 19,256 | 18,097 | 16,835 | 15,927 | 13,953 | 11,948 | 11,107 | 10,186 |
| Lines/Employee | 102 | 104 | 122 | 154 | 190 | 238 | 315 | 358 | 386 |
| Lines in Service/100 Inhabitants | 12.6 | 12.6 | 14.1 | 16.4 | 18.8 | 20.9 | 22.8 | 23.4 | 22.9 |
| % Digital of Network | 18.1 | 24.0 | 38.2 | 52.9 | 70.8 | 77.8 | 90.1 | 100.0 | 100.0 |
| Public Telephones Installed | 14,642 | 20,686 | 24,027 | 31,671 | 41,434 | 47,810 | 55,686 | 66,343 | 97,663 |

*Source: Telefónica de Argentina Annual Reports*

unions and the imposition of performance standards on the operators, the owners of Telefónica de Argentina and Telecom Argentina proved successful at creating and capturing value. In the next two chapters, we will examine how incumbents attempt to manage opportunity and risk in the new market economy.

# 4 ✦ *Transforming Corporate Governance and Strategy*

*Deregulation and privatization* offer extraordinary opportunities for incumbent enterprises confronting the reform bargain's new landscape. For owners and managers, the task of transforming these established firms may appear similar to engineering the turnaround of a corporation whose fortunes have languished under some combination of poor leadership and changing market conditions.[1] Yet, as we shall see in this chapter and the next, the transformation of incumbent enterprises after deregulation and privatization involves challenges that go well beyond those of a typical turnaround situation.

In the first place, the magnitude of the task is often formidable. Most incumbents' governance system, top management, organizational structure, internal systems, and other human and material resources are ill-suited for meeting the commercial opportunities and risks posed by liberalization. In some cases, operating and financial performance was so poor under the old system that the firm's ability to thrive in a more market-oriented environment may be highly questionable.

A second, and often more crucial, issue is the challenge of managing the evolution of the reform bargain itself. Although the reform bargain changes the rights and obligations of the incumbent and the state in significant ways, implementation and enforcement of the new arrangement is as yet untested. Indeed, parties that perceive themselves as losers in the new environment may strive to shape the bargain over time in ways detrimental to the incumbent. Conversely, if the incumbent's own fortunes wane in the new environment, *it* may seek relief through changes in the reform bargain's implementation or terms. Ultimately, incumbents' actions not only in the political arena—for example, lobbying and public relations activities—but also in the market—pricing, procurement, employment, and production policies—are likely to affect the bargain's evolution. Too often, however, incumbents tend to underemphasize the need to manage their reform bargain due to the immediacy of problems and opportunities in the commercial sphere and the mistaken belief that deregulation and privatization eliminate the need for political engagement. Although managers in traditional turnaround situations also need to consider the implications of their actions with respect to the state, these executives rarely face the degree of change and uncertainty characteristic of the early stages of market reform.

Not only is understanding the challenges of corporate transformation under the reform bargain important for owners, investors, and managers of incumbent enterprises, it is also highly relevant for actual and potential competitors, suppliers, customers, and other parties affected by the incumbents' activities in the market.[2] This second group of players may incorrectly assume that deregulation and privatization have little direct impact on their business and thereby overlook critical opportunities and risks associated with reforms.

In this chapter and the following, we draw on the case of National Power PLC,[3] a privatized British power generator operating in a deregulated market, to illustrate the key challenges of transformation faced by firms in the new market economy. This chapter focuses on challenges related to corporate governance and strategy, including government and public relations. In chapter 5, the transformational challenges posed by operating issues (human resources, technology and production, procurement, sales and marketing, and finance and control) are explored.[4] The analysis in both chapters includes comparative examples from the experiences of incumbents active in geographic and product markets beyond those of National Power. These examples, selected from among the most difficult situations confronting incumbents under the reform bargain, provide valuable insights into the experience of established firms after liberalization.

## THE BRITISH POWER SECTOR REFORM BARGAIN

During the 1930s and 1940s, the British government consolidated the nation's fragmented electric utility industry.[5] Power generation and transmission activities were placed under a single state-owned firm, the Central Electricity Generating Board (CEGB), while local distribution and sale of electricity was organized under twelve regional SOE monopolies known as area boards. During the late 1980s, the Thatcher government proposed that the industry be restructured and privatized and that the power generation market be deregulated. This initiative followed the privatization of a number of SOEs during the 1980s—British Leyland, British Telecom, British Airways, and British Gas, for example. The government's principal objectives in these sales included improving state finances, raising operating efficiency, and building broad-based public support for capitalism through individual ownership of shares in the former SOEs.

In 1990 the government sold its shares in the area boards through public offerings. Under this reform bargain, the area boards—renamed regional electric companies (RECs)—were granted joint ownership of the transmission system, the National Grid.[6] The government also established a new government body, the Office of Electricity Regulation (OFFER), to regulate prices charged for electricity transmission and distribution.[7] The nonnuclear plants of the former state-owned firm were divided into two companies—National Power and PowerGen; the government sold 60 percent of these companies' shares to the public in March 1991.[8] The CEGB's nuclear power plants were combined to form a new SOE, Nuclear Electric.[9] Under the reform bargain, the three incumbent generating companies plus new entrants would sell power into a national power pool at prices determined through half-hourly competitive bidding.[10] The new government body, OFFER, did not have the authority to regulate the wholesale price of electricity—that is, the price of power sold through the pool prior to transmission and distribution.

The reform bargain included several key transitional provisions. In March 1990, contracts locking in minimum power-sales volumes and target prices through March 1993 were established between individual power generators and the RECs. These "contracts for differences" were essentially hedging arrangements protecting each party from volatility in pool prices. They required compensating payments from the RECs to individual power generators when the target price exceeded the pool price, and from generators to the RECs under the opposite conditions. The generators and state-owned British Coal also signed three-year contracts, which specified declining minimum purchase volumes and prices in coal supply arrangements over time.[11] Finally, the British government was able to block unwanted takeovers of privatized power generators and RECs through its possession of a "special share" in each company. The terms of the special share gave the government the right to prohibit shareholdings above 15 percent in any of the firms, through March 1995 in the case of the RECs and indefinitely in the case of the power generators.

The terms of National Power's enterprise bargain and the bargains of other parties associated with the British electric power market shaped the opportunities and risks facing the privatized company following sector reforms. In subsequent years, National Power emerged as a highly profitable corporation with business activities extending increasingly beyond the borders of England. Yet the British government constrained the firm's freedom of strategic choice in various ways, and in 1997 required National Power to pay a windfall profits tax of £266 million. In addition, problems in its international diversification efforts and the resignation of the firm's chief executive in 1999 raised additional concerns regarding National Power's future prospects.

## GOVERNANCE AND LEADERSHIP

Broadly speaking, incumbents confront two principal challenges relating to governance and leadership under reform bargains in the age of the new market economy. First, the boards of these enterprises tend to face the demands of representing a new set of owners and forging strategy in markets in which the terms of the enterprise bargain and the bargains of other affected parties have undergone significant change. In this context, some or all members of the enterprise's prereform board of directors and top management may not match the firm's postreform governance and leadership needs. In particular, the increasing commercial opportunities and risks enterprises face under privatization and deregulation often imply that at a minimum, the composition of the board and top management should be adjusted to include individuals with greater expertise in the areas of commercial strategy and organizational restructuring. To the extent that the enterprise looks to expand (or contract) its activities with respect to other product or geographic markets—that is, to revise its corporate strategy—additional changes in governance and top management may be advisable in the postreform environment.

The second major challenge is a critical counterpart to the first: ensuring that the firm's board and top management not lose sight of the evolving nature of its enterprise bargain. Ultimately, the firm's long-term performance is influenced as much by the terms and enforcement of its bargain over time as by its actions in the marketplace. In effect, the firm's direct governance mechanism—typically a board of directors—is accountable not only to the firm's shareholders, but to all parties with the potential of shaping the evolution of the bargain. Thus, paradoxically, a governing board and top management team that does not integrate the interests of other affected parties into strategy design and implementation often fails to deliver the best long-term results for its shareholders. This situation is frustrating and confusing for boards and managers who view deregulation and privatization as sending the signal that commercial skills—as opposed to political skills—are keys to success in the new market economy. In the end, both are critical for the firm's long-term success. In the case of National Power, unfavorable shifts in its bargain with the British government, as well as its bargains in several foreign markets, raised concerns regarding the sustainability of its positive financial performance in the initial period following the reform bargain.

As is typical under reform bargains, privatization and deregulation created strong incentives for National Power to focus its strategy on maximizing profits. Private shareholders would evaluate National Power's performance based on measures such as share price appreciation and dividend yield, and not on other indicators important to previous government owners—such as job creation, regional development, and the viability of the British coal industry. Although the British government retained a 40 percent shareholding in National Power through March 1995, it did not attempt to use its minority holdings to influence company strategy.

The British government selected National Power's board members prior to privatization.[12] There were seven executive directors,[13] primarily senior managers from the CEGB, and six nonexecutive directors, primarily chief executives from other British corporations. National Power's first chief executive was John Baker, managing director of the CEGB from 1986 to privatization and a member of the CEGB board since 1979.

From a shareholder perspective, the composition of National Power's board embodied potential strengths and weaknesses. The considerable experience of the firm's executive directors at the CEGB—especially John Baker—suggested that these directors could leverage their knowledge of the organization to identify opportunities for efficiency improvements.

In addition, given their familiarity with the organization's culture and its human and material resources, these executives might be able to implement strategy more effectively than could executives drawn from outside the CEGB. Conversely, there was a risk that the former CEGB executives would lack both the toughness to implement necessary changes within the organization and the vision to design appropriate value-maximizing strategies for the firm in the postreform environment. The presence, however, of nonexecutive directors from outside the industry offered a counterweight to these concerns. Also, the threat of competitive pressures in the power market and investor pressure in the capital markets would tend to impose discipline on the board and top management.

The membership of National Power's board—particularly its executive directors—remained stable in the initial years after privatization. In the short term, the firm raised the efficiency of its operations and boosted its profitability. By the mid-1990s, however, National Power, faced with a stagnating share price and relatively limited growth opportunities in the home market, decided to accelerate its expansion into international power markets. John Baker became board chairman in April 1995, and Keith Henry, former CEO of the international engineering contractor Brown & Root, was named chief executive. By August 1996, the remaining (original) six executive directors had been replaced by a younger group of managers with considerably more international commercial experience. These changes reflected the board's desire to bring on a top management team better equipped to meet the demands of the revised strategic vision. Within four years of Henry's arrival, National Power's international investments rose from £147 million to £1.2 billion, while its British business remained profitable.

Eastern Electricity, one of the privatized regional electric companies (RECs), initially pursued a governance strategy similar to National Power's, naming the person who was its managing director under state ownership as its chief executive and filling other executive directorships with former area board managers. In the year following privatization, however, Eastern's operating and financial performance was disappointing, particularly when compared to that of other RECs; its share price lagged relative to this peer group. Under pressure from large institutional shareholders, Eastern's board replaced its chief executive with an outsider—John Devaney—experienced in corporate restructurings. Devaney subsequently assembled a new top management team, consisting primarily of executives drawn from outside Eastern, which succeeded in reversing the firm's lagging performance. As such, the Eastern case reveals the powerful impact of share price comparisons on spurring change in the governance of privatized enterprises—including monopolies not subject to direct competition in the (product) market.[14]

Corporate governance issues may be more complicated for the incumbent following the reform bargain if government entities retain a majority of shares in the enterprise. For example, a number of privatizations in Malaysia and elsewhere have involved the sale of only a minority of the firm's shares in a public offering. In 1992 Malaysia sold 25 percent of the shares in the national electric utility Tenaga Nasional Berhad in a public offering.[15] The remaining shares were held by various government entities, including the finance ministry (18 percent), the ministry of industry (17 percent), and state-owned banks and pension funds (40 percent). Under this ownership structure few changes initially emerged in the composition of Tenaga's board of directors and top management. In principle, the visibility of Tenaga's share price exerted pressure on the firm to focus on value creation and capture; the government, as majority owner, however, was able to pursue a broader range of objectives—including job preservation and gradualism in business redesign and organizational restructuring. Ultimately, the catalyst for change in Tenaga's leadership occurred in August 1996, when most of Malaysia experienced a sixteen-hour electricity blackout. Three weeks later, Tenaga's board brought on a new chief executive from outside the industry, with a reputation for rejuvenating government organizations, who proceeded to implement changes designed to improve both operating and financial performance.

Majority government ownership following the reform bargain does not inevitably create tensions between commercial and noncommercial objectives. When the German government prepared state-owned Deutsche Telekom (DT) for privatization, it created a new supervisory board of directors consisting of executives from the private sector and representatives from the public sector. Ron Sommer, former COO for Sony Corporation of America and Sony Europe was named chief executive, and initiated major reforms in the firm's strategy and organization prior to the government's sale of 25 percent of DT's shares to the public in November 1996. Ironically, in the period following the January 1998 deregulation of the German telecommunications market, Sommer complained that German regulatory authorities, under the strong influence of the new Social Democratic government, favored entrants at the expense of Deutsche Telekom, thereby subjecting the firm to considerable pressure in both its product and capital markets. The DT example shows that the multiple institutions of the state do not always act monolithically.

Some SOE reform bargains involve changes in governance but do not anticipate that even a minority ownership stake in the firm will be privatized. In New Zealand, the 1986 State-Enterprise Act required that state-owned entities providing commercial services be organized as corporations with a commercially oriented board of directors. The act also mandated entry deregulation in markets that the SOEs served and eliminated these firms' rights to operating subsidies from the state. In the years following passage of the legislation, the composition of the boards of directors of these SOEs changed dramatically, and even those enterprises remaining under state ownership achieved significant improvements in operating and financial performance.[16]

Despite the successes of corporatized SOEs in New Zealand, economists generally maintain that private ownership tends to provide superior incentives for operating efficiency, innovation, and overall value creation.[17] This prediction is supported, in fact, by evidence from New Zealand where corporatized companies, such as New Zealand Rail and Telecom Corporation of New Zealand, achieved significant additional gains in efficiency and profitability following privatization.

Under some privatizations, restrictions are placed on maximum or minimum shareholdings of particular owners—for example, foreign investors. Such restrictions may complicate the firm's governance and adversely affect operating and financial performance. Yet, ownership limits can serve a useful role in helping the firm internalize the interests of various parties affected by market reform. Argentina requires that 10 percent of the shares of a privatized firm be distributed to the company's workers, who are typically represented on the board of directors by a union official. The participation of local partners as minority shareholders in privatized firms such as Telefónica de Argentina and Telecom Argentina helps sensitize the firm to issues relating to national sovereignty.

At the same time, the general public may be more likely to support the interests of firms if it holds shares, either directly or indirectly through pension funds. Margaret Thatcher, for example, placed great emphasis on purchases of shares in privatized firms by the general public and customers of these enterprises. Although this approach did not result in a uniformly favorable evolution of British reform bargains—witness the windfall profits tax—the overall sustainability of these bargains has been impressive, even after the 1997 electoral victory of the Labor Party.

In sum, the above examples of corporate governance and leadership under the reform bargain suggest several conclusions. Reform bargains involving variations of privatization and deregulation tend to shift the composition of an incumbent's governing body (typically a board of directors) and its executive management to include a greater proportion of individuals with private sector commercial experience. Yet markets in which most reform bargains occur include features that, for the incumbent, make a purely commercial orientation problematical. Where issues of market power, basic goods access, and/or national security are widely perceived to be important, social expectations translate into explicit and implicit constraints on company behavior, even under the reform bargain. Explicit constraints include various restrictions and requirements regarding ownership, which can be seen as a means for shaping behavior through the structure of corporate governance. Alternatively, explicit limits on company strategy or profitability may appear as obligations in the reform bargain. For their part, implicit constraints are, in effect, invisible boundaries, which, once transgressed, trigger pressures from affected parties to modify the reform bargain's terms or enforcement. As such, designing and implementing a commercial strategy in the shadow of these implicit constraints is perhaps the greatest management challenge under the reform bargain—and one that ultimately tests the vision and leadership of the firm's board of directors and top executives.

## CORPORATE STRATEGY AND
## ORGANIZATIONAL STRUCTURE

At the time of liberalization, incumbents often find that the scope of their business activities and the structure of the enterprise are ill-suited for meeting the opportunities and risks of the reformed market. Many state-owned enterprises, for example, are sprawling organizations at the time of reform, having expanded in size and scope over time to create jobs and to reduce their dependence on supplier and other supporting markets by pursuing such activities in-house. Thus, prior to privatization, the Telecom Corporation of New Zealand built many of the chairs, tables, and desks used in its facilities.[18] Some SOEs likewise address the social needs of their employees or local communities, providing such things as housing, food services, and recreational activities as an adjunct to their primary commercial activities.

Incumbents used to operating in traditional regulated industries may also find themselves with bloated organizations at the time of the reform bargain, attributable, for example, to years of operating under reasonable profit guarantees and/or protection from competition. At the same time, the scope of the incumbents' operations in various geographic or product markets may have been significantly constrained under the old system. For example, until recently, commercial banks in the United States were not permitted to open branches outside of their home state, or offer investment banking, insurance, and a host of other financial services.[19] SOEs may also face restrictions on the scope of their business activities, particularly in foreign markets.[20]

Thus, incumbents typically confront competing tensions in defining the scope of their business at the time the reform bargain comes into force. First, the board and top management often perceive the need to focus on defining the core business (or businesses) and adjusting the organizational design of the company to improve efficiency and profitability. Implementing the firm's strategy in this area frequently requires divesting lines of businesses outside the core. It also tends to involve restructuring the core business—for example, shifting from organizational structures based on functional or geographic divisions to profit or cost centers organized around specific products and/or customer segments. This effort may also lead to outsourcing certain activities formerly provided in-house. At least in the short term, an emphasis on the core business often means shrinking the incumbent's workforce and physical assets.[21]

Rarely, however, will the incumbent's long-term strategic vision be confined to retrenchment. In some cases, the firm will seek to increase sales of its traditional goods and services, leveraging off improvements in operating efficiency. The incumbent may also build on its existing resources and capabilities to expand the scope of its activities.[22] If the incumbent faces increased competition in its core business under the reform bargain, an extension in the range of activities can be seen as having both defensive and offensive motives.

Once again, the experience of National Power illustrates issues related to business definition. Recall that prior to liberalization, National Power was part of a state enterprise that produced and transmitted virtually all of Britain's electric power; after privatization, four enterprises emerged, each with a narrower scope of business than its SOE predecessor. National Power started out with a single line of business: generating electric power for the British market via nonnuclear (primarily coal-based) production technology. Initially, the firm worked to improve the efficiency of its core generation business, making progress far beyond the gains projected at the time of privatization. It shut down or sold off over one-third of its generating capacity and reduced its workforce by 60 percent during its first three years after reform. Over time, however, National Power broadened the scope of its business in three directions, expanding into (1) natural-gas-fueled generation, (2) power generation outside the United Kingdom, and (3) retail power sales. Although National Power's move into gas-fueled generation could be considered an extension of its core business, the expansions into international markets and retail sales represented more fundamental attempts to diversify beyond the core business.

American Airlines also pursued a "retrench, then build" strategy following U.S. airline deregulation.[23] Recall from chapter 2 that this large incumbent lost over $100 million in early 1980, as the second international oil shock and the surge of competition exposed the inefficiency of American's operations. In response, CEO Bob Crandall terminated service along a number of far-flung routes so as to concentrate more than two-thirds of the carrier's traffic through its Dallas/Fort Worth Airport hub. American rationalized its administrative operations as well, selling its expensive New York City flagship building and consolidating its staff in a new Dallas/Fort Worth headquarters. Throughout the early years of the reform bargain, American continued to invest in its SABRE computer reservation system—a business highly complementary to its transport activities—which Crandall viewed as integral to the carrier's long-term success. Only after returning to profitability in 1983 did American begin to expand its route system in the United States and, later, into an increasing number of international markets.

An extreme example of an incumbent's business and structural transformation is provided by the state-owned Argentine oil company YPF SA.[24] In 1990 Argentine president Menem appointed former Baker Hughes executive José ("Pepe") Estenssoro to prepare the nation's largest enterprise for privatization. Estenssoro saw tremendous potential in the company, despite its dubious distinction of being among the world's few money-losing oil companies, having amassed deficits of $6 billion during the 1980s. One of his earliest initiatives was to divest the assets the enterprise had accumulated over the years that were tangential to its vertically integrated petroleum business—such as real estate, hotels, and miscellaneous manufacturing and service operations. Estenssoro went even further, however, selling off oil exploration and production assets viewed as holding little long-term strategic value. During this period, Estenssoro also restructured YPF's core business operations, dividing the firm's upstream (exploration and production) and downstream (distribution) activities into separate business units to enhance effectiveness in planning, implementation, and performance evaluation. Ultimately, these structural adjustments paved the way for extensive changes in YPF's personnel and systems. The impact of this transformation was demonstrated vividly by the nearly 90 percent reduction in YPF's workforce from 1990 to 1993 and by the $3.04 billion paid by investors in a June 1993 public offering of 44 percent YPF shares. Again, as in the case of National Power and American Airlines, only after an initial period of retrenchment did YPF begin to expand the scope of its business, particularly into international markets.

YPF's decision to create separate divisions for its upstream and downstream operations is typical of vertically integrated incumbents following the reform bargain. The Malaysian electric utility Tenaga, for example, created three separate divisions for its generation, transmission, and distribution activities at the time of privatization. Similarly, as part of its process of corporatization, Deutsche Bahn, the German state-owned railway, replaced an organizational structure based primarily on geographic regions with a holding company structure consisting of four major business units, including one cost center—Rail Infrastructure—and three profit centers: Freight Transport, Long Distance Passenger Transport, and Local Passenger Transport.[25] Similarly, the regional structure of Telstra, the former state-owned Australian telephone company, was reorganized into a network division plus three separate divisions serving residential, business, and large corporate customers. In general, incumbents often adopt new organizational structures that permit more effective management of costs, on the one hand, and more effective segmentation of customers, on the other.

The state restructures some enterprises at the time of the reform bargain, often as a means for reducing their postreform market power. Probably the most extreme example of this type of restructuring involved British Rail. Not only was the gateway monopoly of tracks and stations, RailTrack, separated from the rest of the enterprise, but the remainder of the SOE was divided into almost seventy entities at the time of privatization. The individual pieces consisted of companies in the train/locomotive leasing business (rolling stock companies—ROSCOs), freight transport franchisees, passenger transport franchisees, and rail and station maintenance companies.[26] This extraordinary restructuring allowed for focused management of the many activities formerly provided by the British Rail monopoly. In contrast, all of the restructuring carried out by Deutsche Bahn took place within the firm under a corporatized governance structure. Although the German approach had the potential advantage of preserving cost advantages of scale and scope economies in the business, the British approach tended to harness the power of the profit motive and benchmark competition to improve efficiency.

From the perspective of the evolving bargain, restructuring that occurs prior to the full implementation of market reform tends to produce a more stable bargain over time, but typically at the cost of a slower process of change. Structural change within Deutsche Bahn, for example, has taken place thus far under government ownership. Although the pace of change as measured by the speed of layoffs, asset disposals, efficiency improvements, and profit increases has been slower than that associated with the former British Rail, the process has been subject to far less public acrimony. Disputes regarding profiteering, erosion of service quality, and adequacy of investment have clouded the legitimacy of the British rail-industry reform bargain following privatization and have led to changes in terms and enforcement over time. Tensions such as these are particularly common when the incumbent produces a basic good or service and continues to possess a substantial degree of market power under the reform bargain.

## Diversification

We have seen that similar to many firms in turnaround situations, incumbents often initially need to focus on achieving efficiency improvements in their core business. This process typically entails the divestment of unrelated businesses or other assets not considered central to the firm's new mission. Subsequently, however, the slimmed-down firm frequently will expand into other product and geographic markets. This progression is quite common among established enterprises under reform bargains, particularly as a result of newfound strategic freedom, significantly enhanced financial position, and the glow of success from improvements achieved in the core business. In addition, incumbents' desire to explore opportunities in other product and geographic markets may be spurred by increased competition in its core market or by restrictions on its right to expand its horizontal and vertical reach within its traditional sector.

However, though some incumbents' diversification efforts have been extremely successful, many have ended in failure—or at best with mixed results—in large part because the costs and risks associated with these initiatives have not been fully appreciated. These costs include not only direct financial losses, but also indirect costs associated with a shift in management's attention away from core business operations. In addition, negative reactions by the general public or government officials to diversification efforts can lead to unfavorable changes in the reform bargain.

The relationship between the incumbent's corporate strategy and its evolving bargain with the state, therefore, often entails a number of tensions and trade-offs. Incumbents' right to pursue mergers or acquisitions with other firms operating in the same market is usually conditioned on some form of antitrust review. Although the incumbent may have a strong argument for its strategy based on anticipated gains in scale and scope economies, its potential gains in (and exercise of) market power may pose too great a threat to government concerns regarding concentration of economic and political power. These concerns tend to be even stronger when the incumbent is foreign-owned. The incumbent's attempts to pursue vertical integration also will tend to face explicit or implicit restrictions under the reform bargain if vertical restructuring played a critical role in the initial reform program.

A government tends to be particularly wary of an incumbent's attempts to leverage market power associated with control over monopoly infrastructure by expanding its scope of activities to include goods and services that are difficult or impossible to provide without access to the monopoly infrastructure. For example, the U.S. Baby Bells' attempts to leverage their near-monopoly control of local telephone networks to enter the long-distance business have met stiff resistance from long-distance telecommunications firms and government institutions. Often, the challenge for incumbents in these instances is to provide credible evidence that other politically influential parties will also benefit (or at least not be net losers) from extensions of horizontal and vertical scope. In late 1998, the Baby Bells secured support for their attempt to expand their scope of activities from a major group of communications equipment manufacturers and, in 1999, Bell Atlantic was granted the right to sell long-distance services in New York.

Even if an incumbent with control over critical infrastructure secures approval to extend the scope of its activities, it may be required to create separate organizational units for the provision of monopoly versus competitive services. This practice is referred to as "ring fencing," for example, in the British water industry. In this context, the incumbent faces a distinct set of rights and obligations with respect to local monopoly water system assets, as opposed to other businesses, such as the sale of household water filtration systems and investments in international water systems. If the incumbent is seen as abusing its monopoly position following the adoption of the reform bargain, the firm will often incur penalties under terms of the existing bargain or face revision of the terms of the bargain to its disadvantage.

The enthusiasm with which many incumbents have plunged into new businesses and geographic markets under the reform bargain is perhaps best conveyed by the metaphor of "the kid in the candy store." The case of CSX Corporation, a U.S. railroad, provides a vivid example of this phenomenon.[27] CSX was formed in 1980 as a merger of two railroads at the time of U.S. deregulation of the interstate rail transport and motor carrier markets. CSX focused initially on achieving operating improvements in its core rail transport business and successfully increased cash flow and profitability. Yet over time, the firm's top management came to view the railroads as a mature industry that offered few investment opportunities commensurate with the firm's cost of capital. The executives became increasingly intrigued with the firm's freedom, under the terms of its reform bargain, to expand the scope of its business outside the rail industry. By 1986 CSX had expanded into a number of other businesses selected on the basis of their high historical returns and anticipated synergies with the firm's expertise in the areas of long-distance transportation and facilities management. Yet the resulting acquisition of a natural gas pipeline company, participation in the development of a fiber-optic network, and investments in real estate proved disastrous. By 1989 CSX had divested these businesses and used the proceeds to repurchase 38 percent of the firm's outstanding shares.[28]

The CSX story, although perhaps an extreme example of corporate strategy run amok under the reform bargain, is not unique. International diversification is another area rife with peril for incumbents.[29] In the early 1990s Thames Water PLC, the parent holding company of the privatized British utility Thames Water Ltd., reasoned that its success in improving the operating efficiency and financial performance of the London water system made it eminently qualified to build and operate water systems in other countries. Yet its initial strategy of pursuing international business through contracting subsidiaries based outside the United Kingdom ended in failure. In 1993, the firm took a £25 million write-off on Egyptian contract work performed by its U.S.-based subsidiary Portals Water Treatment (PWT). By 1996 poor results at PWT and Thames Water's German Utag subsidiary resulted in the sale of these and several smaller entities, a £95 million write-off, and the resignation of the firm's chief executive.[30] The retreat of the U.S. utilities Entergy and PacifiCorp from their domestic and international diversification strategies in the late 1990s provides additional examples of questionable efforts to expand the scope of an incumbent's business under the reform bargain.

Top managers of established enterprises sometimes justify their expansion into new product and geographic markets under the reform bargain by arguing that this strategy will allow the firm to diversify its risks. It is unclear, however, why individual shareholders in these firms would not be able to diversify risk through less costly means—and in a manner reflecting their own preferences for risk—by investing in a diversified portfolio of financial assets. Paradoxically, it would appear that diversification into areas where the incumbent lacks expertise along one or more critical dimensions—including management of government and public relations in the target market—may actually *increase* the risks faced by the firm. Although these potential pitfalls of diversification apply to any firm, postreform incumbents are particularly susceptible to these problems given the typical contextual factors mentioned above: greatly enhanced opportunity combined with inexperience.

Some incumbents argue that performance problems associated with initial diversification efforts may obscure the important learning benefits of these investments. Based on experiences gained in its early investments abroad, for example, Thames Water has refocused its diversification efforts under a new management team, participating in consortia focused on building and operating international water infrastructure projects. Although the results of this revised strategy appeared very encouraging through early 2000, only time will tell if the long-term returns on this incumbent's diversification strategy will be sufficient to recover the initial losses.

In another example, American utilities acquiring British RECs have argued that a portion of the return on these investments will take the form of lessons learned in the more deregulated British market that can be applied in the United States when comparable changes are implemented in the home market bargain. Yet the value of these anticipated benefits is difficult to quantify and may take years to emerge.

In contrast to these more questionable cases, a relatively successful example of international diversification is found in the experience of the former state-controlled Spanish telephone company, Telefónica de España (TdE).[31] TdE's first significant foray abroad was in 1989 with the purchase of a 10 percent share of the Chilean international telephone company, Empresa Nacional de Telecomunicaciones de Chile. In 1990, TdE acquired 50 percent of Compañía de Teléfonos de Chile, the former state-owned local telephone monopoly, from Bond Corp. International. That same year, TdE took the lead role in the consortium awarded a controlling share in the privatized Telefónica de Argentina. A number of factors contributed to TdE's subsequent success in these ventures, including its knowledge of the Latin American context and the region's telecommunications sector through its relationship as an equipment supplier to the former state-owned telephone companies. The strong historical ties between Latin American and Spanish governments, as well as the common linguistic, cultural, and legal traditions of the countries appeared to play important roles in ensuring the favorable evolution of TdE's bargain and performance in these markets. TdE subsequently built on its experience in Chile and Argentina, taking stakes in privatized telephone companies in Puerto Rico, Peru, and Brazil. In early 2000, the firm consolidated its position in the region by purchasing all outstanding shares in its principal Latin American ventures.[32]

In some instances, incumbents have created successful product diversification through innovative use of physical assets in alternative applications. Several railroads, including Deutsche Bahn, the French SNCF, and New Zealand Rail have used internal communications systems and rights of way along rail properties to offer bulk telecommunications services, typically in joint ventures with entrants in deregulated national telecommunications markets. Similarly, the British National Grid PLC formed a new telecommunications firm, Energis, upgrading its existing communications assets and rights of way along its electricity transmission network. In these situations, incumbents have typically captured the value created by these unrelated diversifications by spinning off the new business instead of attempting to manage them over the long term. For example, National Grid sold 25 percent of Energis in 1997 in an initial public offering for £220 million. Even after selling an additional 25 percent in January 2000 for £1 billion, National Grid's remaining shareholdings in Energis accounted for 78 percent of the parent firm's market value.[33]

Privatized and corporatized airports have also demonstrated creativity in capturing value from physical assets under the reform bargain. BAA, the former British Airports Authority, recognized the tremendous potential for transforming underutilized areas within airports into premium retail space. BAA, in effect, became part luxury mall developer, leasing space in its airports to Hermes, Bally Shoes International, and other well-known retailers. The strategy has been extraordinarily successful with retailers such as Bally achieving higher sales per square foot in London's Heathrow Airport than at any other of the firm's outlets.[34] The corporatized Auckland Airport Authority initiated a series of joint ventures with private companies to develop retail and industrial space on land owned by the airport but apart from the terminal building, runways, and other traditional facilities. To support this effort, it also entered into a joint venture with the local municipality to develop a second access road to the airport.[35]

As for National Power, its corporate strategy proved largely disappointing by the end of the 1990s. Regarding its international strategy, one of the firm's most difficult experiences has been in Pakistan, where a power purchase agreement signed with a prior government came under dispute in 1998 with officials in the subsequent administration. The new regime claimed that the terms of the original bargain were unenforceable since the negotiations allegedly were tainted by corruption. Because Pakistan's judicial system lacks significant independence from the sitting government, the efforts of National Power and its consortium partners to resolve the dispute remained fruitless through early 2000. Other international diversification efforts, although less problematic, had yet to make a substantial contribution to National Power's bottom line by the end of the 1990s relative to the investments incurred.

In the home market, the British government, concerned about market power, blocked National Power's initial attempt at vertical integration into regional electricity distribution in the mid-1990s. In 1999, however, the government permitted National Power to purchase the electricity supply business of the REC Midlands Electricity. Approval was apparently granted as a quid pro quo for National Power's surprise offer to divest its largest generating facility, the 4,000 MW Drax plant, which represented about 40 percent of the firm's remaining generation capacity.[36] During this period, National Power also acquired Calortex, a retail supplier of natural gas, and attempted, but failed, to negotiate a merger with United Utilities, a distributor of electricity and water. In the words of one observer, "National Power's strategy appeared increasingly incoherent to City investors,"[37] who questioned the firm's diversification moves within the United Kingdom and abroad. In April 1999 chief executive Keith Henry resigned. Sir John Collins, who had succeeded John Baker as National Power chairman in June 1997, became acting chief executive while the firm searched for new executive leadership. Meanwhile, National Power announced that it would reduce its 2000 dividend and implement an austerity program to reduce operating costs.

As the preceding discussion suggests, National Power's postreform strategic options and, ultimately, its performance continued to be affected significantly by its relationship with government institutions and the general public. In the following section, we will explore the management challenges associated with government and public relations under the reform bargain—in general, and with respect to National Power.

## GOVERNMENT AND PUBLIC RELATIONS

Under the terms of the reform bargain, the mix of incumbent's rights and obligations is altered, typically in ways that enhance freedoms in the marketplace, while reducing restrictions, requirements, and entitlements. The reform bargain also includes mechanisms to interpret and enforce the adapted rights and obligations. A critical challenge for the incumbent is managing the evolution of its reformed enterprise bargain, particularly since many of the rights, obligations, and enforcement mechanisms will be new, or at least untested in their reconfigured form. This shift may confront the incumbent with new or unfamiliar government institutions, or new rules within established institutional arrangements.

With respect to the institutions responsible for interpreting and enforcing the reform bargain, the incumbent may face three alternative situations. First, the firm may confront a newly created regulatory body with jurisdiction over certain rights and obligations. National Power, for example, found that OFFER (the Office of Electricity Regulation), a government institution established at the time of the reform bargain, was authorized to take actions to "promote competition in the generation and supply of electricity."[38] The breadth and vagueness of this mandate, however, left considerable room for interpretation as to the types of restrictions or requirements that OFFER could impose on firms such as National Power. Although OFFER's newly appointed chief, Professor Stephen Littlechild, was a well-known scholar of economic regulation,[39] the institution was effectively a blank slate at the start of the reform bargain. In fact, the creation of new regulatory bodies to oversee the operation of privatized firms is quite common, particularly in telecommunications, public utility, and transport markets.

A second situation faced by many incumbents involves interaction with established regulatory bodies, previously irrelevant to the incumbent, that obtain authority over certain rights and obligations under the reform bargain. Antitrust (competition) agencies often fall into this category since prior to the reform bargain, incumbent's pricing, merger, and acquisition activities usually are controlled directly by the government owner (in the case of an SOE) or an industry-specific regulatory body (in the case of a private company). The British Monopolies and Mergers Commission (MMC) and the Office of Fair Trading (OFT), for instance, took on relevance for National Power following privatization since British antitrust laws defined the basic limits on a firm's behavior with respect to market competition. Although National Power's predecessor, the CEGB, had little experience with this institution,[40] the MMC would prove quite important under the reform bargain in light of frequent allegations of anticompetitive behavior on the part of British power generators (discussed in more detail below). Recall that American Airlines' reform bargain significantly increased the relevance of antitrust oversight by the U.S. Department of Justice and the Department of Transportation.

A third challenge for the incumbent may involve dealing with a familiar government institution that is responsible for enforcing revised terms under the reform bargain. The CEGB, for example, reported to the secretary of state for energy, which held the authority to regulate virtually every aspect of the enterprise's behavior. Following privatization, the authority of the secretary of state for trade and industry (the successor to the secretary of state for energy) over National Power's bargain was much more indirect, ruling for instance on appeals of decisions by the MMC. In the United States, deregulation has modified the rights and obligations enforced by certain government institutions in the areas of pricing and profit. For example, state regulatory bodies with jurisdiction over local telephone companies now employ price caps or other forms of incentive regulation in evaluating incumbent's pricing behavior, as opposed to the rate-of-return approach central to most prereform bargains in the sector. A comparable change has also affected many incumbents in the local gas distribution and electric utility markets. In all of these cases, despite a perhaps long-standing relationship with the government institution, the incumbent still may find it challenging to assess the potential risks and opportunities associated with the new terms of the reform bargain under the institution's jurisdiction.

Occasionally, a regulatory institution is actually eliminated under the reform bargain. The U.S. Airline Deregulation Act, for example, phased the Civil Aeronautics Board (CAB) out of existence. Although the CAB's demise reflected the removal of explicit entry barriers and pricing restrictions on domestic flights, the reform bargain linked carriers to a number of other government institutions including, for example, the Federal Aviation Administration, the Departments of Transportation and Justice, the court system, municipal governments, and even the presidency.

Whether incumbents face new or unfamiliar government institutions, or simply confront changes in the terms of the bargain under well-known regulatory bodies, these enterprises are operating under conditions that are new and untested. In this context, it may be difficult to predict how these institutions will interpret, and how effectively they will enforce, the terms of the bargain. In fact, the institutions charged with implementing the bargain may possess considerable discretion in carrying out their responsibilities, as suggested above in the case of OFFER. By ignoring these institutions, the incumbent may miss opportunities for shaping a more favorable environment for its interests, while at the same time risk the adverse consequences that may flow from active pressure of competitors, suppliers, buyers, and external parties on these governmental bodies.

The risks tend to be particularly salient for incumbents operating in markets in which concerns about market power, sovereignty, broad-based access, or safety are present at the time of the reform bargain, or are likely to emerge. The experience of Yorkshire Water,[41] a British SOE privatized in 1989, provides an example of these risks.

Following privatization, Yorkshire Water established a regulatory affairs function to manage its relationship with the newly created government body, Ofwat (Office of Water Regulation). Under the reform bargain, Ofwat was authorized to set a cap on annual changes in the prices charged by the privatized water companies over a ten-year period, which in Yorkshire's case amounted to an annual increase of 3 percent plus the rate of inflation.[42] Although Yorkshire Water did engage in limited outreach to local environmental groups during its early years under privatization, its strategy was mostly inward-looking, directed at achieving increases in productivity and profitability under a top management team almost entirely held over from the SOE era.

In 1995 the Yorkshire region experienced a drought of historic proportions.[43] In early summer, Yorkshire Water imposed hosepipe bans (restrictions on outdoor water usage) and urged customers to reduce their indoor water consumption. As the crisis mounted, the firm encouraged local businesses to reduce water usage by limiting factory washdowns and employee showers, extending staff holidays, and shifting production to sites outside the Yorkshire area. These suggestions were met with outrage from business leaders, one of whom described the proposal as "impractical and an affront."[44] Meanwhile the firm announced that if water consumption was not reduced by 25 percent, it would be necessary to implement rotating twenty-four-hour cutoffs, supplemented by emergency water access via standpipes placed throughout the community. The firm's growing public relations nightmare only became worse when Yorkshire Water's managing director declared in September that "I personally haven't had a bath or shower now for three months, and nobody has noticed. You can wash adequately in half a bowl of water."[45] Within twenty-four hours, he clarified that he had not taken baths at home, but instead with relatives living outside Yorkshire. Consumers found the company's growing admonitions against water "wastage" particularly galling, since approximately one-third of the water entering Yorkshire's distribution network was lost in leakage.[46]

Several additional factors predating the drought contributed to the local community's cynicism toward the company. Yorkshire Water's workforce was cut back substantially after privatization, while its executive compensation, profits, and dividends increased significantly alongside higher water rates. At the same time, Ofwat criticized the firm for the increasing frequency of water supply interruptions. In 1994 the company angered certain community and small shareholder groups by successfully opposing the candidacy of Diana Scott, former chair of Yorkshire's Community Services Committee of Ofwat, to the board of Yorkshire Water PLC.[47]

In the fall of 1995, with a full-fledged crisis looming, Yorkshire Water adopted extraordinary measures to avert service curtailment, trucking in over 70,000 tonnes per day of water during the worst of the shortages and spending a total of £47 million on these and other emergency activities. To provide relief from future droughts, the firm constructed two new pipelines designed to connect rivers in the eastern portion of the county to dry towns in the west. The pipelines were completed in record time at a cost of £110 million.[48]

In January 1996 Yorkshire's board of directors commissioned an independent inquiry into the company's response to the drought under the direction of John Uff, a fellow of the Royal Academy of Engineering and a professor of law at London University. While the investigation was under way, Yorkshire Water PLC's chairman, Sir Gordon Jones, was replaced by Brandon Gough, former chairman of Coopers & Lybrand, and managing director Trevor Newton was replaced by Dr. Kevin Bond, former chief executive of the National Rivers Authority.[49] In addition, Yorkshire Water's board was expanded to include additional members, such as a director of communications with extensive public relations experience hired during the drought.

The firm took full responsibility for the deficiencies presented in the Uff Commission's final report, which criticized Yorkshire Water and its regulators for their contributions to the crisis and offered a number of recommendations.[50] Bond himself apologized to the public for the inconvenience caused by Yorkshire Water's actions and for the firm's failure to consult and communicate adequately with the community. Bond also noted that many of the report's recommendations were already being implemented.[51] Ofwat subsequently penalized the firm the equivalent of £40 million by reducing its allowable rate of return for the following year. The regulator also imposed a number of additional conditions, including the appointment of two nonexecutive directors with relevant experience and understanding of customers' interests to Yorkshire Water's board of directors.

Meanwhile Yorkshire Water began rebuilding relationships with local municipalities throughout the service territory, in effect renewing ties that had existed during the era of state ownership, when municipal representatives had held seats on the SOE board. These relationships, designed to improve the two-way flow of information and facilitate contingency planning, would have proven extremely valuable during the drought. Within the firm, more emphasis was placed on training in the area of customer relations. Yorkshire Water's new communications strategy entailed much greater openness with the media, including greater accessibility of the managing director. This enhanced openness was extended as well in the firm's relationship with Ofwat.[52]

During the years following the drought, Yorkshire steadily rebuilt its reputation in the community. More important, it appeared that the firm was much better positioned to deal with contingencies, whether in the form of major external shocks, such as droughts, or more day-to-day concerns of affected parties and regulators, such as progress on investment programs and water quality improvements.

Many of the actions taken by Yorkshire Water following the drought simply represented good management practices. Yet its efforts in the area of government and public relations were particularly important given the number of "hot button" characteristics of its market and product from the standpoint of the public. These features included the absence of competition, the service's status as a basic necessity, and the critical nature of product quality. Ultimately, if the firm could not allay the public's concerns in these areas—in other words, fulfill its explicit and implicit obligations under the reform bargain—it was unlikely that it would be able to sustain its right to earn a reasonable return on its long-term sunk investments. The irony of Yorkshire Water's position was perhaps most succinctly described by British environment secretary John Gummer: "Privatization subjects companies to public control."[53]

Three years after Yorkshire Water's drought crisis, a privatized firm halfway around the world grappled with an external shock of similar proportions. Light Serviços de Eletricidade SA, the former state-owned electricity distributor for the Brazilian state of Rio de Janeiro, was overwhelmed by the effects of a record heat wave that led to widespread power blackouts and brownouts over several months. In the face of sub-stantial opposition spearheaded by public sector unions, the Brazilian government had sold a majority stake in the enterprise in 1996 to a four-firm consortium including Electricité de France, U.S.-based Houston Industries Energy and AES, and the Brazilian steel giant, Companhia Siderúrgica Nacional SA.[54] Fears that the foreign owners would exploit their monopoly position and Brazil's weak regulatory system to profit at the expense of the Brazilian people seemed to many to be borne out by the repeated service failures during the heat wave.

In their defense, Rio Light's owners asserted that the condition of the distribution system was in much worse shape than they had realized at the time of the purchase. In fact, they believed that the extent of the blackouts would have been even more extreme if Rio Light had con-fronted the heat wave under its previous state ownership. Yet the owners lost the battle of public opinion. As a result of the service failures, Rio Light was fined the equivalent of $1.8 million and required to accelerate its investments in the distribution system.[55]

One of the ironies for Rio Light's foreign owners was that the very fea-tures that initially attracted them to the privatization—the opportunity to purchase a controlling stake in an underperforming company operating as a monopoly under a new, weak regulatory system at a very attractive price—all became liabilities in the midst of the crisis. Rio Light became iso-lated and a perfect target for the wrath of frustrated electricity consumers, workers laid off from privatized enterprises, and members of the general public who resented the sale of national assets on the cheap to foreigners. Still, the venture's fate would probably have been much worse were it not for the participation of a local partner, Companhia Siderúrgica Nacional SA, Brazilian government entities, and Light employees in the privatized firm's ownership structure. In fact, after the initial furor of the blackouts died down, Rio Light was able to steadily rebuild its reputation with sub-stantial improvements in reliability achieved during the following year.

In National Power's case, tension with government institutions and the general public resulted not from issues relating to quantity or quality of production, but instead to prices. Under the reform bargain, Britain's power pool system was expected to result in a highly competitive spot market for electricity. In theory, power companies would identify (on a half-hourly basis) their lowest cost generation options at various levels of production. The pool price paid to the generators for power during a specific half-hour interval would reflect the cost of the most expensive source required to meet actual demand. The price would also include an additional fee (the "capacity charge") compensating the companies for the availability of backup capacity during periods of high demand. Given the presence of excess generating capacity at the time of privatization, the deregulation of entry in the power generation sector, and the emergence of low-cost CCGT technology, spot prices for power were expected to decline steadily and significantly over time.

In fact, spot prices exhibited a surprising trend: initially falling, but then rising after the first few months of trading. This trend spurred an investigation by Stephen Littlechild of OFFER, who was concerned about the effects of these unregulated prices on the final rates paid by retail customers.[56] Although the contracts for differences offset increases in pool prices to some extent, these prices were still relevant for two reasons. The initial contracts for differences were valid for only three years, and thus would have to be renegotiated. Presumably the higher the pool prices, the higher the hedged price the generators would be able to secure with RECs (or other buyers) in the terms of the new contracts.[57] Also, some buyers purchased power directly at the pool price without the use of long-term contracts.

In theory, National Power and PowerGen could manipulate pool prices in several ways.[58] The generators might declare usable low-cost plants unavailable at certain times, so that the pool price would be determined by the (higher) operating costs of less efficient plants.[59] They might also retire capacity prematurely so as to exaggerate capacity constraints and increase compensation for the availability of backup capacity. Alternatively, the generators might simply overstate the costs associated with marginal capacity. After investigating National Power's and PowerGen's actions relating to the pool, Littlechild threatened, in February 1994, to refer the companies to the MMC for further investigation unless (1) average pool prices declined during the following two years and (2) the generators sold 6,000 MW of capacity to rival firms.

During subsequent years, the power generators and Littlechild played a game of cat and mouse. Average pool prices declined somewhat, as did retail prices to consumers. However, unusually high spikes in pool prices emerged from time to time, causing Littlechild to threaten unspecified actions. After some delay, the generators sold 6,000 MW of capacity to the REC, Eastern Electricity. However, the complex terms on which the deal was structured did not appear to increase competition in the pool, at least in the short term.[60]

In October 1995 National Power made a bid to acquire the REC Southern Electric PLC. Littlechild opposed the takeover, particularly because it would allow National Power to absorb Southern Electric's current and potential future investments in competing independent power producers (IPPs).[61] The MMC reviewed the merger and in March 1996 recommended that it be permitted, on the condition that National Power divest all of Southern Electric's IPP holdings—a condition accepted by the firm. In a rare move, however, the secretary of state for trade and industry overruled the MMC's recommendation.[62] The minister's decision appeared to reflect broad public opposition to the merger, ranging from consumer advocacy groups to such mainstream observers as *The Economist* magazine.[63] Later that year, U.S.-based Southern Company attempted to acquire National Power, having already purchased South Western Electricity, a REC with holdings in IPP assets. When the British government signaled that approval was unlikely, the Southern Company abandoned its effort, effectively denying National Power's shareholders the opportunity for a substantial takeover premium. It is noteworthy that both of these unfavorable developments in National Power's bargain came under the Conservative government, which had originally implemented privatization and deregulation in the sector. Apparently, given public dissatisfaction with the outcomes of electricity sector reforms, the low standing of the Conservatives in opinion polls, and the prospect of national elections in 1997, the government decided to yield to popular pressure.

The election of the Labor government in 1997 brought new risks and opportunities to National Power's evolving bargain. As promised during the campaign, the new government imposed a windfall profits tax on all of Britain's privatized utilities.[64] National Power moved quickly to build bridges with the government, supporting strategies to benefit the coal industry and agreeing in late 1998 to divest its large Drax generating facility, in exchange for the right to pursue vertical integration through the acquisition of REC supply assets. The government's consent was probably helped by the fact that it was under little public pressure to rebuff the firm—after all, the "pound of flesh" had already been extracted through the windfall profits tax.

With these developments, National Power seemed to have succeeded in transforming its government and public relations strategy from a liability into an asset. Yet, by early 1999 Britain's electricity generators were under attack again—this time from Callum McCarthy, Steven Littlechild's successor at OFFER and soon-to-be head of the new combined gas and electricity regulatory body, Ofgem (Office of Gas and Electricity Markets). McCarthy accused power producers of "gaming" the pool pricing mechanism and threatened aggressive measures if the practices continued.

The examples of Yorkshire Water, Rio Light, and National Power each explored the effectiveness of the incumbent's government and public relations strategy after the adoption of the reform bargain. In some cases, however, the incumbent may be able to influence the terms of the reform bargain through its strategy in the government and public arena during the reform process itself. For example, New England Electric System (NEES), a vertically integrated Massachusetts-based utility,[65] anticipated in the early 1990s that the state government would eventually adopt legislation substantially reforming the terms of enterprise bargains in the state's electricity market.[66] NEES was especially concerned that entry deregulation involving mandatory opening of transmission and distribution systems to competing generators might leave the firm unable to fully recover its prior investments in generation assets—particularly high-cost nuclear facilities.

Instead of waiting passively for the legislature to design the reform bargain, NEES, under the leadership of President and Chief Executive John Rowe, worked to create a model bargain that would address its own concerns, as well as important objectives of other affected parties, including greater ease of entry for competitors, lower consumer prices, and avoidance of environmental quality degradation.[67] In preparing its proposal, dubbed the "Grand Bargain," NEES consulted extensively with former regulators, independent power companies, and environmental groups.[68] Most of the key principles included in the resulting design proposal were adopted in the plan submitted by the Massachusetts Department of Public Utilities (DPU) to the state legislature and passed with only minor amendments in 1997.

Under the terms of the reform, industry incumbents were required to divest all of their generating capacity and reduce retail prices by a minimum of 10 percent. In exchange, incumbents were permitted to recover the full costs of investments made under the prereform bargain in less-competitive generating facilities ("stranded costs") through surcharges on prices charged for transmission and distribution.[69] The basic rates charged for access to transmission and distribution systems would be subject to a form of price cap regulation similar to the system applied to the British RECs. Power generators and power marketers based anywhere in the

United States would be free to offer services to any consumer in competition with incumbents. However, no generator whose production did not meet minimum environmental standards would be allowed to participate in the market. An attempt by several consumer groups to overturn the Massachusetts Electric Restructing Act of 1997 by ballot referendum failed by a vote of 71 percent to 29 percent in November 1998, an indicator of NEES's success in shaping the political dynamics of the reform process.[70]

In December 1998 NEES received a friendly takeover bid from the British National Grid PLC at a 25 percent premium over its share price, which had performed well during the period of regulatory transition. Although NEES's strong performance was attributable to a number of factors—including solid management of operations and a relatively supportive regulatory environment in Massachusetts[71]—its focused political strategy in the area of government and public relations played a key role as well in the years leading up to the reform bargain.

In generalizing from the experiences of Yorkshire Water, Rio Light, National Power, and NEES, it is important to emphasize the interrelationships between the market context, the expectations of parties affected by the reform bargain, and the incumbent's strategy. Expectations regarding postreform outcomes vary widely across reform bargain contexts, but may be shaped before and after the reform bargain by the incumbent through its government and public relations strategy. At the same time, the incumbent's commercial strategy may lead to outcomes that aggravate hot button issues—such as market power, basic goods access, and national sovereignty and security—and differ considerably from prior expectations. Ultimately, the incumbent should develop its commercial and political strategies simultaneously, with careful and ongoing assessment of contextual factors, so as to avoid an unfavorable evolution of the reform bargain in response to pressures from postreform losers.

# 5 ✦ *Transforming Operations*

*Chapter 4 focused on* the challenges established firms face
with respect to corporate governance and strategy following liberalization.
In this chapter, we move the analysis down to the operating level. We will
explore the challenges incumbents encounter in the day-to-day running
of their businesses, specifically in the areas of human resources, technology and production, procurement, sales and marketing, and finance and
control. We examine not only the commercial aspects of strategy design
and implementation but also the political implications of these strategies
with respect to the firm's evolving bargain with the state. As in chapter 4,
we draw liberally on the case of National Power and other incumbents to
illustrate the experience of established firms after liberalization.

## HUMAN RESOURCES

The operational challenges incumbents face at the time of liberalization
are particularly striking in the area of human resources. Issues of workforce
size, employee skills, compensation systems and terms of employment,
and corporate culture must be carefully thought through, not only in light
of postreform commercial opportunities but with respect to the political
and social realities that shape the firm's relationship with the state.

### Workforce Size

It is nearly axiomatic that incumbent SOEs are overstaffed at the time
of liberalization, due to the weak profit motive, strong unionization, and

emphasis on job creation and preservation typical under state ownership. Private incumbents operating under restrictive prereform bargains also tend to be overstaffed, given limited competitive pressure and restrictions on profitability. In either case, the (excessive) size of the incumbent's workforce often reflects the inclusion of employees performing activities in-house that could be outsourced at a lower cost at equivalent or superior levels of quality.

Some incumbents operate under reform bargains in which achieving a significant reduction in the workforce is difficult, if not impossible, in the short term. In Malaysia, for example, privatized firms are barred from carrying out involuntary layoffs during the first five years after privatization. Because Malaysian workers traditionally seek lifetime employment with a firm, and since the Malaysian government does not create special severance funds for privatized enterprises, voluntary layoff programs are difficult to implement. In another example, the reform bargain of the privatized Brussels Airport Authority required the new owners to add to their payroll half of the government employees who were previously responsible for air traffic control. The airport itself remained under state ownership.[1]

Such restrictions to a firm's freedom of action can be viewed as shaping the distribution of costs and benefits associated with the reform bargain in ways favorable to labor. Although the restrictions tend to reduce potential gains in labor productivity—and thus reduce the potential value added as a result of reform—they may enhance the long-term stability of the bargain by reducing workers' incentive to push for changes in the enforcement and terms of the bargain over time. In fact, in some cases the initial reforms might be impossible to secure without restrictions on layoffs as an integral part of the terms of the bargain.

National Power's initial workforce included about 17,000 employees from the former CEGB. The firm's privatization prospectus acknowledged excessive staffing levels and projected that employment could be cut to 12,000 over the five years following privatization.[2] In fact, National Power reduced its workforce to 6,000 employees within three years. The magnitude of the reductions reflected National Power's strategy to shut down one-third of its generating capacity and to raise labor productivity on the remaining capacity in line with leading international benchmarks. Several factors facilitated the program's implementation. The British government provided the firm with £411 million at the time of privatization to fund severance payments and also transferred

sufficient financial assets to fully fund National Power's pension obligations. The severance payments, typically one month's salary per year of
service, were attractive to much of the workforce, whose average age was
fifty-one at privatization. The retirements were voluntary and supported
by the unions.[3]

Of course, even though an incumbent's workforce tends to shrink or
remain flat during the initial years following reform, the trend may
reverse over time.[4] At American Airlines, for example, employment fell
from 43,000 to 41,500 during the carrier's retrenchment phase (1980–
1982), yet had increased to over 100,000 by 1990 as Crandall steadily
expanded operations throughout the remainder of the 1980s. In general,
demand conditions in the incumbent's market play a critical role in shaping employment trends after the initial reform stage. Air and rail transport provide a dramatic contrast in this respect. From 1978 to 1998, air
passenger miles in the United States increased almost threefold, whereas
rail ton-miles rose only 60 percent over the same period.[5] Also, there has
been only a slight reversal in the dramatic employment reductions implemented by incumbent railroads following deregulation.[6]

Even when an incumbent undertakes permanent net job reductions,
the magnitude of the decline may overstate the extent to which the
reform bargain results in job destruction. Divestment by the privatized
Argentine petroleum company YPF of numerous businesses outside its
core oil and gas activities contributed to a dramatic reduction in the firm's
workforce. Yet some employees in these other businesses continued to
work under the new owners.[7] Incumbents may also spin off certain support activities historically performed in-house, but continue to contract
with these same groups or individuals to perform the activities on an
arm's-length basis. For example, the privatized Australian electricity distributor Powercor terminated most of its in-house meter reading and line
maintenance activities, purchasing these services instead from independent contractors, consisting primarily of individual (or groups of) former
employees. From Powercor's perspective, this new arrangement enabled
the firm to enjoy substantial cost reductions through competition in the
market for electricity contract services—a market that previously did not
exist. The potential labor backlash to this change was largely mitigated
by the fact that the electrical workers' union was involved in setting up
many of the independent contractors and even took ownership stakes in
some of these firms.[8]

Despite the range of potential benefits that may accrue to incumbents through workforce reductions, there are also a number of risks associated with the implementation of downsizing programs. Voluntary severance programs may have the unattractive side-effect of encouraging highly capable workers to leave (and perhaps migrate to competing firms), while less-qualified, more risk-averse workers remain. Even if the firm has some discretion in laying off workers, it may be difficult to assess which workers are most and least likely to perform well in the future environment, particularly if performance incentives and measurement systems were limited prior to liberalization. Downsizing may also demoralize the remaining workers, particularly if the process is perceived as arbitrary or likely to be repeated in the future. Ultimately, the incumbent's performance under the reform bargain is shaped not only by the size of its workforce, but also by the skills of these employees, the incentives under which they work, and the broader culture or climate that develops over time in the organization.

## Employee Skills

The skills of the incumbent's employee base at the time of reform—including both managers and workers—is typically inadequate or inappropriate for the attainment of the firm's postreform strategic vision. Skills in sales and marketing tend to be lacking due to the weakness or absence of industry competition under the prereform bargain. Skills in procurement are often deficient given a historical dependence on government procurement officers or requirements to source from a limited number of state-approved vendors. Skills in human resource management, including hiring, compensation design, and career development, are usually inadequate because of the predominant role traditionally played by government civil service departments or unions in these activities. Skills in finance, particularly in the case of SOEs, generally are minimal due to a reliance on the government for capital allocations. Even in the case of private firms, incumbents may lack expertise in financing activities barred under many prereform bargains—for example, mergers, acquisitions, and foreign investments—or, because of the stabilizing role played by regulatory bodies, have less experience in financial risk management. Skills in the design and application of internal control systems typically are lacking as a result of the relative unimportance of profit as an objective and the limited ability of the incumbent to link rewards and punishments to performance. Finally, given restrictions on the scope of business activities before liberalization, or the reliance on government officials to carry out these functions, strategic planning skills at both the corporate and business unit levels are inadequate or nonexistent.

Incumbents also tend to lack certain skills in the area of technology and operations prior to reform. Many incumbents have engineering staffs that are highly competent with respect to technical issues of production and service provision. Yet these firms often lack the ability to translate technical expertise into significant cost-reducing process innovations or customer-driven product and service innovations. In some cases, the incumbent's workforce may lack experience with certain types of technologies due to restrictions included under the prereform bargain—for example, limits on access to foreign technologies.

A final area of expertise deserves special mention: skills in the area of government and public relations. On the surface, it might appear that the incumbent would have little need for such skills—after all, the essence of reform bargains would seem to be a shift away from state involvement. But as we have seen, the reform bargain still leaves the incumbent party with a particular set of rights and obligations, the provisions of which are often governed by both new and existing enforcement mechanisms. An incumbent that focuses exclusively on commercial activities while ignoring government and public relations activities risks unfavorable evolution in the enforcement and terms of the reform bargain. Although the incumbent may retain experience in these areas from its years as a state-owned enterprise or highly regulated firm, these skills and relationships are not necessarily transferable to the context of postreform market dynamics, political dynamics, and the terms of the postreform bargain.

National Power's strategy with respect to skill realignment, particularly among high-level managers, is instructive in light of the potential skill-related problems highlighted above. The process can be seen as falling into two phases. During its initial retrenchment phase, National Power relied heavily on managers retained from the CEGB and several new executives brought on during the period immediately preceding privatization. The sales and marketing director was former executive vice president of British Petroleum's U.S. marketing operations; the finance director, former finance director of a leading British conglomerate; and the operations director, former general manager of Hong Kong's China Light and

Power.[9] Directors retained from the CEGB included chief executive John Baker and the firm's human resource director, technology director, and company secretary/development director.

Although a limited number of lower-level managers and hourly employees were also recruited from outside National Power, the firm relied primarily on the existing workforce during the period of rapid downsizing. In segments of the workforce where the firm saw the need for additional skill development, it initiated internal training programs. Interestingly, National Power's executive management group did not include a director of government affairs/public relations.[10] This omission was not surprising, however, since it appeared that by operating in a deregulated market for power generation, its activities would be of little concern to the government or the general public.

Eventually, as National Power began to expand the scope of its business, its needs for additional expertise expanded. In particular, Keith Henry's appointment as CEO in April 1995 accelerated the development of National Power's international power-generation strategy.[11] Henry proceeded to replace the firm's current executive directors with outside executives, each of whom brought extensive international experience to the table.

When faced with the need to bring additional skills into the organization, incumbents often find it useful to recruit workers with experience in firms that have undergone reforms in other product or geographic markets. For example, Public Service of Colorado, a U.S.-based electric utility, brought in a number of workers with telecommunications industry experience to manage and staff its marketing and customer service departments as part of its transformation under industry deregulation.[12] In late 1995 the corporatized New Zealand power generator, Contact Energy, hired as its chief executive Paul Anthony, a former CEGB and PowerGen executive with extensive experience under British power sector privatization and deregulation in the early 1990s. To head up its generation and business development division, Contact brought in an Australian power industry executive with experience under the electricity industry reform bargains in the state of Victoria.[13]

Mergers, acquisitions, and alliances may serve as an important vehicle for infusing new skills into the incumbent's organization. Thus, if the government chooses to privatize an SOE by selling it to a corporation or consortium—as opposed to selling shares to the public—the acquirer may transfer a number of its own employees into the incumbent organization to provide additional skills critical to success under the reform bargain. When the Central Wisconsin Railway purchased state-owned New Zealand Rail (renamed Tranz Rail) in 1993, it proceeded to transfer expertise developed as an operator of short-line railroads in the deregulated U.S. transport market.[14] The mechanisms for diffusion of skills included frequent visits by Central Wisconsin managers to the New Zealand operations, visits by Tranz Rail managers to the U.S. operations, and the placement of several executives from the parent company on-site in New Zealand during the initial years following the acquisition.[15]

Many of Argentina's privatizations have been structured to bring a range of skills into the incumbent organization through the sale of a controlling share in the enterprise to a consortium of firms with varying types of expertise and other resources. As illustrated by the ENTel case in chapter 3, these consortia typically include an experienced international operator in the industry, a local partner, and in many cases a financial institution. The Spanish firm Telefónica SA not only brought its operating skills to bear through its participation in Telefónica de Argentina, but subsequently leveraged its skills and experience across other privatized, state-owned telephone companies in Latin America in which it acquired ownership stakes.

Acquisitions and mergers also may play an important role in the development and transfer of skills following deregulation. As many traditional barriers to entry have fallen in the U.S. commercial banking industry, large banks and bank holding companies such as Bank One and NationsBank have emerged through extensive merger and acquisition activity in the sector. Although this consolidation can be attributed in part to incumbents' desire to take greater advantage of scale economies and enhance market power, it can also be viewed as a means for diffusing best practices across formerly separate firms. U.S. acquisitions of nuclear power assets in the late 1990s by British Energy, the former state-owned British nuclear power generator, can also be viewed in this light.

Overall, an incumbent's workforce that is infused with new skills may be able to generate and capture significant added value. Yet the costs of acquiring these skills—through hiring new employees, employing outside experts, and (re)training existing workers—may be substantial. The use of expatriates, for example, can be quite expensive as can extensive reliance on consultants. Also, to the extent that new entrants or established competitors in the incumbent's market or firms operating in other markets also seek the same skills, bidding wars for scarce talent may develop. In this context, the incumbent may face the loss to other firms of employees with particularly valuable skills. For example, in the 1980s and 1990s AT&T suffered the defection of a number of senior executives to new and established telecommunications companies. Ultimately, incumbents' ability to attract, motivate, and retain a workforce whose skills meet the needs of the firm's strategic vision will depend to a large extent on the compensation systems, terms of employment, and corporate culture of the organization.

## Compensation Systems and Terms of Employment

Prior to liberalization, incumbents' employee compensation and terms of employment are typically characterized by fixed wages and salaries by job classification, promotion decisions based more on seniority or political considerations than on merit, and the relatively low likelihood of job loss. In the case of state-owned enterprises, these features are linked to the primacy of such objectives as job creation/preservation, fairness in compensation, and political control—as opposed to profit maximization. Private firms whose bargains have limited the range of profitability through guarantees and restrictions have had little motivation to oppose such compensation systems and terms of employment, which tend to be strongly supported by unions.[16]

Reform bargains often enhance the incumbent's freedom to increase profitability, while at the same time threatening to lower profitability through a more vigorously competitive market. In this reformed environment, incumbents often find that significant changes in employee incentives are critical to the firm's effort to create and capture value. National Power's initiatives in this area illustrate a number of important components of strategic adjustment in compensation systems and terms of employment.

Following privatization, National Power introduced major changes in compensation levels and structure. The reform bargain freed the firm from many restrictions on compensation and terms of employment linked to civil service rules and labor contracts, although the firm remained unionized and subject to general provisions of Britain's labor laws. In this new environment, National Power adjusted salary levels for various positions up or down depending on the prevailing salaries for comparable jobs elsewhere in the private sector. Although National Power was able to reduce salary levels for some low-skill positions, it increased salaries for many high-skilled positions to match comparable market averages. The increases were particularly significant for the firm's top managers and directors, whose postreform salaries were adjusted to reflect National Power's ranking among the largest 100 firms listed on the London Stock Exchange. For example, base salary for the chief executive, capped at £89,500 prior to privatization, had risen to £374,000 plus 510,599 share options by 1994.[17]

For some incumbents, however, reductions in compensation for certain employee groups to reflect lower market salaries may be difficult to implement following the reform bargain. At American Airlines, for instance, the terms of union contracts signed prior to deregulation prevented the company from cutting most salaries. Even when these contracts came up for renewal, the carrier risked costly strikes or other impairments to service quality and efficiency if it attempted to impose unilateral changes in compensation. Meanwhile, American faced actual and potential competition from nonunion carriers with much lower compensation levels and less restrictive work rules. As a compromise strategy, in 1983 Crandall developed a two-tier wage system, accepted by American's unions, that allowed the carrier to offer substantially lower salaries to newly hired employees. Above-market salaries were retained for existing employees who, however, agreed to accept less restrictive work rules.[18] Despite easing tensions in the short term, this compromise created new rifts in the firm's workforce.

At National Power, the firm adjusted not only compensation levels under the reform bargain but also the structure of compensation for higher-level managers, replacing fixed salary with a combination of fixed plus variable compensation. Since the amount of the variable component was determined by achieving various measures of operating and financial performance, managers were strongly motivated to engage in activities that raised the firm's profitability. The new compensation system was enhanced by the changes in National Power's organizational structure, discussed above. By creating clearly identifiable cost and profit centers, the firm could rely on performance measures at various levels of aggregation in assessing compensation for managers at different levels in the organization. In addition, by listing its share price on the London

Stock Exchange following privatization, National Power had an important new performance indicator for its compensation system. Since share price reflects the capital market's assessment of the long-term value that the firm will provide to shareholders, changes in share price over time tend to provide a richer measure of overall company performance than single-period changes in accounting profits or cash flow. National Power took advantage of this additional performance measure in several ways. Some executives, for example, received part of their compensation in the form of National Power stock or a cash bonus linked in part to share-price performance. Also, beginning in 1991, all directors received options to purchase a certain number of National Power shares at a fixed price at a future date. Depending on the actual share price at that time, the options ultimately could be either worthless or extremely lucrative. National Power encouraged its employees to purchase shares, thereby providing broad-based incentives for its workforce to contribute to the firm's financial success.

In addition to changes in the levels and structure of compensation at National Power, there were also changes in the dynamics of compensation. Prior to liberalization, employees saw little ability to affect changes in their compensation over time, since promotions and raises were based largely on seniority and the possibility of being fired was remote. Following reform, employees faced a greater range of future compensation and employment scenarios, depending on their contributions to National Power's performance. The "carrot" of rapid advancement and the "stick" of dismissal thus strengthened the workforce's incentive to engage in value-enhancing activities for the firm.

As a result of these changes, average compensation for National Power employees below the director level increased 9 percent per year on average from 1990 to 1994, while average annual compensation for directors rose 27 percent.[19] These changes represented significant increases in real compensation given the low level of inflation during the period—approximately 2 percent per year. Yet National Power's compensation-related expenses fell from £360 million to £220 million—and from 8.8 percent to 7.6 percent of total expenses—driven in large part by the extensive downsizing of its workforce.[20] National Power's overall profitability improved significantly over this period as well, its return on equity rising to 22.6 percent. Its market returns during the first four years following privatization (share-price appreciation plus dividend payouts) increased an extraordinary 33 percent per year. Although it is impossible to prove a direct causal link between changes in employee compensation systems and improvements in the firm's financial performance, it is reasonable to conclude that the workforce, by virtue of new incentives, was strongly motivated to ensure National Power's profitability.

It is important to recognize that changes in the incumbent's compensation levels may have a significant impact not only on the firm's direct performance in the market but for the evolution of its enterprise bargain. Sharp increases in compensation, for example, may generate a political backlash among customers, particularly if they do not perceive to have benefited sufficiently from liberalization in terms of product or service price and quality. In the case of National Power and other firms in the British electricity sector, for example, retail customers complained that privatization and deregulation had primarily enriched top executives and directors as opposed to the public at large, whose electricity rates remained relatively unchanged during the early 1990s. The public's negative reaction was exacerbated by a prior controversy over executive compensation at the privatized British Gas in the late 1980s. This so-called "fat cat" dispute contributed to the eventual imposition of a windfall profits tax on all privatized British utilities in 1997.

The incentives embedded in the firm's compensation system may also have implications for its evolving bargain with the state. To the extent that employee compensation and advancement are tied exclusively to improvements in of operating efficiency and financial performance, the incumbent may neglect to incorporate the indirect impact of the firm's strategy (and the actions of individual employees) on the enforcement and terms of the bargain. In the case of National Power, changes in the firm's compensation system supported the attainment of rapid increases in efficiency and profitability. Yet its very successes in these areas alienated some parties affected by the bargain. This eventually led to unfavorable changes in its bargain with the state, including the mandatory divestment of generating capacity, disallowance of merger attempts, and the imposition of the windfall profits tax. Essentially, the reform bargain removed many explicit restrictions on National Power's commercial strategy, but did not eliminate implicit limits on its behavior and performance. Thus National Power, as well as other incumbents, ultimately faces the challenge of designing incentive systems that reward employees for capitalizing on increased freedom to create and capture value while avoiding behaviors that lead to an unfavorable evolution of the reform bargain.[21]

## Corporate Culture

An almost universal objective among incumbents under the reform bargain is to create a more commercially oriented organizational culture in which employees value and exhibit professionalism, sound business practices, and a concern for the bottom line. Features of this desired cultural transformation include a greater sense of individual accountability, competitive spirit, customer service, entrepreneurship, and flexibility to change. To an extent, the firm can influence the organizational culture through its hiring and firing of particular types of individuals, the design of its compensation system, and its employee training practices. The communications style and skills of the CEO and other top managers, and their leadership by example, tends to have a significant impact on the culture. Nevertheless, there are often substantial obstacles to altering the organization's culture, including basic human fear of and resistance to change.

A risk incumbents face in their efforts to modify the organization's culture is that, in the process, they may destroy beneficial elements of the existing culture. Such values as loyalty, support of fellow employees, and commitment to the broader community may be eroded by a single-minded emphasis on individual contributions to profitability. The loss of such values is particularly problematic for firms operating in basic infrastructure sectors where business activities often remain squarely in the public eye even after reforms have been adopted. Incumbents may also find it difficult to strike the appropriate balance between various elements of the desired culture. Thus, excessive attention to customer service might undermine profitability; a too-aggressive pursuit of entrepreneurial opportunities may distract the organization from its core business activities; and, as suggested earlier, an overemphasis on commercial outcomes may result in an unfavorable evolution of the reform bargain.

In some cases, the terms of the reform bargain constrain the incumbent's ability to achieve significant changes in organizational culture. In Malaysian privatizations, for example, the initial five-year moratorium on involuntary layoffs limits the use of employee dismissals as a means for removing from the organization less desirable workplace attitudes and behaviors. Also, the government's retention of a majority shareholding in these firms in effect constrains the potential infusion of new leadership into the incumbent's organization. Yet this gradualist "pie-sharing" approach to organizational transformation is an explicit objective of the Malaysian government, which fears that changes implemented too rapidly cannot be sustained in a nation with a prior history of violent ethnic conflict.[22]

Even under the constraints posed by Malaysian reform bargains, innovative approaches to cultural change have occurred. In an effort to enhance individual accountability among managers of Tenaga's numerous power generation, transmission, and distribution stations, the chief executive implemented a daily reporting system that identified the ten stations with the most significant operating problems. The reports, assembled and distributed each morning through e-mail, leveraged the power of information and personal pride to accelerate improvements in operating efficiency throughout the organization.[23]

Changes in the incumbent's organizational culture can be shaped as well through changes in the physical environment following reform. New Zealand's Contact Energy worked to build creativity and teamwork in the organization following corporatization by using a specific set of design principles when setting up the head office of the divested power-generation firm. In particular, the firm emphasized a nonhierarchical open floor plan, high ceilings, bold use of color, modern furniture, and other features that distinguished the space from traditional headquarters of state-owned corporations.[24]

In the case of National Power, the terms of its reform bargain enabled it to rapidly shift toward a greater commercial orientation. The firm strongly encouraged employees whose attitudes and skills did not match this new orientation to accept the generous severance terms offered at the time of privatization. The rapid implementation of market-oriented compensation systems facilitated a shift toward a more commercial culture. It is also possible that the cultural shift was expedited as a result of its implementation by a group of executive directors who had previously served as managers in the CEGB. The logic here is that not only did these managers have a deep understanding of the organization but they were able to use this knowledge—and the workforce's receptiveness to familiar leaders—to recast the culture with relatively little resistance. The risk, however, in relying on previous management to implement change is that they may not possess the vision or skills to transform the culture effectively. Eastern Electricity's initial failure to change its culture following privatization illustrates the potential problems of relying on managers from the prereform organization to lead the change.

## TECHNOLOGY AND PRODUCTION

Incumbents may suffer from a variety of problems in the area of technology and production at the time of liberalization. Under the prereform bargain, various limits on the incumbent's freedom of action and profitability often distort the firm's choice of technology employed and the size of its production capacity. The CEGB, for example, was limited by a ban on natural gas-fueled power generation in the United Kingdom. Many SOEs are limited more broadly in their technology choices by obligations to purchase from local manufacturers or politically favored foreign producers. Restrictions on layoffs may lead prereform incumbents to favor less efficient, labor-intensive technologies. For example, Ferrocarriles Argentinos, the Argentine national railway, failed to automate its traffic-monitoring activities while under state ownership, relying instead on visual monitoring by railroad employees through the 1980s.[25]

At the time of the reform bargain, the incumbent's production capacity may be excessive or inadequate relative to the market in which it operates. Excess capacity may be linked to investment subsidies under state ownership or profit guarantees under rate-of-return regulation.[26] This problem may be exacerbated by declines in demand for the incumbent's output due to the emergence of substitute products, changes in consumer tastes, or the arrival of new entrants (including imports). The successors to the CEGB, including National Power, started out with excess capacity under the reform bargain. Their collective generation capacity—60 gigawatts—was considerably higher than the level of peak hourly demand—48 gigawatt-hours.[27] In this case, excess generation capacity could be linked, on the demand side, to increased energy conservation on the part of consumers and enhanced competition from natural gas and, on the supply side, to the CEGB's reluctance to close high-cost plants.[28]

In contrast to National Power's experience, incumbents in many other contexts are confronted with significant shortages in capacity relative to potential demand. Throughout much of the developing world, privatized telephone companies typically confront huge backlogs in demand for installations at the time of reform. Capacity shortfalls typically result from inadequate access to capital in general or foreign exchange in particular. In some instances, the system in place is underutilized because of inadequate maintenance, shortages of parts, or other factors impeding operational effectiveness. Electricity brownouts were a common problem in Argentina prior to the 1993 privatization of the power generation industry, despite the fact that capacity utilization in the industry averaged below 50 percent.[29] As we saw in chapter 3, high opportunity costs associated with inadequate or underutilized production facilities often constitute a strong force motivating the adoption of reform in the relevant sectors.

Regardless of the status of the incumbent's production facilities at the time of liberalization, designing and implementing an appropriate technology and production strategy often poses significant challenges. Since the reform program may lead to changes in the level and growth of market demand, costs of production, and intensity of competition, it may be quite difficult for the incumbent to assess the extent to which it should modify, contract, and/or expand its inherited production capacity.

Despite excess capacity in the British power generation industry, National Power chose to build new generating plants in addition to closing down facilities following privatization. This strategy can be explained by the significantly lower costs associated with combined-cycle gas turbine (CCGT) generation technology as compared with traditional coal-fired thermal plants. Once the British government had opened the door to gas-fired generation, National Power decided that it would be preferable to cannibalize some of its obsolete coal-fired capacity by investing itself in CCGT capacity rather than simply waiting for competitors to do so. At the same time, National Power was able to lower costs at its coal-fired facilities through efficiency improvements and coal price reductions.

Decisions regarding production and technology strategy tend to carry high stakes for firms in industries characterized by substantial long-term investments in fixed assets. National Power mitigated the risks associated with its CCGT investments in two ways. First, the magnitude of the CCGT investments—5,000 MW during the mid-1990s—was more than offset by the incumbent's closure of coal-fired plants. Second, National Power sold the majority of its production on terms established in medium- and long-term contracts with the RECs and large end-users ("contracts for differences") as opposed to relying on the uncertainties of the spot market for electricity (the power pool system) to determine sales volumes and price.[30]

Under the terms of some reform bargains, incumbents are required to meet minimum investment targets over specific periods of time. Such obligations are particularly common when the incumbent retains monopoly status in the market. For example, both Telefónica de Argentina and Telecom Argentina were required to add a minimum number of telephone lines and pay phones, specified annually by individual province in the monopoly service territory of each carrier during a seven-year period. The risks associated with the resulting capital expenditures— more than $600 million per year by each company—were mitigated to an extent by restrictions placed on new firms entering the market during the period.[31]

As an alternative (or supplement) to obligations involving minimum levels of physical investment or capital expenditures, the incumbent's bargain with the state may include requirements relating to service quality or other outcomes that have important indirect implications for investment. Aguas Argentinas, the privatized Buenos Aires water monopoly, was required by the state to meet specific targets for water quality, service availability (percentage of households), and leakage (percentage of water lost in transmission). The firm actually preferred these obligations to physical or financial investment requirements since outcome targets provided more flexibility regarding its investment strategy.[32]

Once again, the incumbent's strategy may have important implications for the evolution of its bargain. Even when incumbents do not face explicit obligations with respect to capital investments, the public visibility of problems associated with inadequate capacity—either in size or quality—may provoke backlash in the political arena. For example, electricity blackouts, busy telephone circuits, water supply interruptions, and rail service delays and accidents place the offending service provider at risk for incurring penalties under existing terms of the reform bargain or unfavorable modifications to the bargain. In some instances, the incumbent may choose to exceed investment obligations specified in the terms of its reform bargain in order to build goodwill among the affected parties. Telefónica de Argentina and Telecom Argentina both exceeded their minimum line expansion requirements and various quality targets during their initial seven-year period of exclusivity. As we saw earlier, these significant improvements helped the operators resist pressures to implement reductions in service prices, which—particularly in the area of domestic and international long-distance services—were among the highest in the world.[33]

## PROCUREMENT

Prior to liberalization, many incumbents operate as monopolies. In principle, these firms are well-positioned to extract highly favorable terms from suppliers. Yet in practice, most prereform incumbents lacked the freedom and/or the incentive to take advantage of their market power. SOEs are often obligated to purchase key inputs from other state enterprises or politically favored private suppliers. The CEGB was required to purchase coal from state-owned British Coal at prices almost double that charged by foreign coal suppliers.[34] The firm was also expected to purchase major capital equipment from British manufacturers, which significantly restricted its procurement options. Private monopolies operating under prereform bargains typically are less subject to the types of restrictions and political pressures in the procurement area than SOEs. Nevertheless, cost-plus or maximum-profit regulation reduces these firms' incentive to negotiate aggressively with suppliers, since shareholders are unlikely to capture benefits from the exercise of market power in procurement.

Following reform, however, incumbents typically enjoy greater freedom and incentives to seek procurement-related cost reductions. In some cases, they will be able to win substantial price concessions from existing suppliers by threatening to switch to alternate vendors. National Power was able to negotiate increasingly more favorable prices from British Coal and its successor companies over the course of the 1990s, given its enhanced freedom to import coal from abroad and its ability to move away from coal-fired generation to CCGT technology. As part of this strategy, National Power invested in the development of port facilities to support the transfer and storage of imported coal. In another example, following corporatization, the German railroad Deutsche Bahn (DB) was able to secure price reductions of about 30 percent to 40 percent from domestic suppliers of locomotives and rail cars.[35]

Some incumbents realize substantial reductions in procurement costs under the reform bargain by eliminating various forms of corruption. For example, the new owner of a major privatized Argentine electricity distribution company discovered that employees responsible for procurement activities had extracted kickbacks and other personal benefits from suppliers. By implementing internal control systems and taking advantage of increased freedom to fire workers, the firm was able to identify and correct these problems.[36]

Postreform incumbents often face the broader challenge of assessing the relative merits of purchasing goods and services from outside suppliers as opposed to producing them internally. We have already noted that as a means of preserving and creating jobs, SOEs often demonstrate a bias toward internal production of raw inputs and intermediate goods. Although some forms of backward integration may well make sense as a means for reducing transaction costs or lowering risk, others—such as New Zealand Telecom's internal production of furniture in the prereform era—do not appear justifiable from a profitability perspective. National Power found that it was able to improve its cost position by contracting out a number of activities formerly performed by its own employees under state ownership.

Up to this point, the discussion might suggest that the incumbent's traditional suppliers lose out following reform. These suppliers, however, may benefit from reform under certain conditions. If the reform bargain leads to a strong expansion in the incumbent's capital expenditures and/or sales, suppliers may enjoy substantial increases in unit sales to the incumbent, even if margins are less attractive than in the past. For example, reform bargains in the railroad sector of the United States, Argentina, Great Britain, Germany, and New Zealand sparked a surge in capital spending by incumbents, substantially increasing demand for locomotives and rail cars, switching equipment, logistics and scheduling software, and so on.

Traditional suppliers may also benefit from the increase in competition that follows many reform bargains. In these cases, the incumbent may find that its increasing freedom and incentives to exercise market power are counterbalanced by a loss in market power resulting from new entry. In the telecommunications sector of many nations, the emergence of new competitors in both the landline and wireless segments following entry deregulation has enhanced the relative market power of leading industry suppliers. Lucent Technologies and Ericsson, for example, have seen their profitability flourish in the wake of reforms in telecommunication services markets.

One additional situation in which the supplier may benefit from reform involves cases in which the incumbent enjoyed access to the supplier's goods or services at below-market prices prior to liberalization. For example, governments sometimes impose controls on prices charged for basic industrial inputs (e.g., oil, steel), which serve as an indirect subsidy for downstream industries. To the extent that these controls benefit the incumbent and are eased or removed in the terms of the reform bargain, the supplier's relative bargaining position improves vis-à-vis the incumbent.

Sometimes incumbents' relationships with suppliers have important implications for the evolution of the reform bargain as well. Following liberalization, National Power faced substantial pressure from British government and mine workers to continue purchasing fuel from the British Coal and its postprivatization successor, RJB Mining.[37] In 1998, as National Power's most recent five-year coal contract with RJB Mining was up for renegotiation, it struck a deal that enhanced the attractiveness of its own bargain, while reducing the attractiveness of the bargains of a number of competitors and potential entrants in the British power sector.[38] Specifically, National Power supported RJB Mining's call for a moratorium on the construction of new CCGT generation capacity in Britain and agreed to purchase substantial volumes of coal from the firm at above-market prices. In exchange, National Power not only enjoyed the benefits of government-enforced barriers to competition, but also found a greater willingness on the part of the British government to look favorably on mergers involving power generators and RECs. This evolution in the reform bargain helped pave the way for National Power's eventual acquisition of Midlands Electricity's (retail) supply business.

## SALES AND MARKETING

Regarding the challenges faced by incumbents vis-à-vis customers following reform, we will look at sales and marketing broadly defined to include issues related to pricing, product quality, and promotional activities such as advertising. Prior to reform, most incumbents charge relatively uniform prices across customer groups, provide a fairly narrow range of product quality/features, and—particularly in the case of monopolies—engage in few promotional activities.

### Pricing

The incumbent's postreform strategy in the area of sales and marketing is typically driven by opportunities associated with greater freedom of action, and risks associated with enhanced prospects of competition. Prior to reform, the incumbent often faces restrictions with respect to both the average level of prices and the structure of prices. Before deregulation, the bargains of private utilities, telephone companies, air carriers, and motor carriers in the United States permitted these firms to charge rates commensurate with (but not exceeding) reasonable returns. Although the average prices charged by some SOEs were sufficient to cover both operating and investment costs, prices sometimes were constrained below this level to promote other government objectives—for example, increasing the affordability of basic services.[39]

National Power's reform bargain was somewhat unusual with respect to pricing freedom. Because the government had established contracts for differences prior to privatization, the price charged for the electricity National Power would sell was effectively fixed over the period 1990–1993 at a level the government regarded as sufficient to allow reasonable profits.[40] An advantage of these terms was that the firm did not face downward pressure on prices from established competitors or entrants, at least in the short term. Yet at the same time, National Power was not able to take advantage of its dominant position in the market to raise prices during these first three years. In essence, National Power faced the equivalent of a price cap which, although constraining its market power, provided a strong incentive to reduce costs, since cost savings would translate directly into higher profits.

For incumbents whose production processes involve a high proportion of fixed costs, the reform bargain tends to have important implications for price structure. Preform bargains of both private and state-owned enterprises often stress price uniformity, even in the presence of substantial differences in the cost of service or price sensitivity[41] across customers. A classic example of uniform pricing is the fixed postal charge in the United States for all first-class letters weighing up to one ounce. Regardless of the distance traveled, remoteness of the place of origination or destination, the volume of mail associated with the sender or recipient, or the customer's willingness to pay, the price is the same. Under this system, the postage paid to deliver certain letters does not even cover the variable cost of providing service. For other letters, the postage far exceeds the variable costs and thus contributes to the fixed costs of the postal system and cross-subsidizes service provided to high-cost customers. Similar patterns prevailed under prereform bargains in other sectors such as telecommunications—where rural households often paid the same fixed monthly fee (or even less) for telephone service as urban business customers—and in air transport, where fares were based on distance traveled, regardless of differences in traffic density, airport capacity factors, or nature of the travel (for example, business versus leisure). Power generators like the CEGB tended to charge the same rate for electricity throughout the year, despite production costs being much higher at peak usage times than at off-peak times.[42]

*Rebalancing.* The easing of limits on freedom of action and profitability creates powerful incentives for incumbents to implement changes in their prereform pricing structure. Ideally, the incumbent would like to engage in a strategy of price "rebalancing." In essence, rebalancing involves raising prices for services that are more costly to provide and for customers whose demand is less sensitive to price while, at the same time, lowering (or not changing) prices for less-costly services and for more price-sensitive customers.[43] If successfully put into place, rebalancing should enable the incumbent to enhance its profitability by (1) abandoning customers unwilling to pay even the marginal costs of service, (2) charging higher margins on sales to customers who place high value on the product and have few, if any, competitive alternatives, and (3) charging lower margins but increasing sales volume to customers who place lower value on the product or enjoy greater competitive alternatives.

Yet implementing a rebalancing strategy may be difficult, particularly if the incumbent does not have a thorough understanding of its cost structure and customers or if the reform bargain continues to include restrictions on pricing and service curtailments. The incumbent may also find that increased entry and competition force it to lower prices to so many of its customers that it is unable to earn acceptable returns in the absence of significant cost reductions. Finally, even if the incumbent is able to implement a successful rebalancing program in the short term, the strategy may not be sustainable if the losers are able to secure changes in the terms of the bargain in their favor. For example, consumers facing price increases may be able to obtain a rollback or restriction on future price increases through activity in the political arena.

National Power pursued several forms of rebalancing under its reform bargain. The introduction of the power pool system allowed the firm to offer its power at higher prices on the spot market when costly peak generating capacity was required, and at lower prices when less costly gener-ating capacity could be employed to satisfy system demand. This arrangement also allowed the firm to enjoy the benefits of customers' higher willingness to pay at peak times. The firm also offered power at lower prices to large industrial customers who bought electricity whole-sale from National Power, as opposed to purchasing at retail through a regional electric company. In general, prices for large power users fell at a faster rate over time than those for residential customers, given large users' greater ability to switch to alternative fuels, produce power in-house, and negotiate one-on-one with power generators. This rebalanc-ing, however, did not go unnoticed by residential consumers, who even-tually used their power in the political arena to press for a more restric-tive enforcement of incumbents' bargains and the punitive adoption of the windfall profits tax.

Deutsche Telekom adopted a rebalancing strategy following its corpo-ratization in the early 1990s. The firm made aggressive price cuts in seg-ments where it faced growing competition in the wake of deregulation—for example, the large business customer market. At the same time, it increased prices in segments where it faced little rivalry, including the res-idential customer and local calling service markets. The terms of its reform bargain, however, continue to place limits on its freedom of action in this area. Deutsche Telekom, like telecommunications incumbents in all other OECD countries, are still required to make basic telephone ser-vice universally available at a "reasonable price."[44] In addition, its price-cutting is subject to challenge by competitors on antitrust grounds as constituting predatory behavior.

The experience of American Airlines suggests that rebalancing may become an ongoing preoccupation for incumbents as opposed to a one-time correction following reform. Following deregulation, American found that it could charge relatively high prices on routes with fewer alternative carriers and to customers with less flexibility in their travel scheduling—for example, business travelers who booked flights on short notice and flew at peak times during the workweek. Yet these higher fares tended to attract additional competition from established carriers and new entrants, leading to downward pressure on prices. At the same time, mergers among carriers and the abandonment of service along particular routes opened the door to price increases for other cus-tomers. In this context, American's extensive investment in regional

hubs, the information-rich SABRE reservations system, and its AAdvan-
tage frequent flier program can all be viewed as strategies supporting its
effort to identify and enhance customers' willingness to pay higher
prices in a complex array of airline markets. Despite these strategic initiatives by American, and similar efforts by other carriers, postderegulation airfares have tended to change dramatically over time and demonstrate wide variation at any point in time. As we saw in chapter 2, this
volatility has led frustrated entrants and consumers to challenge incumbents' behavior.

*Access/Interconnection Pricing.* Following reform, some incumbents
face the challenge of responding to competitors seeking access to infrastructure controlled by the established enterprise. Entry may be difficult or impossible in a market if a vertically integrated incumbent holds
monopoly control over one or more links of the value chain associated
with a particular good or service. For example, if Deutsche Telekom
refused to provide interconnection service to its local network for rival
providers of long-distance, local, or wireless telecommunications services, little if any competition might occur. Yet if Deutsche Telekom
were required by the terms of the reform bargain to offer interconnection service at too low a price, it might find itself in the odd position of
providing competitors with the means to steal away its most attractive
customers. In fact, German regulators interpreted Deutsche Telekom's
reform bargain as requiring it to charge some of the lowest interconnection rates in Europe. As a result, the firm's market share in long-distance
calling fell 30 percent in the first year of deregulation.[45]

Not surprisingly, access to gateway infrastructure—including access
pricing and technical specifications—has become a key battlefield for
competition not only in the telecommunications sector, but in other
sectors involving control over a monopoly link by a vertically integrated incumbent. Whether occurring in telecommunications, electricity, natural gas, water, cable television, rail transport, air transport, or
other sectors—such as computer software—the outcomes of these battles have critical implications both for incumbents and potential
entrants, as well as for customers, suppliers, and other affected parties.
The resolution of each conflict ultimately involves playing off two opposing notions of a free market in the age of the new market economy: the
freedom of the incumbent to determine its actions in the market versus

the freedom—and entitlement—of potential competitors to enter the market. Ultimately, battles over access are played out in both the commercial and the political arenas.

***Bundling.*** The incumbent may be able to take advantage of its control over gateway assets through the use of product bundling under the reform bargain. Bundling involves the selling of two or more distinct products as a single unit, at a price below the sum of the stand-alone prices of the individual items. Thus, a telecommunications incumbent may create a bundle of local, long-distance, and wireless services to sell as a package to consumers at a discount. Even if the incumbent is required to provide access to its network assets to competitors, its bundling strategy may leave rival providers of individual services unable to compete profitably with the discounted package, due either to cost or quality disadvantages related to the terms of access. Actual and potential competitors, however, as well as other affected parties, may challenge the implementation or terms of the reform bargain if the bundling is perceived as a means for leveraging the incumbent's market power in one market into other markets that otherwise would be characterized by active competition.

The case of the U.S. Department of Justice versus Microsoft powerfully illustrates the opportunities and risks associated with bundling. Microsoft stood accused of using its domination of the computer-operating-system market to gain control over the Internet browser market. In effect, Microsoft's Windows operating system constituted a near-monopoly gateway between an Internet browser provider, such as Netscape, and consumers. Microsoft's strategy of developing the Explorer browser, and bundling it as a standard feature in its Windows operating system, created a dilemma for Netscape. Although consumers could still install Netscape's Navigator browser for use with Windows, Explorer offered the advantage of preinstallation. Also, because not all of Windows' proprietary code was available to outside programmers, Microsoft was able to integrate its browser more fully with Windows and other Microsoft program applications than could Netscape or other browser developers. Depending on the outcome of the litigation, Microsoft will either remain free to continue its bundling strategy—thus bolstering its ability to dominate the browser market—or be required to unbundle

Explorer from Windows or separate its operating system and program businesses through mandatory divestitures.

## Product Quality

The quality of a good or service can be viewed along a number of dimensions including, for example, reliability, technological sophistication, and range of features. Prior to liberalization, the quality of an incumbent's products tends to be fairly uniform, in keeping with the relative uniformity of its prices and, in some cases, specific obligations included in its bargain with the state.

Incumbents are often forced to make changes in quality in response to heightened competition following reforms. The lowering of entry barriers in the Argentine steel market, for example, compelled the privatized incumbent Siderar to make dramatic improvements in the consistency and reliability of its production or face the loss of market share to imports.[46] Entry also may exert pressure on the incumbent to adopt a more advanced technological standard for its products. Sprint Corporation's early adoption of a 100 percent fiber-optic network for long-distance telephone service threatened incumbent AT&T with increasing share losses if it continued to rely on a partial copper-wire network.

Regardless of the intensity of entry following the reform bargain, incumbents may be able to create and capture additional value by expanding the range of quality offerings in their product line. Following deregulation, U.S. airline incumbents substantially expanded their range of quality offerings, particularly on the low end—for example, nonrefundable, Saturday-night-layover, hub-connecting, and nonjet services. This approach enabled the carriers to more effectively segment potential travelers, matching prices to an individual customer's willingness to pay, and thus attracting more total customers.

Despite the potential benefits of increased customer segmentation—implemented through rebalancing, bundling, and quality adjustments—most incumbents are woefully lacking in information with respect to their actual and potential customers, information that is necessary in order for them to implement these strategies at the time of reform. Substantial investment in market research is often required to overcome what one executive in a major privatized firm described as "the dangerous assumption that we actually understand the customers that we have served for so many years."[47]

## Promotional Activities

At the time of reform, incumbents often find themselves in a paradoxical position with respect to consumers. Most incumbents, particularly monopolies, engage in little direct marketing prior to the reform bargain—after all, they essentially sell to captive markets. Yet these firms tend to be quite well-known within the market they serve, often owing to their provision of basic goods and services, high levels of employment, and involvement in the civic and political life of the community.

The incumbent's inherited reputation can be both a blessing and a curse under the reform bargain. Although its name/brand recognition is typically high and its historical role in the community viewed as important, the incumbent may have a reputation for inefficiency, lack of innovation, arrogance, poor quality, high prices, and/or corruption. Thus one of the first critical challenges for the incumbent is to implement a makeover of the corporate image while, if possible, retaining the residual name recognition and goodwill. One firm particularly successful at this effort was British Telecom, which prior to its privatization in 1984 was the most hated company in the United Kingdom according to public opinion surveys.[48] At privatization, the firm adopted a sleek new logo and began identifying itself as BT, to distinguish itself from its previous incarnation.[49] More important, the incumbent supported its rhetoric with a series of early service quality improvements and price reductions. British Telecom's revised image proved particularly useful vis-à-vis the new entrant in the market: Mercury Communications. Essentially BT could claim to be both new and improved, yet a bulwark of strength and tradition. Mercury was tiny and untested in comparison. Given that telephone service was regarded as a virtual necessity, British Telecom was able to play off its new image and the risk aversion of the majority of users to continue to hold a dominant share in both the local and long-distance markets. In general, when the reformed market involves goods or services for which reliability is a key consumer concern, incumbents have found it quite useful, in promotional activities, to question entrants' financial and operating capabilities as well as their long-term commitment to the market.

At the same time, a risk incumbents face under the reform bargain is that while customers may enjoy substantial gains in value from the new-and-improved incumbent, they (and other affected parties) may continue to expect firms to maintain certain practices carried out in the prereform era. For example, many prereform incumbents are not aggressive in demanding prompt payment of bills and rarely, if ever, cut off service in the case of nonpayment. Many do not charge explicitly for certain services.[50] Prereform incumbents often provide or contribute financially to a range of social and community services, in the form of direct and indirect job creation, and by providing housing, recreational facilities, community centers, and so on. Postreform incumbents are often eager to abandon such practices in the pursuit of commercial objectives. Yet they should be aware of the potential for backlash leading to an unfavorable evolution in the terms of their reform bargain. This risk may be manageable to some extent through an educational, expectations-setting marketing campaign on the part of the incumbent. Yet ultimately, the incumbent may find it necessary to make adjustments in its commercial strategy as well as engage explicitly in government and public relations activities to maintain and enhance the attractiveness of its bargain.

## FINANCE AND CONTROL

Incumbents face the challenge of developing and implementing a strategy for meeting financing requirements and achieving an appropriate capital structure following reforms. Although incumbents generally enjoy considerable freedom in the area of financial strategy, the reform bargain may contain some restrictions on the firm's financial structure, particularly if part of its business is subject to limitations on investment returns.[51]

Both the opportunity and necessity of engaging directly with the capital markets represent a major change for former SOEs under the reform bargain. Under state ownership, the incumbent typically negotiates with government institutions such as a Ministry of Industry or a Ministry of Finance to establish the level and sources of financing for capital investments and working capital requirements. These interactions also determine the distribution of the SOE's internal cash flow or subsidization of its operating losses. Under the reform bargain, the former SOE typically faces a higher cost of capital, having lost its access to government guarantees and subsidies. Yet this loss is countered by the increased availability of financing relative to the situation under state ownership.[52] The incumbent's actual postreform cost of capital will be affected by the terms of the bargain—in particular, its expected impact on the level and stability of future cash flows.

National Power's financial condition following privatization was quite strong. The British government assumed virtually all of the enterprise's debt as part of the reform bargain. This situation, common to many privatized SOEs, creates both opportunities and risks for the incumbent. A clean balance sheet provides borrowing capacity that, in combination with the firm's internal cash flow, can be utilized to fund capital investment needs that perhaps have long remained unaddressed. Particularly in developing countries, where the need for modernization and expansion of SOE productive capacity is typically high, the incumbent's initial debt-free status can be important. In these cases, the owner(s) of the privatized firm are typically private corporations, which fund a considerable portion of ongoing financing requirements through the parent organization's (consolidated) cash flow or through corporate borrowings.

In National Power's case, however, capital investment requirements for the firm's core business were modest. In addition, its highly successful cost-cutting program led to dramatic increases in earnings and cash flow. Thus, even after healthy dividend payouts, the firm's cash flow continued to mount in the years following privatization. This combination of factors created opportunities for National Power to diversify outside its core business and/or increase payouts to shareholders. In fact, many former state-owned and private incumbents, particularly those firms operating in low-growth industries, find themselves in a similar position following reforms. The advantages in flexibility that such a financial position provides, however, simultaneously create risks for the incumbent.

The risk that a firm flush with financial resources may rush headlong into unwise diversification activity is not unique to postreform incumbents.[53] Yet as we saw in chapter 4, such enterprises are particularly susceptible to this trap given the often sudden freedom to expand into other product and geographic markets, a rapid improvement in financial position, and the arrival of managers eager to prove themselves in the new market economy. On the other hand, an alternative strategy—large payouts to shareholders—can also pose problems for the incumbent, particularly with respect to the evolving bargain. Significant increases in the firm's dividend payout ratio, payment of large one-time special dividends, and major share-buyback programs all may raise concerns among the public that shareholders—who often include the firm's directors and top managers—have reaped the lion's share of benefits following reform. These concerns in turn can trigger pressures for changes in the bargain such as the windfall profits tax levied on privatized British utilities in the wake of major increases in profitability and shareholder payouts by these enterprises.[54] In some cases, firms subject to periodic pricing reviews have timed large shareholder payouts to occur after, as opposed to before, new pricing restrictions have been set by regulators.[55]

National Power responded to its improved financial situation in several ways. As its net income rose from £78 million in 1990 to over £500 million annually by mid-decade, the firm increased its capital expenditures from £206 million to a high of £886 million in 1997, with a growing proportion of this investment supporting international diversification efforts (see table 5-1).

During the first half of the 1990s, National Power appeared to be substantially underleveraged, its net debt to equity ratio remaining about 10 percent. This situation represented an ongoing opportunity cost to the firm, since interest payments, unlike dividend payments, are tax-deductible. Yet a major restructuring of the balance sheet would have increased pressures for additional diversification or large shareholder payouts—each fraught with the risks discussed above. One approach to unlocking the value in an incumbent's balance sheet is for the enterprise to be acquired. National Power was subject to a takeover bid in 1996 by the U.S.-based Southern Company, which had already purchased the REC South Western Electricity. The British government blocked the bid, however, on grounds that the acquisition would have produced anticompetitive effects on the British electricity market. In response, National Power made a special dividend payout of £1.2 billion. This payout, along with an increase in nonrecourse debt for its international projects, boosted the firm's net debt to equity ratio to 88 percent in 1997.

An alternative strategy for creating a more optimal balance of debt and equity is for the incumbent to acquire a highly leveraged firm. The privatized Argentine oil company YPF successfully pursued this strategy in its 1995 purchase of Maxus Energy, a U.S.-based firm engaged in petroleum exploration and production. The principal motivation for the acquisition was the diversification of YPF's oil production properties, which were

Table 5-1   NATIONAL POWER PLC FINANCIAL AND OPERATING STATISTICS, 1991–1999
(fiscal years ending in March; data in millions of British pounds, unless otherwise indicated)

| | 1991 | 1992 | 1993 | 1994 | 1995 | 1996 | 1997 | 1998 | 1999 |
|---|---|---|---|---|---|---|---|---|---|
| *Financial Performance* | | | | | | | | | |
| Total Revenue | 4,378 | 4,701 | 4,348 | 3,641 | 3,953 | 3,948 | 3,535 | 3,354 | 3,009 |
| Net Income* | 206 | 365 | 420 | 522 | 525 | 608 | 584 | 335 | 473 |
| Capital Expenditures | 466 | 555 | 604 | 601 | 366 | 354 | 886 | 474 | 606 |
| of which, International | 0 | 0 | 0 | 147 | 71 | 33 | 670 | 269 | 283 |
| Market Capitalization | 2,804 | 2,492 | 4,288 | 5,764 | 5,101 | 5,312 | 5,897 | 7,458 | 5,823 |
| Common Shareholder Equity | 1,778 | 2,027 | 2,314 | 2,643 | 2,548 | 2,666 | 1,935 | 1,951 | 2,487 |
| Return on Sales (%) | 4.7 | 7.8 | 9.7 | 14.3 | 13.3 | 15.4 | 16.5 | 9.7 | 15.7 |
| Return on Assets (%) | 5.5 | 9.0 | 11.0 | 12.8 | 12.2 | 14.2 | 14.2 | 7.4 | 9.5 |
| Return on Equity (%) | 10.6 | 19.2 | 20.7 | 22.6 | 19.9 | 23.9 | 21.9 | 16.9 | 24.2 |
| Net Debt/Equity, including nonrecourse debt (%) | 13.3 | 11.1 | 13.0 | 13.0 | 9.0 | 14.0 | 88.0 | 83.0 | 71.0 |
| *Operating Performance* | | | | | | | | | |
| Output (domestic sales, terawatt hours) | 121.8 | 117.1 | 108.6 | 94.6 | 92.3 | 90.8 | 69.4 | 60.3 | 62.5 |
| Installed Capacity (domestic megawatts) | 28,666 | 26,623 | 24,094 | 21,235 | 20,243 | 19,635 | 15,721 | 16,113 | 15,954 |
| Market Share (% of total UK power generation) | 45.5 | 43.5 | 40.9 | 35.0 | 34.0 | 32.0 | 24.0 | 21.0 | 21.0 |
| Employees at year end (thousands) | 14,513 | 11,421 | 7,377 | 6,064 | 5,447 | 4,848 | 4,474 | 4,348 | 4,445 |

*Source: National Power PLC Annual Reports*

*Net income affected by restructuring costs of £137 million in 1991 and a windfall profits tax of £266 million in 1998.

concentrated in Argentina.[56] Also, YPF's management felt confident that it could apply its experience with the transformation of YPF's organizational structure and systems in the early 1990s to Maxus, which appeared to be suffering in large part from weak management. The acquisition of Maxus's $1 billion in debt as part of the purchase was, in a sense, a bonus. These terms enabled YPF to increase its leverage (and tax benefits) indirectly, as opposed to borrowing from international lenders at relatively high rates, given the market uncertainties that characterized the early stages of Argentina's reform process.

As suggested earlier, the successful design and implementation of the incumbent's financial strategy may require hiring individuals with specialized expertise in investor relations. In addition to formulating a strategy for meeting the firm's capital requirements, the incumbent also typically must revise and enhance existing systems for internal financial control. Under the prereform bargain, these systems tend to be fairly rudimentary and designed primarily to fulfill government-mandated reporting requirements. Following the introduction of reforms, the incumbent has the opportunity to create control systems that facilitate the analysis of product costs and profitability, provide measures of employee performance, generate information critical to the planning process, and produce data required for external audiences, including private investors and regulatory bodies. In some cases, these systems also may play a critical role in identifying and deterring various forms of theft and corruption that may have existed prior to reform.

## THE TRANSFORMATION OF NATIONAL POWER

National Power's performance during the first four years after privatization was impressive in many respects. The company made significant improvements in return on sales, return on assets, and return on equity (see table 5-1) and achieved substantial share-price gains relative to market averages during this period (see figure 5-1).[57] Thus National Power provides a clear illustration of the incumbent-on-top pattern of short-term market dynamics following reform. Interestingly, National Power's strong performance during this period mirrored that of the privatized electricity sector as a whole, as shown in the figure.

National Power's early successes can be attributed to several factors. Under the reform bargain, the firm's market power relative to suppliers

Figure 5-1 **APPRECIATED VALUE OF NATIONAL POWER PLC: COMMON EQUITY RELATIVE TO BENCHMARK INDEXES, 1991–1999**

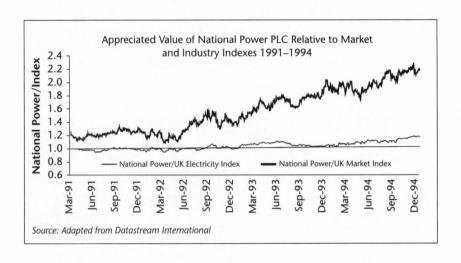

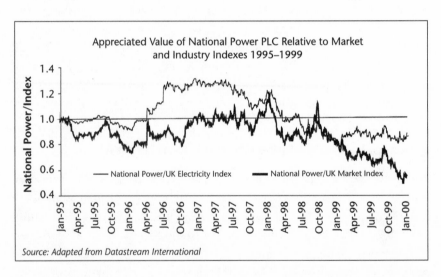

Note: Appreciated value incorporates stock price appreciation, dividends, and the starting value of the stock or index. For example, if the value of National Power equity increased 50 percent over a given period, while the value of a benchmark index remained the same, the appreciated value of National Power equity relative to the index would equal (1.50/1.00)=1.5.

(including labor) increased significantly with the easing of restrictions on freedom of action. Profit deregulation provided broad incentives to take advantage of this market power, and changes in compensation systems provided inducements to individual directors and managers to squeeze down costs. At the same time, sales prices and volumes were essentially fixed through the contracts for differences, neutralizing the ability of buyers to play incumbent generators off against each other and discouraging new entry. Thus despite industry overcapacity, cost reductions translated into gains for shareholders (through higher profits) as opposed to gains for consumers (through lower prices).

In principle, the expiration of the initial contracts for differences in March 1993 opened the door for buyers to extract significant price concessions in their new contracts. Yet the incumbent generators' negotiating position was strong—pool prices had steadily increased and no competing power generators of significant size had emerged to challenge the dominance of National Power and PowerGen, who were unlikely to engage in a price war during contract renegotiations. Finally, under the terms of the reform bargain, the major buyers of wholesale power, the RECs, simply passed along the cost of power to their captive customers and, therefore, had little incentive to demand significant price concessions from the generators.[58] Thus, the new contract prices did not threaten National Power's profitability. In fact, the firm achieved impressive gains in accounting returns and market returns during its 1994 fiscal year.[59]

National Power's performance during the second half of the 1990s was less impressive in comparison. Although accounting returns remained fairly strong, market performance stagnated, apparently in response to the increasingly hostile regulatory and public relations environment and skepticism over the firm's international and domestic diversification strategy. Whereas National Power's market value appreciated at a much greater rate than the U.K. market average from 1991–1994, this pattern reversed in subsequent years, leaving the firm approximately where it started, in relative terms, by the end of the decade (see figure 5-1). National Power's market returns during the second half of the 1990s were also below those of other firms in the British electricity sector.

During this period, National Power's bargain evolved in unfavorable ways as losers among the affected parties—principally retail consumers—

pressed for tough enforcement of restrictions on anticompetitive behavior. DGES Littlechild, whose personal reputation as one of the chief architects of the reform bargain was on the line, responded forcefully to these pressures, mandating capacity sales and pool price declines. These obligations, combined with Conservative government opposition to National Power's merger and acquisition plans, suggest that the firm had overplayed its hand in seeking to capture for itself, through deft use of market power, the lion's share of value created through the reform bargain. National Power appeared to reach an accommodation with the Labor government in the late 1990s, but only after taking the hit of a windfall profits tax and moving to divest its largest generating plant.

National Power's long-term fate remained highly uncertain at the beginning of the new millennium. In late 1999 the firm announced its intent to carry out a demerger by splitting its domestic and foreign operations into "npower" and "International Power" respectively. In February 2000 National Power named new officers for these two companies, stating that its current executive chairman, chief operating officer, and chief financial officer would retire upon completion of the demerger. Thus, the era of the incumbent-on-top appeared to be on the wane, as National Power grappled with the prospects of increasingly effective competition in the markets in which its more focused successor companies would operate.

# 6 ✦ Competing Against Incumbents

$O$*ne of the hallmarks* of the new market economy is the easing of limits on freedom of entry. Two general types of entry opportunity are associated with liberalization. The first involves the opportunity to compete against one or more industry incumbents. The deregulation of the British power generation sector, for instance, opened the way for independent power producers (IPPs) to compete against former state-owned incumbents National Power, PowerGen, and British Energy.[1] Similarly, deregulation of U.S airline markets paved the way for competitive entry along city-pair routes by start-up carriers and by established carriers formerly restricted to serving other routes.

The second type of entry opportunity involves contracting with a government institution to provide goods or services in sectors that previously excluded private enterprises. These opportunities include, for example, concessions to build and operate new toll roads, light rail systems, power plants, pipelines, and mining facilities.[2] Typically, such concessions are themselves monopolies awarded through a process of competitive bidding. Variations of this form of entry involve contracts to provide social services (housing, incarceration, and trash disposal services, for instance) and intermediate services to government enterprises or agencies (such as management and outsourcing of support services).

The opportunities and risks associated with entering the marketplace to compete against incumbents are explored in this chapter. Chapter 7 focuses on the challenges of entry through concessions and other forms of contracting with a government entity.

## COMPETITIVE ENTRY AND THE REFORM BARGAIN

Many of the challenges faced by prospective competitors in sectors under-going deregulation and privatization are similar to those confronted by a potential entrant into any preexisting market.[3] The entrant, for example, must devise a strategy for attracting existing customers or new buyers by offering price/quality combinations superior to those provided by incumbents.[4] Devising a strategy that is sustainable will be difficult unless the entrant possesses competitive advantages that incumbents cannot easily replicate. Even if the prospective entrant does have some unique advantages, it may face substantial hurdles in overcoming other advantages that incumbents hold, such as strong brand names, supplier relationships, and distribution systems.

Competitive entry under a reform bargain, however, may pose special challenges. To begin, the high cost structure, poor or erratic product quality, and limited product variety often associated with incumbents at the time of deregulation and privatization may appear to offer an extremely attractive opportunity for entry. Yet, as we have seen, the easing of limits on freedom of action and profitability often enables incumbents to implement dramatic improvements in operating efficiency, quality control, and marketing. Also, an incumbent's size may allow it to leverage scale and scope economies to bring its costs below those of the new competitor. The danger for a potential entrant, therefore, is to underestimate the extent and speed at which incumbents can execute their transformation under the reform bargain. The risks associated with misperceptions in this area are particularly high if the entry opportunity involves high up-front investments with long payback periods.

A second challenge often faced by potential entrants is the threat of price rebalancing by dominant incumbents, discussed in chapter 5. At the time of the reform bargain, an entrant may find certain customer segments much more attractive to serve than others at the price(s) the incumbent charges, leading the entrant to adopt a niche strategy targeting the "cream of the crop." Yet, when a relatively high proportion of the costs incumbents incur is fixed, the easing of price restrictions often leads the established firm to rebalance its price structure; it may shift the recovery of fixed costs away from customers easily targeted by entrants and onto less accessible or otherwise less attractive consumers. Thus, an apparent price arbitrage opportunity for the competing entrant may be narrowed or eliminated completely as the incumbent abandons the price-averaging and cross-subsidization common prior to reform. In the extreme, the entrant may be unable to survive unless (1) its full costs of serving its target customer segment(s) are less than the incumbent's marginal costs of serving these same customers, or (2) its product is sufficiently differentiated from the incumbent's to shift the basis of competition away from price alone.

A third challenge competing entrants often face is access to gateway infrastructure owned or controlled by the incumbent.[5] Without access to these assets—for example, a local telephone network or electricity transmission system—the potential entrant in the associated market will be unable to offer service without duplicating the gateway assets or utilizing an alternate technology that allows it to bypass the infrastructure completely. These alternatives, however, might be prohibitively expensive or physically impossible to carry out. Of course, the entrant may be entitled to access the incumbent's infrastructure under the terms of the reform bargain. But, as we will see below, the price and quality of the access may still leave the entrant at a considerable competitive disadvantage relative to the established firm. Furthermore, the incumbent may be able to extend the reach of its gateway assets through bundling strategies that place entrants attempting to provide any combination of products or services at a competitive disadvantage. Even if the incumbent has not traditionally engaged in these practices, its incentive to do so is likely to be much greater under the terms of the reform bargain.

In sum, the position of a potential entrant under the reform bargain is somewhat paradoxical. The lifting of limits on the freedom of entry and the weak state of many incumbents would appear to signal vast opportunity for would-be competitors. Yet without special entitlements in the terms of their bargains, prospective competitors may face impenetrable barriers to entry in practice, or achieve a Pyrrhic victory that cannot be sustained.

In this chapter, we illustrate key challenges of competitive entry with the case of Clear Communications Ltd., a start-up venture facing a privatized incumbent in New Zealand's deregulated telecommunications market. As in chapters 4 and 5, we will draw on a number of comparative examples from the experiences of entrants in other geographic and product markets to provide insights for firms operating across a wide range of markets and conditions.

## CLEAR COMMUNICATIONS VERSUS
## TELECOM CORPORATION OF NEW ZEALAND

Clear Communications Ltd. (CCL) was established in 1990, following deregulation of the New Zealand telecommunications market during the prior year.[6] CCL was a joint venture of three private firms—Bell Canada, MCI, and Todd Corporation (a privately held New Zealand conglomerate)—and two state-owned enterprises—New Zealand Rail and Television New Zealand. CCL was attracted to New Zealand's telecommunications market not only because of the rapid growth in demand for telecommunications services, but also because of the nation's reputation as a leading proponent of free market principles.[7] New Zealand's philosophy of light-handed regulation, which rejected the use of industry-specific government regulatory bodies, appeared to offer welcome relief from bureaucratic interference in the affairs of private enterprises.

Historically, the state-owned New Zealand Post Office provided telecommunications services in New Zealand as a protected monopoly. In 1987 the New Zealand government split off the Telecom Corporation of New Zealand Ltd. (TCNZ) from the post office as part of a national program to improve the efficiency of state enterprises.[8] Prior to its sale in 1990 to the U.S. Baby Bells Ameritech and Bell Atlantic, TCNZ adopted a process of organizational transformation under new management. The privatized TCNZ was required to offer universal service and was prohibited from raising the price of local residential telephone service above the rate of inflation. No other price controls were included in the reform bargain.

Clear Communications Ltd. saw an opportunity to establish itself as an alternative telecommunications carrier through the unique combination of resources contributed by its joint venture partners. New Zealand Rail's internal communications network, which ran along its national track infrastructure, formed the initial backbone of the system, along with certain microwave transmission assets owned by Television New Zealand. Bell Canada and MCI brought international telecommunications expertise to the venture, while Todd Corporation contributed financial resources and familiarity with the local market. CCL planned to target business users of long-distance services in its initial phase of entry, then gradually expand its coverage to include residential users and local services.

At least initially, CCL would depend on access to TCNZ's local telephone network to connect callers to its own network and to complete the final routing of each call to its destination. Under the terms of New Zealand's 1986 Commerce Act, firms with a dominant market position were prohibited from restricting entry into that market. Thus TCNZ was obligated to offer interconnection services to CCL, but the price of access was subject to negotiation. The firms reached an interconnection agreement in March 1991 as CCL was finalizing its initial network build-out. CCL began offering service one month later, and by the end of the year had captured a 10 percent share of the long-distance market.

In 1992 CCL sought to expand into the local services market, but was unable to negotiate an acceptable interconnection agreement with TCNZ.[9] CCL sued the incumbent for violating the Commerce Act, and litigation and subsequent appeals continued for three years. The final outcome favored TCNZ, permitting it to charge access prices that appeared to include monopoly profits. The government of New Zealand, perplexed by the long-running dispute, threatened to intervene if the parties did not reach an agreement. In March 1996 an agreement was signed. The following year CCL, unhappy with the terms for local interconnection, began withholding payments to TCNZ, leading the latter to initiate a new round of litigation. CCL then sued to block TCNZ from leveraging its local network monopoly through proposed investments in pay television services. Additional rounds of litigation followed and, by the end of the 1990s, the concept of free markets in the New Zealand telecommunications sector was ambiguous at best.

## ASSESSING THE ENTRY ENVIRONMENT

Unlike incumbents, prospective entrants can choose whether or not to participate in a market under the reform bargain.[10] It may be difficult, however, to accurately assess the attractiveness of the entry opportunity at the time of the reform. Demand projections based on preform prices, product offerings, and macroeconomic conditions[11] may be highly inaccurate. Predictions of incumbents' strategy based on their preform behavior may also be wide of the mark. Assessing the evolution of the reform bargain itself may be extremely challenging. Of particular importance is the evaluation of enforcement mechanisms associated with entrants' rights—and incumbents' obligations—related to competition. The prospect of entry by other parties eager to serve the deregulated market may complicate this analysis even further. Not surprisingly, potential entrants often look to the outcomes realized under reform bargains in other product and geographic markets to obtain insights into opportunities in newly reformed markets. For example, prospective entrants in deregulated European airline markets often look to the experience of U.S. airline deregulation in evaluating opportunities and risks of entry in European Union member markets.

The potential competitor's assessment of the market and political environment should reveal strengths and weaknesses of alternate entry strategies in terms of partnering, scale, scope, and timing. Partnering—for example, forming a joint venture—may provide important benefits following reforms.[12] Incumbents' historical relationships with customers, suppliers, and government institutions—as well as their often large, installed asset base and financial resources—tend to confer built-in advantages to these firms within both the commercial and the political sphere, even if they face major short-term transformational challenges. Partnering may help entrants overcome incumbents' advantages more effectively or more rapidly by combining strategic resources not held by any single party. Thus, the CCL joint venture brought together preexisting telecommunications infrastructure, expertise in local and competitive long-distance telephone system operations, local and international financial resources, and commercial experience within the New Zealand private and public sectors. In another example, the largest independent power plant in England, the Teesside facility, combined the international IPP development expertise of U.S.-based Enron Corp. with the customer base and political relationships of four British regional electric companies.[13] A potential drawback, however, of joint ventures is the possibility of governance problems. These are explored in more detail below.[14]

Decisions relating to the scale, scope, and timing of the entry investment may be closely linked to the terms of the reform bargain. For example, if access to gateway assets owned or controlled by the incumbent is critical for reaching customers in the market, the entrant may hesitate to build capacity on a large scale until the interpretation and enforcement of the reform bargain's access terms have been tested. If access proves to be prohibitively expensive, or problematic from a technical standpoint, the potential entrant may face the choice of bypassing the incumbent's infrastructure—which may entail major investments—or forgoing the entry opportunity. For example, competitive entry into local telephone markets in the United States has been extremely difficult, despite provisions in the Telecommunications Act of 1996 that require the Baby Bells to provide access to their local networks. As a result, several entrants, such as MCI/WorldCom, have adopted the strategy of constructing or acquiring their own local switching and transmission networks in major local markets. The scope of these investments is much broader than what would have been required if entrants had found it attractive to lease capacity on the local incumbent's switches and transmission lines, as originally envisioned under the reform legislation. In other cases, entrants provide a close substitute to the incumbents' product as a form of bypass. In late 1998 Southwest Airlines announced that it would begin providing service to and from the New York City area through the use of Long Island's MacArthur Airport. This strategy permits Southwest to avoid LaGuardia and Kennedy airports, where incumbent carriers maintain tight control over gates and landing and takeoff slots. Of course, consumer demand for service through this alternative airport may differ considerably from demand for flights through the traditional sites.

Even if the potential competitor does not face infrastructure access problems, its ultimate success may depend heavily on the terms of the reform bargain related to antitrust (competition) policy. An assessment of these terms and their likely evolution may provide critical input to the entrant's decisions regarding the magnitude and timing of its investments. Within the context of the European Union, for example, EU member nations are being required to adopt competition policies relatively more favorable to entry than in the past. In particular, a series of EU directives adopted during the 1980s and 1990s has gradually led to the opening up of national markets in the telecommunications, energy, and transportation sectors. As these directives have taken effect, greater authority for enforcing restrictions on anticompetitive behavior has shifted to the EU's competition commissioner, whose vigorously procompetitive positions to date have created a more favorable environment for entry in the affected sectors over time.

Given the high degree of uncertainty of market and political dynamics at the time of liberalization, would-be competitors may be tempted to adopt a wait-and-see attitude, updating their assessment of the entry environment as events unfold. Yet this more cautious approach also has drawbacks. If the new investment's minimum efficient scale is high relative to market demand, opportunities for entry may be very limited, perhaps to a single first mover. In the case of New Zealand's telecommunications market, for example, the limited size of the population—about 3.4 million—made it unlikely that more than one broad-based fixed-wire entrant could compete profitably against the incumbent. Although New Zealand's model of light-handed regulation was virtually untested at the end of the 1980s, CCL's joint venture partners were optimistic about the prospect of competing successfully in the market. TCNZ's chairman, Sir Ronald Trotter, had assured government officials that "interconnection would be provided to competitors on a fair basis and that the relationships between Telecom companies would not disadvantage competitors."[15] Furthermore, the provisions of the Commerce Act, in conjunction with New Zealand's independent judicial system,[16] appeared to offer a reasonable process for challenging the incumbent if problems arose. CCL decided to move quickly to preempt other possible entrants, applying for a license to be a telecommunication network operator as soon as the relevant legislation took effect, and initiating construction of its network soon thereafter.

## CORPORATE CHALLENGES OF ENTRY

Once a potential entrant has decided to compete against the market incumbent(s) under the reform bargain, it faces another set of challenges. Drawing on the categories introduced for incumbents in chapter 4, we explore the challenges of competitive entry from the perspectives of governance and leadership, corporate strategy and organizational structure, and government and public relations.

### Governance and Leadership

Whereas most incumbents grapple with governance and leadership issues related to transforming large, often inefficient organizations, entrants typically confront challenges related to the start-up of a new organization. The ownership structure of entrant enterprises is often complex, reflecting the need to assemble a variety of resources seen as critical to the venture's success, including, for example, managerial, technological, and financial resources. In many cases, the inclusion of other affected parties, such as suppliers and customers, as well as entities with experience and credibility in the relevant public and government arenas may be considered desirable or necessary for entry. The examples of CCL and the Teesside plant illustrate variations on these joint venture structures.

An obvious danger to including multiple parties within the enterprise's ownership structure is fragmentation in objectives and strategic decision-making. This problem may be exacerbated if participants in the joint venture are themselves subsidiaries of larger parent organizations with corporate objectives potentially in conflict with the more focused mission of the subsidiary. These underlying tensions may generate instability in the entrant's ownership structure over time and, in extreme cases, lead to the entrant's dissolution. The case of competitive entry in the German telecommunications market vividly illustrates these difficulties in ownership structure and governance.

In the early 1990s several German industrial conglomerates looked toward the telecommunications sector for diversification opportunities outside their slow-growth core businesses. Opportunities in various segments of the market emerged over time as a series of EU telecommunications directives compelled Germany and other members of the European Union to open national markets to competition. During this period RWE, Germany's largest utilities and energy conglomerate, consolidated a number of small investments in telecommunications ventures within and outside of Germany in a wholly-owned subsidiary, RWE Telliance.[17] One of these investments was a 25 percent shareholding in Communications Network International (CNI), a joint venture with financial services giant Deutsche Bank (25 percent) and the conglomerate Mannesmann (50 percent), a coowner of Germany's second largest cellular telephone company.[18] CNI was established in 1993 to develop fixed-line telecommunications services in competition with Deutsche Telekom.[19] RWE's extensive electricity transmission system—covering about 40 percent of German territory[20]—would provide CNI access to the firm's internal communications network and rights-of-way for additional construction of backbone infrastructure.

In 1995 RWE pulled out of CNI due to a fundamental disagreement with its partners' objective of focusing exclusively on corporate telecommunications networks.[21] In contrast, RWE wanted to build a full-service telecommunications company offering local and long-distance services to business and residential consumers. As an alternative to CNI, RWE began to form a series of smaller joint ventures with other electric utilities to link their internal communications systems to its own. In March 1996 RWE Telliance announced that it was joining forces with VIAG Interkom, a joint venture between the German utilities and energy conglomerate VIAG and British Telecom. By combining RWE's northern network and

VIAG's southern network, the new joint venture would cover over 70 percent of German territory. Yet by October, the venture had fallen apart over disagreements concerning strategy for both the fixed-line business as well as the cellular business, which VIAG Interkom hoped to enter through a bid for Germany's fourth cellular telephone license.

RWE's split with VIAG Interkom was followed almost immediately by the news that it was entering a joint venture with yet another utilities and energy conglomerate, VEBA,[22] which had formed its own telecommunications subsidiary in 1994. In that year, VEBA Telecom joined forces with German steel-giant Thyssen and U.S-based BellSouth to bid successfully for Germany's third cellular telephone license.[23] In 1995 Cable & Wireless (C&W), an international telecommunications firm based in the United Kingdom, bought a 45 percent share in VEBA Telecom, while VEBA purchased a 10 percent share in C&W. During 1996 VEBA Telecom signed long-term agreements with several natural gas transmission and distribution companies to gain access to internal communications networks and rights-of-way.

The new joint venture between RWE (37.5 percent), VEBA (40 percent), and C&W (22.5 percent), named "o.tel.o," combined the firms' German fixed-line telecommunications assets with VEBA's cellular telephone, satellite telephone, and cable television assets.[24] RWE was given principal responsibility for managing o.tel.o's network, while VEBA was to take the lead on the services side.[25] This venture, however, also proved unstable. C&W chairman Richard Brown had initiated a sweeping review of the firm's worldwide activities after his appointment in June 1996. In early 1997 he announced that C&W would withdraw from o.tel.o, shifting its continental European focus to the Global One joint venture between Deutsche Telekom, France Telecom, and U.S.-based Sprint Corporation. C&W's shares were sold to VEBA, which placed them in a trust for a future international partner. Meanwhile another complex telecommunications joint venture, Mannesmann Arcor, emerged in 1997. This fixed-line competitor was created as a merger between CNI and DBKom, the internal communications subsidiary of the German railroad Deutsche Bahn.

When the German telecommunications market was opened to full competition in January 1998, o.tel.o struggled to gain market share against an increasingly aggressive Deutsche Telekom, which had been partially privatized in November 1996,[26] and a number of other new and recent entrants, including Mannesmann Arcor.[27] O.tel.o's initial growth was slowed by delays in bringing its services to market and its more cumbersome customer registration procedures.[28] Also, its heavy investment in infrastructure placed it in a high cost position relative to lean entrants such as MobilCom that relied heavily on lines leased from Deutsche Telekom to provide retail services. In August, o.tel.o's CEO, who had come from the VEBA side of the partnership, was fired and replaced by a leading executive from RWE. For the year as a whole, o.tel.o's revenues were less than half its projections and its losses were estimated at DM 2.2 billion ($1.4 billion).[29]

Many observers attributed o.tel.o's disappointing performance under the reform bargain to ongoing instability and tension in the venture's ownership and governance, which took a toll on its ability to design and implement a successful strategy in the rapidly changing German environment.[30] These problems had adverse implications for its international strategy as well. In September 1998 BellSouth, which had been on the verge of purchasing the stake in o.tel.o previously held by C&W, walked away from the deal.

In April 1999 Mannesmann Arcor acquired o.tel.o, ending the efforts of VEBA and RWE to diversify into the German telecommunications market.[31] As the year progressed, Mannesmann continued its aggressive expansion in the European telecommunications sector, increasing its shareholdings in the Arcor venture and acquiring the British cellular operator Orange. Yet the company's ambitions were thrown into disarray when Vodafone, the British wireless giant, initiated a hostile takeover bid for the German firm in December 1999. By that point, the only thing that appeared certain was continued instability in the German telecommunications sector.

Challenges of governance and leadership may also be exacerbated by ongoing pressures for consolidation among entrants confronting large incumbents under the reform bargain. In the early 1990s entry accelerated in the British cable television market due to changes in the industry bargain that (1) lifted restrictions on ownership by non-EU corporations and (2) freed cable television operators to offer telephone service.[32] Cable operators bid for nonexclusive seventeen-year franchises to serve specific geographic areas. Although these entrants rarely faced direct competition from other cable operators,[33] they encountered indirect competition from Britain's satellite television incumbent, Ruport Murdoch's BSkyB, and the telecommunications incumbents BT and Mercury.

Over time, consolidation increased among cable operators, who hoped to gain scale and scope economies that would allow them to compete more effectively against the incumbents. On the cable side of the business, consolidation would help the entrants increase their bargaining power in negotiating fees for programming, much of which was controlled by BSkyB. On the telephone side, consolidation would help entrants increase the reach of their telecommunications networks and thus reduce the extent (and expense) of interconnection with the networks of incumbents or other entrants. Consolidation might also allow the entrants to take advantage of scale economies in other areas such as marketing, equipment procurement, and government and public relations.

One of the first major consolidations in the British cable television industry involved the 1991 establishment of Telewest through the merger of systems owned by two U.S.-based companies: the Baby Bell U.S. West[34] and cable giant TCI. Telewest's assets grew rapidly in the early 1990s through investment in distribution infrastructure and acquisition of existing systems. The contrasting corporate cultures and organization of the parent companies, however, posed challenges to Telewest's governance and leadership. In particular, U.S. West tended to adopt a more centralized approach in contrast to TCI's more decentralized management philosophy. Beyond these tensions, both parent companies found that their experiences in the U.S. cable television and telecommunications markets could not be translated easily into the British context, given the significant differences in the terms of British reform bargains in these sectors and differences in demographics, consumer tastes, and preexisting industry structure.[35]

To help finance rapid growth, Telewest sold 26.2 percent of its equity in a 1994 share offering, adding public shareholders to its ownership structure.[36] In 1995 the firm continued its consolidation drive, merging its operations with those of SBC Cablecomms, a British cable operator owned by the U.S. corporations SBC (the Baby Bell formerly known as Southwestern Bell Corporation) and cable operator Cox Communications. Although the merger reinforced Telewest's position as the U.K.'s largest cable operator, it introduced new complexities and tensions into the firm's governance, since both Cox and SBC received equity stakes and board representation.[37] In 1998 Telewest's acquisition of Britain's fourth largest cable operator, General Cable, brought a fourth major partner into the firm's ownership structure: Vivendi, the diversified French utilities company formerly known as Générale des Eaux.[38] Throughout this period, Telewest continued to run financial losses due to its heavy investments in infrastructure and its difficulties in winning customers away from the incumbent satellite television and telephone companies.

Telewest experienced considerable volatility in leadership from 1994 to 1998, as the firm changed its chief executive three times during this period of rapid consolidation, shifting governance structure, and continuing financial losses. In 1998 U.S. West moved to gain greater control over the firm, purchasing SBC's Telewest shareholdings in September. Subsequently, both Vivendi and Cox sold their shares to institutional investors. These moves left Telewest under majority control of U.S. West's MediaOne subsidiary (30 percent) and TCI (21 percent). Analysts were hopeful that under its more focused ownership structure, considerable scale, and new chief executive—an outsider with strong marketing skills—Telewest was poised to overcome its tumultuous past history as an entrant. Yet ownership changes continued to affect the firm as AT&T acquired TCI and as Microsoft made an offer for MediaOne's Telewest shares, subject to EU regulatory approval.

In contrast, the evolution of Clear Communications's ownership was less problematic during its initial years of operation. CCL was established in October 1990 when separate joint ventures led by Bell Canada (with Television New Zealand) and MCI (with New Zealand Rail and Todd Corporation) merged to form a stronger competitor vis-à-vis the privatized TCNZ. Initially each partner held an equal 20 percent shareholding in CCL, whose first CEO was George Newton, a thirty-year veteran of Bell Canada. Eventually CCL's New Zealand Rail's shareholdings were replaced by lease arrangements that gave CCL access to the firm's telecommunications assets. Bell Canada and MCI experienced little conflict in establishing the firm's strategic direction, and Television New Zealand and Todd Corporation remained largely passive investors in the firm. In 1996 British Telecom (BT) purchased Bell Canada's share in CCL—a change in ownership that created even closer congruence in governance. BT and MCI were already working closely together in international markets through their joint venture Concert, which offered telecommunications services to major multinational business customers.[39]

CCL's leadership remained relatively stable during the early years of the joint venture. Newton served as CEO until late 1993, when he returned to Canada. His successor, Andrew Makin, was a British citizen who since 1990 had served as chief executive of the corporatized state-owned enterprise responsible for New Zealand's air traffic control system. One advantage of Makin's selection was that it transcended the individual interests of the joint venture partners. In addition, the appointment placed a widely respected executive with local experience in bridging the New Zealand public and private sectors at the company's helm. Makin provided strong leadership through the summer of 1997 when, due to illness, he stepped down.

Makin's departure marked the beginning of a period of instability in leadership and governance at CCL, however. His interim successor, a British Telecom executive, was transferred after six months in office. CCL's technology director briefly became acting CEO and was succeeded in March 1998 by Tim Cullinane, whose past positions included chief executive of the computer firm ICL New Zealand and the corporatized state-owned Forestry Corporation. Meanwhile, the relationship between CCL's foreign owners began to fray as BT's attempted merger with MCI was thwarted by WorldCom's successful counteroffer. As MCI withdrew from Concert, and as BT teamed up in an international joint venture with AT&T, BT's and MCI's mutual interests in CCL eroded. During this period, CCL's profitability declined as TCNZ initiated aggressive price cuts and as newer long-distance entrants increased their market shares. Also, an opportunity for CCL to acquire BellSouth NZ, TCNZ's leading cellular competitor, was forgone as CCL's foreign partners apparently were unwilling to pursue the deal in the midst of uncertainty over their long-term strategic interests in the New Zealand market.

By the summer of 1999 BT had successfully negotiated with MCI, Television New Zealand, and Todd Corporation to buy out their ownership stakes in CCL. By taking sole control of the venture, BT hoped to provide more focused leadership to CCL in the challenging New Zealand telecommunications market.

## Corporate Strategy and Organizational Structure

In chapter 4 we saw that at the time of liberalization, incumbents often grapple with the unwieldy or inappropriate scope of their business activities and organizational structure. In contrast, entrants typically start with a blank slate or, in some instances, key assets that form the core of the initial entry opportunity—for example, the telecommunications assets of New Zealand Rail and Television New Zealand in the case of CCL.

Over time entrants often weigh opportunities to expand into or withdraw from certain lines of business or geographic regions. In addition, the entrant may consider merger and acquisition opportunities involving competitors, as demonstrated in the cases of o.tel.o and Telewest presented above. The impetus for expansion may be grounded in the prospect of achieving greater economies of scale or scope in production, marketing, administration, or even in government and public relations activities. The firm may also hope to increase its bargaining power relative to suppliers, buyers, and external parties. In cases where incumbents control access to gateway infrastructure, the entrant may be particularly interested in pursuing forms of vertical or horizontal integration that allow it to bypass or at least improve the terms of access to these assets. The entrant's strategy in this area, however, may be constrained by government competition policy under the reform bargain. For example, it is not clear whether the British government will ever permit the consolidation of the nation's joint cable television/telephone entrants into a single enterprise.[40]

Selected divestment or abandonment of business activities may allow the entrant to enhance its financial position and achieve greater focus in its operations and sales and marketing efforts. This pullback strategy may be particularly relevant for firms that adopt an aggressive broad-based entry strategy as the reform bargain comes into place, but are unable to compete profitably across multiple lines of business, customer segments, and geographic regions over time.

## Government and Public Relations

Entrants often find themselves in a paradoxical position vis-à-vis the state under the reform bargain. On the one hand, their mere existence can be attributed to the willingness of the state to ease restrictions on freedom of entry. Yet the adoption of laissez-faire bargains throughout the reform sector may leave entrants unable to compete profitably, especially when industry incumbents control access to gateway assets or other critical resources. Thus entrants often want the state to ensure their freedom to enter while simultaneously guaranteeing their right to access facilities controlled by the incumbent. Entrants also desire the right to protection from anticompetitive behavior, such as predatory pricing, on the part of incumbents. Of course, the presence of these rights in entrants' enterprise bargains implies corresponding obligations in the terms of incumbents' bargains.

CCL's CEO Andrew Makin described entry deregulation in the tele-communications sector as follows: "The paradox of the telecommunications market is that it isn't free until someone intervenes to make it free."[41] Over time CCL found, much to its surprise, that its performance was affected as much—if not more—by its evolving bargain with the New Zealand state as by the commercial aspects of its strategy. However, the importance of the terms, interpretation, and enforcement of its bargain— as well as TCNZ's bargain—was largely unrecognized at the time of entry. In effect, CCL assumed that light-handed regulation would provide an ideal environment for competitive entry.

CCL's decision to locate its headquarters in Auckland, as opposed to New Zealand's capital city Wellington, was emblematic of its focus on the commercial, as opposed to the political, aspects of its entry opportunity. The firm's initial successes in the long-distance market probably reinforced the notion that the state was largely irrelevant in the privatized, deregulated environment of New Zealand's telecommunications market. Thus, when CCL was unable to negotiate an acceptable local service interconnection agreement with TCNZ, it found that it had few levers to pull within the New Zealand government for relief. Unlike virtually all other nations implementing reforms in the telecommunications sector, New Zealand did not create a sector-specific regulatory body. At the same time, the New Zealand Commerce Commission, the nation's principal antitrust body, had limited powers of investigation and enforcement. In fact, the New Zealand High Court found that the Commerce Commission's general inquiry into the evolution of competition in the telecommunications industry, released in early 1992 and largely critical of TCNZ, exceeded the commission's statutory powers of investigation.[42] CCL also found little support from Minister of Communications Maurice Williamson, who tended to view the rights of entry in the New Zealand telecommunications sector in terms of freedoms, as opposed to entitlements.[43]

Ultimately, then, battles over the interpretation and enforcement of CCL's and TCNZ's bargains were fought in the judicial system. So, from 1991 on, a steady stream of litigation relating to detailed technical and financial terms of interconnection, the use of product bundling, advertising practices, and other actions emerged in claims and counterclaims filed by the two companies. In the battle for public opinion, CCL accused TCNZ of suffering from "acute monopolitis," while TCNZ dubbed the entrant a "law firm with an antenna."[44] Litigation related to local interconnection lasted three years and involved two reversals on appeal, with CCL losing the final round in a decision by the London Privy Council, the highest appellate court in the British Commonwealth system. Testimony in the trials included arcane economic analyses, presented and debated by experts from New Zealand and abroad.

Although the Privy Council found that TCNZ had not abused its dominant position in its terms of interconnection, it noted that the New Zealand government, through its minister of industry, had the authority under the Commerce Act to impose price controls "in circumstances of reduced competition."[45] CCL, portraying itself as the industry underdog and emphasizing TCNZ's increasing profitability,[46] appealed to the government to intervene. The leader of New Zealand's left-wing Alliance Party supported CCL's position, accusing TCNZ of earning excessive returns. Support from the Alliance Party was a mixed blessing, however, for CCL since the party's anticommercial views could prove problematic for the firm at some future stage. Ironically, neither CCL nor TCNZ could appeal to the public's sense of nationalism, since each was 50 percent owned by foreign telecommunications companies. Eventually, the New Zealand government took a middle-of-the-road approach, threatening possible intervention if the two parties did not reach an interconnection agreement, but remaining purposely vague as to the possible timing and form of such intervention.[47]

CCL and TCNZ reached a comprehensive interconnection agreement in March 1996. Although CCL obtained more favorable terms for long-distance interconnection than in its 1991 agreement, the terms for local interconnection did not appear to provide much opportunity to profit in local calling markets. After TCNZ began offering special local business calling plans priced below CCL's interconnection costs, CCL sued TCNZ for abusing its dominant position and began withholding 15 percent of its interconnection fees. TCNZ countersued. CCL initiated additional litigation as well, suing TCNZ for alleged anticompetitive product bundling and suing the New Zealand government for failure to enforce TCNZ's 1988 pledge to provide "fair, consistent, non-discriminatory and cost-based" interconnection charges.

Alongside its litigation, CCL sought to influence public and government opinion by commissioning the Todd Telecommunications Consortium to study the New Zealand telecommunications market. The Todd report, whose lead author was one of New Zealand's most respected accountants, was released in a press conference in November 1998 as part of a public relations campaign led by Telecom's former PR agency. The report concluded that TCNZ, whose return on equity exceeded 40 percent during 1997 and 1998, was extracting $382 million annually in excess profits from New Zealand consumers. It also accused TCNZ of consistently responding to competition with predatory pricing or litigation. The results of the Todd report complemented those of a report by an Australian analyst released one month earlier, which concluded that TCNZ's dominance had discouraged investment in New Zealand's telecommunications sector and had made New Zealand a less attractive global location for multinational businesses.[48]

The Todd report was endorsed by a range of firms dependent on interconnection agreements with TCNZ including fixed-wire, cellular, and cable television companies. CCL hoped that pressure from this informal coalition, in combination with support from consumer groups, would encourage the government to adopt legislative reforms strengthening the terms of the Commerce Act to enhance the scope of, and penalties associated with, alleged anticompetitive behavior. Nevertheless, it remained unclear at the close of the 1990s whether the government would respond to pressures to modify the principal underpinnings of the nation's model of light-handed regulation. Meanwhile, the Commerce Commission revealed that it was considering strengthening disclosure requirements to compel TCNZ to produce a separate financial statement for its local calling business so that the costs associated with interconnection services in this area could be more easily analyzed.[49]

CCL's experience in the area of government and public relations highlights the challenges facing many entrants under reform bargains. Despite a desire to focus on the commercial demands associated with entry, entrants' success may be determined as much by the evolving terms of competition—including rights, obligations, and enforcement mechanisms—as by technological innovations or clever marketing campaigns. In this respect, entrants, ironically, may find a strong regulator to be their greatest asset following deregulation.

## OPERATIONAL CHALLENGES OF ENTRY

Entrants competing with incumbents face a number of challenges related to the design and implementation of strategies at the operating level. We will look at these using the same categories employed in chapter 5 in the analysis of incumbent strategy: human resources, technology and production, procurement, sales and marketing, and finance and control.

## Human Resources

The broad challenge for most entrants in the area of human resources is building a new organization. At least in the initial stages, entrants owned by firms operating in other markets may be able to draw on individuals within the parent organization(s) to fill key management positions, either on a permanent or temporary basis. As the hiring effort is expanded, however, the entrant often faces a number of trade-offs involving skills, cost, and speed. In essence, the entrant confronts two competing pressures. On the one hand, it may be anxious to build up its organization rapidly so as to offer credible competition to the incumbent(s), whose size and established presence may provide important advantages from both a production and marketing perspective. Speed may also be viewed as critical in establishing a preemptive first-mover advantage in relation to other potential entrants. Yet the faster the ramp-up of the organization the more costly the effort is likely to be, given characteristics of the relevant labor pool at the time of the reform bargain.

Ideally, the entrant would like to hire managers and workers with strong functional abilities, knowledge of industry best practices, language skills, and attitudes aligned with the desired organizational culture. Such ideal employees, however, tend to be in short supply, particularly immediately following reform. Typically, most potential hires in the local market with industry knowledge are current or former employees of incumbent enterprises—workers often unfamiliar with best practices or lacking the motivation and workplace attitudes sought by the entrant. The most qualified of these potential employees may be costly to identify and compensate. Yet the entrant may be in a strong position to attract the more entrepreneurial members of this pool of potential employees. Mercury Communications, for example, found that its status as the first firm permitted to compete with incumbent British Telecom piqued the interest of a number of talented BT employees anxious to work in a smaller, less bureaucratic environment.

Besides drawing on employees of incumbent firms, entrants must often build their workforce by hiring individuals with industry experience in other geographic or product markets. But the associated relocation and training expenses may be substantial. In addition, the entrant faces the risk that once investments in human capital have been made, these employees will become more desirable to other entrants and even the incumbent in their own recruiting efforts. Hence, the very characteristics that may have attracted the entrant to individual hires in the first place— flexibility, entrepreneurship, willingness to take risks—tend to make these workers more susceptible to poaching by other firms. Mercury, for instance, found its best employees targeted aggressively by combination cable-telecommunications entrants and new long-distance competitors after the deregulation of the British telecommunications duopoly in 1991.[50]

The design of compensation systems may be challenging for entrants, particularly in the initial phase of entry. Heavy start-up losses may result from up-front investments in fixed assets and marketing expenses as the entrant works to establish itself in the marketplace. Under these circumstances, it may be difficult to reward managers based on traditional profitability measures. Since many entrants do not have their own publicly traded shares, at least in the early stages of entry, compensation based on market returns is less common among these firms.[51] Yet it may still be possible to create incentives in the form of shares (or share options) for employees of entrants that plan to issue shares publicly at some point in the future. For high-flying entrepreneurial entrants, the use of these financial incentives may be a particularly attractive carrot for recruiting and retaining managers willing to take the risk of joining a new firm. For example, start-up Qwest Communications lured AT&T executive Joseph Nacchio away to be its CEO in January 1997 with a compensation package that included 6.3 million options on Qwest shares, worth an estimated $227 million in late 1998.[52]

In one sense, it might be easier for a new entrant to establish a culture consistent with the postreform competitive environment than for an incumbent, which may retain considerable baggage from the prereform era. Yet the discussion of governance above suggests that clashes often emerge in the organizations of joint venture entrants if substantial differences exist in the cultures of the parent organizations. Cultural challenges also may emerge over time, as entrants pass through various stages of postreform market evolution. Mercury Communications, for example, found it difficult to make the cultural transition from an entrepreneurial start-up in the early 1980s to a more established service provider—in fact an incumbent—when further entry deregulation opened the door to a new set of entrants beginning in 1991.

## Technology and Production

Technology may work to the advantage or disadvantage of the entrant. Some entrants are able to leapfrog the incumbent in technological sophistication by installing a newer generation of equipment or an alternative production process. For example, independent power producers have taken advantage of combined-cycle gas turbine technology to compete against incumbents reliant on higher-cost coal-, oil-, or nuclear-based generation technologies. Likewise, especially in the United States, satellite television companies have used digital signal transmission—which produces a higher-quality picture resolution and sound—to compete against cable television systems, most of which continued to rely on analog transmission in the 1990s.

The entrant, however, may face important technological disadvantages relative to the incumbent, particularly if there are significant scale or scope economies in the production process. Few airline entrants have been able to compete successfully over time with established carriers that leverage extensive hub-and-spoke systems to offer a wide variety of routes and departure times to fliers. Also, even if the entrant initially introduces a superior technology into the market, the incumbent may have the resources and, particularly under the terms of the reform bargain, the incentives to adopt the technology itself in a relatively short period of time. National Power, for example, was quick to embrace CCGT technology following privatization and deregulation of the British power-generation market.

An entrant may face challenges balancing demand for its products and services with its ability to supply them, particularly if capacity can be added only in large increments. It may be difficult to project not only the overall growth in market demand for new or existing services, but also consumers' willingness to switch to the entrant from the incumbent(s). Also, changes in the effective size and utilization of incumbents' capacity may be difficult to predict at the time of reform. Entrants in the Argentine power-generation sector, for instance, failed to project the rapid increases in capacity utilization achieved by incumbent generators under the reform bargain and thus overinvested in new production capacity. This misstep proved unfortunate for many of the new competitors since entrants tended to be highly dependent on electricity spot markets for their sales.[53] In contrast, incumbents' prices and sales volumes were largely hedged through long-term contracts signed with distributors at the time of privatization.[54]

In postreform markets where a competing incumbent controls critical gateway assets, entrants' choice of technology may be shaped significantly by the terms of access to the gateway under the reform bargain. If a potential entrant is able to obtain access to some or all of the assets at favorable wholesale prices, it may decide to invest in few fixed assets of its own, relying instead on the use of the incumbent's gateway as a key input for the provision of goods and services. Yet if the price or other terms of access are unattractive, potential entrants are faced with either developing a means of bypassing the incumbent's gateway—through similar or alternative technologies—or forgoing the entry opportunity.

In the case of the New Zealand telecommunications market, CCL was able to compete successfully in the long-distance market by constructing and utilizing its own telecommunications network for the segment of each call transmitted between cities, while paying TCNZ a fee to carry the segments of each call transmitted within cities. But CCL was unable to replicate this strategy to compete within local markets due to the unfavorable cost of partial access to TCNZ's local networks. One alternative strategy for CCL—the construction of a duplicate local network—appeared prohibitively expensive. Faced with comparable difficulties in competing in local markets in the United States, AT&T acquired cable giant TCI in 1998 with the aim of adapting the technology in TCI's local cable television systems to bypass the Baby Bells' local telecommunications networks.

## Procurement

Many of the resources entrants require, such as labor, capital, equipment, and raw materials, are available through competitive markets. In some cases, however, the entrant may enjoy less favorable procurement terms relative to the incumbent due to smaller size or other factors. For example, large incumbent airlines typically possess greater bargaining power relative to aircraft suppliers than do small start-up entrants. Yet there are situations in which an entrant may enjoy the more favorable procurement position. For example, a large multinational firm such as Enron—an IPP entrant in a number of countries—is often able to extract better terms from equipment and raw material suppliers than incumbent power producers against which it competes. The entrant may be able to combine its procurement strategy with its marketing strategy to provide a differentiated product for consumers. Some entrants, for example, are able to reach an exclusive agreement with the manufacturer of a component used in the service provided by the firm—for example, a distinctive cellular telephone associated with a wireless telephone entrant.[55]

In some cases, as we have seen, incumbents control access to resources sought by entrants. The incumbent's control may be indirect—for example, through exclusive contracts with key suppliers—or direct, through ownership of the resource itself. Entrants' dependence on incumbents for access to important resources tends to be particularly common under reform bargains, due to the technological features of many of the sectors and the long-standing relationships that often exist between incumbents and suppliers. Yet the extent to which the incumbent's control of key resources acts as a barrier to competition will depend on the terms and implementation of the reform bargain.

The deregulation of the U.S. cable television industry in the early 1980s posed several access-related challenges for competing entrants. The first involved programming. A number of popular cable TV channels—such as Home Box Office (HBO) and Entertainment Sports Programming Network (ESPN)—were owned by large incumbent cable TV operators. These multiple systems operators (MSOs) each provided monopoly service to a number of local communities prior to deregulation. The MSOs' vertical integration into programming appeared to make good business sense, since the availability of a greater volume and variety of programming would presumably enhance demand for cable television service. Yet these ownership relationships posed problems for competitive entry into local cable TV markets, particularly those served by vertically integrated MSOs. Entrants often faced difficulties obtaining not only programming controlled by the MSO incumbent operating in the target market, but also programming controlled by other MSOs.[56]

Repeated complaints to the Federal Communications Commission and the U.S. Congress by frustrated entrants eventually led to changes in the terms of the reform bargain: specifically, the 1992 Cable Television Consumer Protection and Competition Act required program owners to provide access to their products on a nondiscriminatory basis. Similar access problems confronted cable television entrants in the 1990s in Britain, where Rupert Murdoch's BSkyB satellite TV service controlled exclusive rights over key sports programming.

At the time of deregulation, U.S. cable TV entrants also faced problems accessing physical infrastructure controlled by incumbents. Cable entrants hoped to avoid wiring houses, apartment buildings, and commercial establishments where wires had already been installed by the incumbent. Yet incumbents were rarely willing to provide access to their physical infrastructure, whether located within or outside the customer location. In response to litigation brought by a number of entrants and property owners, the U.S. judiciary determined that property owners held the ultimate right to determine the use of wiring installed on their premises.[57] This clarification of the terms of the reform bargain proved particularly valuable for entrants serving markets with a high proportion of multi-unit housing.

As we have seen, incumbents' control over telecommunications networks, electricity transmission and distribution systems, natural gas pipelines, water and sewer systems, rail systems, and airport gates and takeoff slots raises the question of whether the mere removal of limits on freedom of entry will be sufficient to attract entry in practice. Yet even when the reform bargain includes incumbent obligations (and thus entrant entitlements) with respect to access, entry may still prove difficult or impossible.

Sometimes incumbents are able to influence the costs and quality of access to physical infrastructure in ways unanticipated at the time of the adoption of the reform bargain. For example, incumbent U.S. local telephone companies have found many creative techniques for reducing the attractiveness of access to their networks to competing service providers, who have accused the Baby Bells of delaying negotiations, imposing arbitrary fees, and setting Byzantine technical requirements.[58] Entrants may also be vulnerable to capacity shortfalls associated with the infrastructure. Entrants and incumbents alike often invoke legal challenges in areas related to access following the adoption of the reform bargain. As the interpretation, enforcement, or terms of access evolve over time, the relative competitive position of incumbents and individual entrants may shift dramatically, as we saw, for example, in the case of the German telecommunications sector.

## Sales and Marketing

Entrants possess both advantages and disadvantages from the perspective of sales and marketing. Since the incumbent often begins with a reputation for poor service, high prices, or both, buyers may be quite receptive to a new producer or service provider at the time of reforms. On the other hand, consumers may be wary of particular entrants with respect to technical qualifications, financial resources, or long-term commitment to the market. Risk-averse buyers may simply remain with the incumbent, preferring the devil they know to one that they don't. Also, to the extent that the incumbent's performance begins to improve at, or even prior to, the time of entry, consumers may not perceive significant long-term benefits to switching.

Establishing credibility in the marketplace often takes on particular importance for competing entrants under the reform bargain, since incumbents in the relevant industries often provide goods and services perceived as basic necessities by households and/or businesses. Concerns regarding reliability and, in some cases, safety may lead consumers to be especially wary of newcomers. Thus, Enron Corporation entered the California retail electricity market as it was opened to competition in the late-1990s, but it failed to attract more than a small fraction of the state's household consumers despite spending an estimated $5 million to $10 million in a statewide advertising and marketing campaign.[59] Enron's worldwide assets totaled $30 billion in the late 1990s, but its experience in retail electricity markets was limited and the firm was virtually unknown to California consumers at the time of entry. Ultimately, Enron concluded that the cost of overcoming consumer resistance was too high to enable the firm to operate profitably as an entrant in the sector, particularly given the low margins embedded in the regulated wholesale power rate it paid to incumbents under the terms of the reform bargain.

Start-up airlines typically face the challenge of convincing the consumer that they are both safe and financially secure. The bankruptcy of numerous entrants in the U.S. airline market since deregulation has left fliers wary of being stranded at critical travel times and perhaps unable to collect hundreds of dollars paid in advance for fares. The fatal crash of a ValuJet airplane in Florida in 1996 confirmed travelers' worst fears that new entrants lacked the experience and financial strength to ensure proper maintenance and operation of their equipment. Following the crash, demand fell sharply not only for ValuJet's flights, but also for the flights of other recent entrants. ValuJet's reputation was so damaged by the accident that it was able to begin a credible recovery only after changing its name to AirTran, a small carrier that it acquired in 1997.

Foreign-owned entrants tend to have both strengths and weaknesses with respect to credibility.[60] On the plus side, foreign firms often bring extensive experience in serving the relevant product market in their home country and perhaps in other countries as well. They may also bring a reputation of greater technological sophistication than that of the local incumbent(s). Yet consumers may worry that the foreign entrant's commitment to and knowledge of the local market is weaker than the incumbent's.

Entrants can sometimes build credibility by securing high-profile customers. WorldCom, for example, secured a contract in 1995 to provide telephone service to the German parliament buildings in Bonn.[61] This widely publicized deal was both an embarrassing loss to Deutsche Telekom and a boon to WorldCom's strategy of building a customer base among large users.[62] Entrants may also seek to enhance credibility through partnerships that combine a variety of resources, such as those found in the CCL joint venture. In some cases, competitors may avoid postentry credibility risks by partnering directly with customers, such as in Enron's Teesside IPP joint venture with several British RECs.

A notable appeal that entrants bring to the market—the novelty factor—can be a double-edged sword. In the early stages of entry, a subset of the potential customer base may be quite willing to buy from the new competitor out of curiosity or of boredom with the incumbent—even if the entrant does not offer significantly greater value in terms of lower price or higher quality. But over time, these same customers often prove more likely to shift their patronage to other, perhaps second generation, entrants or respond favorably to new-and-improved incumbents. In fact, Mercury Communications' customers were aggressively targeted by firms entering the British telecommunications market following the end of the duopoly period in 1991.[63]

The nature and severity of switching costs incurred by customers moving from incumbents to entrants is often highly influenced by the terms of the reform bargain. In many telecommunications markets, including New Zealand's, consumers that wish to use an alternative long-distance carrier must formally request a change in service provider and dial a special access code before placing each long-distance call. Under these terms, customers may be reluctant to formally sever their relationship with the incumbent provider and may find access code requirements burdensome. Some reform bargains are designed to reduce these switching costs by allowing customers to choose their long-distance provider on a call-by-call basis. In Germany, for instance, callers may retain Deutsche Telekom as their default carrier, yet select among an array of long-distance entrants, each with its own access code, for individual calls.[64] Chile has gone one step further in reducing asymmetry between incumbents and entrants by requiring the use of an access code even when placing a long-distance call through the incumbent. At the opposite extreme, British customers were required to purchase special telephones in addition to requesting a change in carrier to switch service from British Telecom to the entrant Mercury Communications at the time of entry deregulation. Not surprisingly, entrant market shares have increased more rapidly following reform bargains in Chile and Germany than in the United Kingdom and New Zealand.

Some reform bargains have included a transition process designed to facilitate switching to a new entrant through a balloting procedure. Under this process, retail consumers in sectors such as telecommunications, electricity, and natural gas are asked to select a provider from a ballot that lists preapproved firms (incumbents and entrants) by name.[65] This procedure tends to raise the likelihood of switching by increasing consumers' awareness of entry deregulation in the market and by providing additional information on specific entrants. Also, by requiring customers to decide whether to remain with the incumbent, as opposed to retaining the relationship on a default basis, the tendency to stay with the incumbent through inertia is reduced.

The issue of number portability has played an important role in shaping switching costs in local telephone markets undergoing entry deregulation. Telecommunications entrants face substantial difficulties attracting customers if callers are not able to retain their existing telephone number when shifting to a new carrier—in other words, if the number is not "portable." Traditionally, incumbents have controlled the allocation of telephone numbers. Incumbents would enjoy a strong competitive advantage over entrants if they retained this right under the reform bargain. On the other hand, if the incumbent was required to provide number portability free of charge, it could find itself at a competitive disadvantage due to the costs incurred in rerouting service to a new entrant on the customer's behalf.[66]

In practice, the costs associated with number portability—and the decision as to which party is responsible for paying these costs—has often led to sharp controversy. In New Zealand, for example, the incumbent TCNZ charged a flat flee of NZ$17.50 (US$10.40) plus 0.5 NZ¢ per minute of usage to customers that wished to retain their telephone number, but switch local service to the entrant CCL.[67] These fees, which were upheld in a legal challenge by CCL, created a dilemma for the entrant. If CCL absorbed these costs on the customer's behalf, its ability to offer profitable service would be impaired. Yet, if customers faced these costs directly, the demand for CCL's service would be adversely affected. These switching costs, in combination with the interconnection charges levied for terminating or originating calls over TCNZ's network, rendered CCL's attempt to enter local telephone markets in the late 1990s unsuccessful.

Deutsche Telekom announced at the time of entry deregulation that it would charge DM 95 ($52.80) to any customer switching to another carrier, whether for long-distance service, local calling, or both. The carrier proposed an additional charge of DM 52.9 ($29.40) for customers wishing to retain an existing phone number. Germany's new entrants challenged these fees as excessive under the terms of the 1996 Telecommunications Act, which restricted switching and interconnection charges to levels commensurate with "reasonable costs." As a result, Deutsche Telekom was forced to reduce its total switching charge per line to DM 26.8.

*Pricing.* Some reform bargains include restrictions on pricing to end users, particularly for services where the incumbent is seen as retaining substantial market power. Examples of such restrictions include the price caps faced by incumbent telephone companies and local distributors of electricity, natural gas, and water even in the presence of entry deregulation in the United Kingdom and the United States. Although these obligations typically affect the incumbent's enterprise bargain, their indirect implications for entrants may be profound.

Paradoxically, although price caps and other forms of maximum price controls tend to directly reduce incumbents' market power relative to consumers, they may discourage competition by reducing the attractiveness of entry, and thus indirectly reinforce the market power of established firms.[68] For example, in late 1997, the Rhode Island Public Utilities Commission required the state's incumbent electric utilities to reduce their prices by 3 percent to 10 percent, depending on customer type.[69] This was highly damaging to New Energy Ventures, the most successful entrant following deregulation of the market for industrial power users. New Energy Ventures, which had previously won over thirteen of the state's thirty largest industrial power customers, found itself unable to operate profitably, either as a power reseller or as an independent power producer. In the short term, the entrant decided to pay rebates to customers to maintain relationships with its large buyers. However, without a future easing of price restrictions or unexpected improvements in its cost position, the firm eventually pulled out of the market.[70]

In contrast, Clear Communications appears to have benefited from the minimal restrictions on pricing to end users in the New Zealand telecommunications market. Although the incumbent, TCNZ, was restricted from raising the price of basic local residential service faster than the rate of inflation, it faced no explicit controls on pricing of other services. The price of domestic long-distance service in New Zealand was quite high at the time of CCL's entry—NZ 86¢ per minute versus the equivalent of NZ 41¢ in the United States.[71] During its initial entry period, CCL offered long-distance service below TCNZ's price umbrella, capturing a 10 percent market share within a year. At first, TCNZ was reluctant to respond with price cuts since the cost of losing a small portion of the market appeared much lower than the cost of reducing prices on its entire long-distance calling base. Yet over time, it became concerned with CCL's rapid gains in market share and did reduce prices. After a brief price war in the mid-1990s, long-distance prices stabilized at about 25 percent below levels prevailing at the time of deregulation.

Pricing challenges are often complicated by the bundling of multiple products—an issue discussed at some length in chapter 5. The entrant may be able to compete successfully against the incumbent head-to-head in offering a single good or service even if the entrant relies on access to a gateway asset of the incumbent as a key input. However, if the incumbent can bundle the product with other goods and services, it may be able to offer a combined price that the entrant cannot meet, even if it could obtain the other goods and services at costs comparable to the incumbent's.[72] In the mid-1990s, for example, CCL alleged that TCNZ was using its dominant position in local telephone markets to create product bundles—including various combinations of local fixed-wire, long-distance, wireless, Internet-access, and pay television services—that would weaken the entrant's long-term ability to compete successfully in the long-distance business.

*Customer-Related Issues.* One important disadvantage that entrants often face under reform bargains is a lack of customer-related information. Incumbents often possess extensive data on the buying behavior of individual customers, including their creditworthiness. The entrant's asymmetric position in this regard can create a range of problems. When local telephone competition was introduced in Rochester, New York, for instance, the incumbent provider, Frontier, happily informed its least attractive customers—in particular, delinquent payers—that alternative providers, including AT&T and Time Warner, were also offering local services.[73] In general, incumbents that were monopolists under the prereform bargain also have the advantage of knowing exactly which customers defect to new entrants following reforms. Competitors claim that British Telecom has used this knowledge along with other information to target the most attractive of these customers through "win back" programs.[74]

The possession of detailed customer information, in combination with the underlying customer relationships, has led some incumbents to offer additional products to the same customer base. Thus, as the retailing of natural gas and electricity has been opened to entry in the United Kingdom, traditional natural gas and electricity distributors have begun to compete in each other's markets. In some cases, however, the terms of the reform bargain may restrict the use of customer information for certain purposes—for example, barring the transfer of customer data from a firm's traditional regulated businesses to its "unregulated" affiliates.

Finally, cultural factors, as well as restrictions under the terms of the reform bargain, may constrain entrants' ability to interact with potential customers. For example, following entry deregulation in British natural gas retail markets, a number of entrants owned by U.S.-based firms were surprised to find strong resistance among the British public to door-to-door sales techniques. In Germany, entrants in the deregulated telecommunications market have had to comply with basic restrictions on telephone soliciting that apply to all firms operating in the nation.

## Finance and Control

Entrants under the reform bargain often face the same kinds of financial challenges confronted by any start-up organization. However, the magnitude of capital investments—and thus funding needs—tends to be particularly high in the reform sectors, and payback periods may be quite long. For example, wireless telephone service entrants cannot expect to earn profits for a number of years after sinking the initial investment. As discussed in the section on corporate governance and leadership, many entrants are financed initially through one or more parent companies that may be incumbents in other markets. Over time, entrants may find it possible to secure their own financing in the capital markets through public equity and debt offerings, such as in the case of Telewest. Public share listings may also provide indirect benefits in the form of additional performance measures to which compensation can be tied. Yet the cost of capital may be relatively high for these new entrants, given the established role of incumbents and the uncertain future path of consumer demand and the reform bargain.

Even if the entrant successfully weathers the start-up phase, it may face ongoing financing challenges. The incumbent may become a much more efficient producer and a more aggressive competitor over time. Also, other entrants may emerge as increasingly effective competitors. Financing pressures may be exacerbated further if the entrant continues to expand its operations in an increasingly competitive environment, for example, to achieve greater economies of scale and scope through internal growth or acquisition. In some cases, entrants eventually become overextended and are forced to downsize, merge with another firm, or face liquidation. Many start-up airlines have experienced this cycle including, notably, People's Express and New York Air.

Internal financial control systems may play a critical role in the entrant's ability to manage organizational growth. Given the natural inclination of the entrant to focus on the build-up of productive capability and sales, it is important that cost-related data be collected and monitored carefully at the same time.

CCL's initial funding requirements were met by its parent companies. Given the relatively small size of the New Zealand market and CCL's limited expansion beyond long-distance service, capital expenditures during its first seven years were fairly modest—NZ$340.2 million. In contrast, TCNZ's capital expenditures over the same years amounted to NZ$4.07 billion.[75] CCL also began to generate funds internally early on in its history due to the fact that it faced only moderate competition from TCNZ in the long-distance market and experienced little in the way of competition from other entrants.

## CLEAR COMMUNICATIONS AND
## THE CHALLENGE OF ENTRY

CCL's performance as an entrant in New Zealand's deregulated telecommunications market is rife with contradictions. On the one hand, the firm's initial performance in the long-distance market was impressive. In fact, CCL increased its market share to 20 percent faster than any other long-distance entrant in any national long-distance market up to that time. It also showed a profit in its third year of operations—an impressive result by international standards. By 1996 the firm was earning a respectable (after-tax) return on sales of 8.8 percent, return on assets of 10.3 percent, and return on equity of 17.6 percent[76] (see table 6-1). These positive results appeared to be driven by a variety of factors, including CCL's strong governance and leadership, the high margins prevailing in the long-distance sector at the time of deregulation, and TCNZ's reluctance to compete aggressively in the long-distance sector. To an extent, TCNZ probably welcomed CCL's successes in the long-distance market since the presence of a profitable entrant undermined criticism of the incumbent's behavior as anticompetitive.

Despite CCL's successes, its performance was disappointing in other respects. The firm made little progress in penetrating local calling markets, even after years of litigation in support of its efforts. In essence, TCNZ remained the incumbent-on-top. Also, CCL's performance in the long-distance market came under increasing pressure from new entrants—in particular the Australian carrier Telstra and a number of smaller competitors—and more aggressive price cutting on the part of TCNZ. As a result, CCL's revenues began to level off and net income declined in both 1997 and 1998. By 1999 CCL was running a loss and

Table 6-1  CLEAR COMMUNICATIONS LTD. FINANCIAL STATISTICS, 1991–1999
(fiscal years ending in March; data in millions of New Zealand dollars, unless otherwise indicated)

| | 1991 | 1992 | 1993 | 1994 | 1995 | 1996 | 1997 | 1998 | 1999 |
|---|---|---|---|---|---|---|---|---|---|
| Revenue | NA | NA | NA | 185.5 | 240.4 | 266.4 | 273.8 | 292.2 | 273.7 |
| Operating Profit | −8.5 | −30.0 | −2.5 | 7.6 | 30.8 | 38.9 | 35.7 | 20.9 | 12.3 |
| Net Income | −7.6 | −31.1 | −5.9 | 5.5 | 29.0 | 23.4 | 20.8 | 9.2 | −1.0 |
| Capital Expenditures | 66.8 | 46.4 | 26.9 | 38.5 | 39.9 | 44.8 | 76.9 | 61.8 | 81.6 |
| Assets | 102.1 | 156.8 | 158.9 | 201.0 | 220.0 | 226.2 | 271.5 | 299.6 | 323.0 |
| Equity | 63.2 | 69.3 | 65.0 | 139.8 | 121.7 | 133.2 | 142.0 | 139.1 | 133.6 |
| Operating Margin (%) | NA | NA | NA | 4.1 | 12.8 | 14.6 | 13.1 | 7.1 | 4.5 |
| Return on Sales (%) | NA | NA | NA | 3.0 | 12.1 | 8.8 | 7.6 | 3.1 | −0.4 |
| Return on Assets (%) | −7.4 | −19.8 | −3.7 | 2.7 | 13.2 | 10.3 | 7.7 | 3.1 | −0.3 |
| Return on Equity (%) | −12.0 | −44.9 | −9.1 | 3.9 | 23.8 | 17.6 | 14.6 | 6.6 | −0.7 |

*Source: CCL Annual Reports filed in the Companies Office of New Zealand.*

*NA = not available*

the company's future trajectory remained uncertain in the face of ongoing disputes over terms of interconnection. Yet BT's consolidation of CCL's ownership, and the announcement of an alliance between CCL and Vodafone New Zealand Ltd. (BellSouth NZ's successor) in early 2000, provided hope for a possible turnaround as CCL entered its second decade.

# 7 ✦ Concessions and Contracting Out

*In contrast to chapter 6*, which examines entry challenges involving competition against incumbents, chapter 7 explores entry opportunities involving various forms of contracting with a government institution for the provision of goods or services—usually in markets in which the state has previously excluded private enterprises from participation. Such arrangements include concessions to build and operate toll roads, light rail systems, power plants, pipelines, and mining facilities.[1] These typically take the form of monopolies awarded through a bidding process. In some cases, all of the firm's output is purchased by government entities, whereas in others, the goods and services are sold to end users or private intermediaries. Examining these cases is particularly valuable given the richness and complexity of associated opportunities and risks.

Variations of this form of entry include contracts to provide social services (housing, incarceration, and trash disposal services, for instance) and intermediate services to government enterprises or agencies (e.g., management and outsourcing of support services). Although these entry opportunities do not generally involve investments on the same scale as those associated with large infrastructure concessions, they often pose similar challenges from the perspective of managing complex contractual relationships with the state over time.

Enterprise bargains associated with contract entry typically include many deal-specific terms, although the initial reform bargain often provides a general structure of rights, obligations, and enforcement mechanisms. For example, Mexican legislation establishing the right of private enterprises to build, operate, and hold equity stakes in toll highways, adopted in 1990, created a framework within which the terms of individual concessions were developed. Thus, all bargains required that the concessionaire own a minimum equity stake of at least 25 percent of the total capital invested in the concession, although any individual deal might require a higher ownership percentage.

Forces for the adoption of reform bargains in the area of public concessions and contracting often include inefficiency, underproduction, and a lack of innovation arising under monopoly government production. Most of the resulting reform bargains are designed to generate economic value by enhancing the role of private ownership to improve incentives for cost reduction,[2] and by leveraging competition at the contract bidding stage to limit the entrant's ability to exercise market power.

Of course, contractual arrangements between government entities and private enterprises are not, in and of themselves, a radical concept. Under Mexico's traditional highway construction model, for instance, the ministry of transportation and communications contracts with privately owned construction companies to build public roads.[3] Similarly, state-owned vertically integrated electric utilities often purchase major capital equipment such as power generation turbines from private vendors. Public school boards typically purchase furniture and textbooks from private firms and contract with private firms to construct school buildings. The key difference between these traditional arrangements and contract-entry reform bargains is that under the latter, the role of private firms expands beyond that of a mere supplier of inputs or construction services to that of a developer, financier, operator, and/or owner of the production facility itself.[4] This shift in roles of the state versus private firms in the market creates opportunity and risk for both parties.

These challenges are shaped by the high degree of mutual dependence that remains between the state and the entrant under the reform bargain, despite the potential illusion that the state has simply stepped aside in favor of private enterprise. This dependence is typically driven by some or all of the following factors:

+ a long, but fixed, time frame associated with the concession/contract;

+ a high degree of specialized assets associated with the entry opportunity;

+ the importance of noneconomic outcomes;

+ difficulties in the areas of performance measurement and monitoring;

+ the inevitable emergence of unforeseen economic, political, and social events;

+ problems associated with recontracting and contract renewal.

As a result, the entrant may face extraordinary challenges in managing its relationship with the state prior to, during, and after closing the deal.

In the sections below, we evaluate the challenges associated with contract entry with the experiences of four corporations drawn from a range of concession/contract settings. The cases include Empresas ICA, as a concessionaire in the Mexican toll highway program; Enron Corporation, as a producer of power for the Indian state of Maharashtra; the Correction Corporation of America (CCA), as a provider of incarceration services for U.S. federal and state governments; and Education Alternatives Inc. (EAI), as a contract manager of public schools in several U.S. cities. Despite obvious differences in the product and geographic markets served by these contract entrants, we will see that they face a number of similar challenges in exploiting opportunity and sustaining success under their respective reform bargains.

## EMPRESAS ICA AND THE MEXICAN TOLL HIGHWAY PROGRAM

Empresas ICA, one of Mexico's largest engineering and construction firms, was founded in 1947.[5] Throughout the 1950s, 1960s, and 1970s, the firm thrived as a traditional contractor to private and public sector clients. A portion of its public sector business included road construction. Historically, ICA bid for road contracts on a unit-cost basis under which it was compensated according to the volume of inputs used—for example, materials and labor- and equipment-hours—times the relevant unit costs, including a profit markup. The volume and profitability of ICA's road-building activities was often affected by government budget cycles, which at times led to payment delays and project cancellations.

The Mexican foreign debt crisis and peso devaluation of 1982 ushered in years of austerity and slow growth under President Miguel de la Madrid.

The construction industry was hit very hard during this period as traditional sources of private and public sector demand contracted. Although ICA diversified into a number of new business areas, including manufacturing and hotel development, its financial performance languished. ICA's fortunes, however, appeared to brighten significantly when an ambitious new private toll highway program was introduced in 1990 under newly elected President Carlos Salinas.

Under the highway concession program, Mexico's secretariat of transportation and communications (SCT) developed a master plan for the development of 4,000 kilometers of high-performance roads, divided into a number of individual routes. In contrast to traditional road development programs, in this effort private enterprises would be responsible not only for construction activities but also for financing,[6] operating, and maintaining these toll highways during the concession period. For each concession route, the SCT developed detailed technical specifications, established a maximum toll level,[7] and determined minimum traffic volumes for which it would provide guarantees. The government also assumed responsibility for securing rights of way along concession highway routes through its power of eminent domain. Private concessionaires were entitled to all toll revenues collected during the concession, plus additional compensation when traffic fell below SCT-guaranteed volumes.[8] Individual concession routes were awarded to the bidder that offered to hold the concession for the shortest period of time.[9] At the end of the concession period, all rights and obligations related to the toll highway would revert to the state, with no compensation to the concessionaire.

From the concessionaire's perspective, this reform bargain appeared to offer very attractive business opportunities. The concessionaire for a particular route, typically a subsidiary of a construction company[10] aligned with a partner financial institution,[11] would profit from participation in two ways. During the construction phase, the concessionaire would contract construction business from its parent company, paying for these services primarily out of loans from the financial partner.[12] During the operating phase, the concessionaire would earn returns on its equity investment in the form of toll revenues less debt service, operating expenses, and maintenance costs.[13] Certain rights in the terms of the reform bargain enhanced the attractiveness of these deals, including government guarantees to secure rights of way and to offset the effects of traffic shortfalls and inflation. Competitive bidding could reduce the potential profitability of participation in these bargains. Yet most Mexican construction firms were capital-constrained after a decade of austerity and only the largest had the capability to undertake a lead management role in sophisticated highway projects. Furthermore, foreign construction firms were either reluctant or unable to participate in the program, which kept the potential pool of qualified concessionaires relatively small.[14]

From the government's perspective, the reform bargain also appeared to offer important economic value-creation benefits relative to the traditional approach. First, the concession mechanism seemed to provide strong incentives for improving highway development efficiency. Since private concessionaires held equity in the concession, the profitability of their ownership stake would depend critically on their success in controlling costs. Second, the reform bargain seemed likely to reverse years of underinvestment in Mexico's highway infrastructure by removing a major impediment under government-financed development—access to capital.[15] In addition, the fixed length of the contract period offered concessionaires powerful incentives to complete the construction of the toll highways in a timely fashion, avoiding delays typical under prereform bargains. The competitive-bidding terms of the reform bargain seemed to allay distribution-related concerns that private concessionaires might earn substantial monopoly profits from the program. Also, since all toll highway routes were designed to run in close proximity to a preexisting free road, no motorist would lose access to affordable road service as a result of contract entry—a key fairness-related consideration.[16]

Opportunities for innovation, however, were limited to a large extent by the detailed technical specifications and toll structure prescribed in advance by the SCT for each concession route. For example, the SCT specified such factors as highway path, locations of interchanges and toll booths, number of lanes, and minimum quality of construction materials. In contrast, some countries, such as Malaysia, encouraged would-be concessionaires to propose highways along routes and with designs of their own choosing. Although this alternative approach allowed for greater innovation, it took away the government's ability to engage in a competitive bidding process for concessions that allowed for apples-to-apples comparisons of alternative bids. In addition, this alternative approach tended to conflict with the desire of many governments to coordinate the development of an integrated route structure with relatively uniform standards across its various segments.

A number of problems emerged early in the Mexican toll roads program. First, a number of concessions experienced extensive construction cost overruns. In principle, the concessionaire was responsible for all construction costs, particularly given the potential for cost-padding in its purchases of construction services from its parent firm. Under the terms of the reform bargain, concessionaires were entitled to receive compensation for cost overruns only when these were caused by inaccuracies or changes in the SCT's original technical specifications.[17] Yet because of the unique features of each highway, and the associated difficulties in measuring and monitoring the physical and financial impact of deviations from technical specifications, it could be quite difficult to distinguish among the various drivers of cost overruns in any particular case.

In the case of the Cuernavaca-Acapulco highway, the largest of the early concessions, cost overruns eventually reached almost 100 percent. Soon after construction began, it became clear that the technical specifications, extrapolated by the SCT from a small segment of the entire route, were substantially flawed. The SCT compensated the concessionaire—a joint venture of Mexico's three largest construction firms—indirectly by having three government entities make capital contributions to the concession equal collectively to 30 percent of total equity.[18] Also, the terms of the concession were renegotiated, extending the duration of the concession period.

The second major problem emerged during the operating period of many of the concessions. Actual traffic volumes were often below the minimum levels projected (and guaranteed) by the SCT—in some cases, by over 50 percent. The SCT had clearly been far too optimistic about motorists' willingness to pay tolls that averaged about 500 pesos per kilometer (US$0.28 per mile)—five to ten times the levels charged for most toll roads in developed countries—especially given the availability of parallel free roads. The SCT had purposely set tolls at these high levels in order to minimize concession periods. Short concession periods implied a faster payback for concessionaires and lenders—a desirable goal for encouraging large investments in specialized assets.[19] Yet concession extensions, the only compensation the state offered for the traffic shortfalls, pushed financial returns even farther into the (uncertain) future.

From 1989 to 1991 Empresas ICA became a leading investor in Mexican toll roads, participating both as a solo concessionaire and in joint venture consortia. The firm earned extremely attractive profits on the construction business its highway concessionaires contracted during these years: operating margins on ICA's concession-related construction exceeded 38 percent in 1991, as compared with margins of 8 percent on its other construction activities.[20] Yet a substantial share of these profits were plowed back into equity investments in concessions which, by the end of 1991, accounted for almost one-third of ICA's total assets. The returns on these assets were minimal due to toll revenue shortfalls (from low traffic volumes) and the first-claim status of debt service on whatever revenues were available. Nevertheless, ICA remained optimistic about the toll roads business given the government's flexibility in renegotiating terms of problem concessions, sharp improvements over time in the accuracy of SCT's design specifications and traffic projections, and the Mexican economy's continued growth. To obtain capital to participate in additional concessions, ICA raised $450 million in a 1992 international IPO. Over the course of the following two years, international investors shared ICA's optimism regarding its contract entry opportunities in the toll highway sector, pushing its share price from $17 at the time of the IPO to over $30 in 1994.[21] Then came the Mexican peso crisis, during which the peso lost over half its value relative to the U.S. dollar.

The unanticipated shock of the peso crisis created numerous problems for the toll highway concessionaires. The accompanying rise in Mexican interest rates significantly increased the capital costs of the concessions, since most of their financing continued to come from short-term bank lending.[22] Recessionary conditions reduced demand for highway usage, yet tight government budgets left little room for subsidizing concessions in financial distress. Most construction firms, including ICA, were left with sizable concession-related receivables and large investments in concession equity that earned few returns. A planned second phase of highway concessions was canceled in the wake of the crisis, leaving no opportunity for ICA to offset its weak financial position with construction contracts on new toll roads. Although most existing concessions were renegotiated to extend the concession length, this evolution of the bargain offered no short-term relief from the heavy burden of nonperforming assets. ICA, whose share price on the New York Stock Exchange fell to $3, pursued a product and geographic diversification strategy while urging the adoption of a new reform bargain that would help resolve the difficulties associated with its toll road concessions.

In August 1997 the Mexican government announced major changes in preexisting highway concessions designed to alleviate the considerable costs associated with these problematic bargains. Under the new reform bargain, the government would take over distressed concessions—about 80 percent of all private toll highways. The state would assume responsibility for 60 billion pesos in debts (mostly bank loans and payables to construction companies), but also obtain the rights to toll revenues on these roads,[23] resulting in an expected net cost to the government of 19 billion pesos (about US$2.4 billion). The construction companies were required to write off all of their investments in these concessions but were compensated fully for the receivables due from the concessionaires. ICA, for example, wrote off 7.2 billion pesos in concession investments but received 4.7 billion pesos for receivables, resulting in a net loss of 2.5 billion, or 23 percent of the book value of its equity.[24] As part of the bailout, the government also announced that it would implement toll reductions of 15 percent to 30 percent on the acquired highways to make the roads more affordable for motorists.

The saga of the Mexican toll highway concessions illustrates the potential perils of contract entry opportunities involving large investments in specialized assets with long payback periods. In this case, it appears that concessionaires relied complacently on guarantees included in the terms of their bargains, without challenging fundamental assumptions related to technical specifications and traffic projections. Although the entrants did receive various forms of relief as the bargains evolved over time, they ultimately were required to share the costs of the program's failures. Yet the important role played by these large construction firms in the broader Mexican economy apparently served as a form of protection against incurring an even greater share of these costs.

This case also demonstrates the complexity facing governments that attempt to meet noneconomic objectives while simultaneously pursuing increases in economic value creation through contract entry privatization. The Mexican government's emphasis on relatively short concession periods (in part to minimize private control over strategic assets) and its insistence on the availability of parallel free roads (to promote fairness with respect to access) impaired the financial viability of many of the highway concessions. By the end of the 1990s, the legacy of the Mexican toll highway program was a twofold paradox: government bailout and ownership of private roads, and the lowest usage on the nation's highest-quality (and highest-capacity) roads.

## ENRON AND THE DABHOL POWER CORPORATION

Halfway around the world from Mexico, a different contract entry opportunity emerged in the early 1990s in the Indian state of Maharashtra.[25] In this case, the opportunity took the form of a twenty-year power purchase agreement between Enron Development Corporation (EDC) and the Maharashtra State Electricity Board (SEB) that would entail power generation investments totaling almost $3 billion.

EDC, a subsidiary of U.S.-based Enron Corporation,[26] sought opportunities to develop power plants and provide electricity, particularly in developing country markets where infrastructure and energy needs were underserved. In the early 1990s EDC entered into projects in Argentina, China, Colombia, Guatemala, India, the Philippines, and the United Kingdom. All of its projects involved long-term contracts in which prices were agreed upon in advance and revenues were protected against foreign currency risk. Each deal relied on a project-finance structure under which lenders had recourse only to the assets of the project itself as collateral.

Enron's entry opportunity in India emerged during a period of substantial political and economic change. Elections in May 1991 brought to power a coalition of parties that put into place the "Liberalized Economic Policy," which removed entry restrictions in many sectors. In early 1992, for example, the government adopted a reform bargain for the power generation sector. The underlying legislation codified a framework for power purchase agreements, which, for the first time, permitted 100 percent foreign equity in power plants and repatriation of dividends in foreign currency. All power sales under these agreements were to be made to government-owned state electricity boards (SEBs)[27] for downstream transmission and distribution to end users. Rate of return on equity was fixed at 16 percent, based on a plant load factor of 68.5 percent.[28] This new framework was designed to help relieve the nation of chronic power shortages in the face of 10 percent annual growth in electricity demand.

In 1992 India's power secretary paid a visit to Enron's headquarters during a trip to the United States to encourage foreign investment in India. A team of EDC executives eventually made their way to the Indian state of Maharashtra, where the combination of a relatively creditworthy state electricity board and a progressive state government appeared to offer an attractive investment locale for Enron. In addition, by 1995 power demand was expected to outstrip supply in the state. In December 1993 an agreement involving a $2.85 billion power project was signed between the Maharashtra SEB and the Dabhol Power Corporation (DPC)—a joint venture owned by Enron (80 percent), equipment manufacturer General Electric (10 percent), and the engineering/construction firm Bechtel (10 percent), formed to develop and manage the project.[29] Lenders to the project included the U.S. Export-Import ("Exim") Bank,[30] the Overseas Private Investment Corporation (OPIC),[31] the Industrial Development Bank of India (IDBI),[32] and Bank of America.

From the start, Enron had proposed that the generation facilities employ the highly efficient and relatively clean-burning combined-cycle gas turbine technology. An unusual aspect of the project design was that it did not rely on local sources of fuel but instead on liquefied natural gas (LNG)[33] imported from the Middle Eastern nation of Qatar.[34] Since Indian natural gas supplies were limited, and controlled by a single government-owned enterprise, Enron argued that only through imports could reliable fuel deliveries be assured for the twenty-year period of the power purchase agreement. The use of LNG, however, required the additional development of a regassification facility. The overall construction program was divided into two stages, including a $992 million, 695 MW[35] plant (phase 1) and a $1.93 billion, 1,320 MW plant plus regassification facility (phase 2).[36]

According to the terms of the deal—in this case the power purchase agreement (PPA)—the Dabhol Power Corporation was required to complete phase 1 of the project within thirty-three months. The state government of Maharashtra was obligated to provide land for the facility as well as power, communications, water, and approach roads during the construction period. The Maharashtra State Electricity Board (MSEB) was responsible for building transmission lines from the plant to its power grid and was required to buy a minimum of 90 percent of the facility's output under the price structure included in the PPA (see below). The government of Maharashtra and the Indian national government, both led at the time by a Congress Party coalition, provided guarantees on the MSEB's financial and material commitments.

The pricing structure consisted of a complex mix of fixed charges (mostly capital-related) and variable charges (mostly fuel-related) that resulted in an initial power price of 2.40 rupees (US$0.07) per kilowatt hour (kWh). Based on projections of inflation associated with the various rupee- and dollar-based price components, the price per kWh was estimated to increase over the course of the contract to $0.114. The MSEB was required to bear all exchange-rate risks associated with the relevant price components. In 1993 the actual retail prices per kWh paid by end users in Maharashtra, some of which were heavily subsidized by the government, varied from 0.18 rupees for farmers to 1.70 rupees for industrial users.

A point of contention during the PPA negotiations was the estimated 26.5 percent return to Dabhol Power Corporation's equity holders implicit in the project's initial financial assumptions. Enron Development Corporation, under the vigorous leadership of CEO Rebecca Mark, argued that the return was appropriate for projects of this type in developing countries. Maharashtra's finance minister, however, argued that any return above 20 percent was unacceptable. Mark countered with an offer to lower the return to 25.2 percent, and noted that the firm's U.S. after-tax return on the project would be only 17.2 percent. After threatening, on several occasions, to abandon the negotiations, Mark obtained sign-off on the revised financial terms from the Maharashtra state government.

The construction of the phase 1 facility proceeded on schedule during 1994 and early 1995. The project encountered serious problems, however, in March 1995, when a coalition of opposition parties won the Maharashtra state elections. The new SS-BJP government,[37] whose members had been fierce critics of the PPA, ordered an inquiry into the power project. The investigatory committee criticized the process by which the deal was reached, in particular the lack of transparency and absence of competitive bidding.[38] Both the state government and the national government were found to have relaxed regulations and ignored required clearances to accelerate project approval. The committee also condemned many of the terms of the PPA itself, particularly the high and rising power price levels and the mandatory purchase requirements imposed on the MSEB.[39]

In August 1995 the coalition government canceled the Dabhol power project. Maharashtra's chief minister declared, "The deal is against the interests of Maharashtra. Accepting this deal would indicate an absolute lack of self-respect and would amount to betraying the trust of the people."[40] The action, which received nationwide attention, became a rallying cry for national BJP leaders, one of whom declared, "We will not be dictated [to] by giant powers or power giants."[41]

Rebecca Mark responded swiftly to the contract cancellation, initiating arbitration proceedings in London (as specified in the terms of the PPA) to recover the $300 million already invested in the project, plus delay costs of $250,000 per day. The Maharashtra government countered, filing suit in the Bombay High Court challenging Dabhol Power Corporation's right to arbitration in London. The U.S Department of Energy had weighed in even before the filing of lawsuits, warning that "failure to honor the agreements between the project partners and the various Indian governments will jeopardize not only the Dabhol Project but also the other private power projects being proposed for international financing."[42]

Shortly before arbitration proceedings were to begin, a high-level meeting between Maharashtra's chief minister Manohar Joshi, Enron chairman Kenneth Lay, and Rebecca Mark led to the reactivation of negotiations. By early 1996 a compromise acceptable to both parties was reached. Under the terms of the revised PPA, the initial power price for phase 1 production was reduced to 2.03 rupees (US$0.06) and would be reduced further to 1.86 rupees (US$0.05) when the phase 2 facility came online.[43] Since the lower prices were made possible by a range of cost savings,[44] however, the returns to the Dabhol Power Corporation remained virtually unchanged. Under the revised terms, the MSEB obtained the right to purchase a 30 percent equity stake (from Enron's share) in the DPC. Also, the DPC agreed to pay for a number of environmental quality testing and remediation activities near the plant and to absorb the costs of delays resulting from the cancellation and renegotiations.

The Maharashtra government declared the revised agreement a great success and in May 1996, the central government gave final approval to the revised PPA. Construction resumed by the end of the year with strong support from the SS-BJP government. Occasional protests continued at the plant construction site, which received protection from the Maharashtra state police. This protection, however, led eventually to a second controversy involving the Dabhol Power Corporation. Just as the DPC was about to commence production in January 1999, New York–based Human Rights Watch released a 166-page report accusing the Maharashtra state police and DPC security personnel of human rights abuses in over thirty incidents of brutality against protesters at the plant. Although the report placed primary blame on the police, Human Rights Watch executive director Kenneth Roth insisted that "corporations cannot look the other way when protesters are being beaten right outside their front gates. Enron has been shirking its responsibility to behave as a decent global citizen."[45] As the DPC finally entered its operating phase, Enron wondered what impact, if any, this latest controversy would have on its evolving bargain in the Indian power market.

Unlike Empresas ICA's "black-hole" experience in the Mexican toll highway program, Enron's contract-entry opportunity in Maharashtra appears to have remained attractive over time despite the emergence of a major political shock and a significant evolution in the terms of its original bargain. Superficially, Enron appeared to be quite vulnerable over time to unfavorable shifts in its bargaining position as it sank more and more capital into specialized assets in a foreign country.[46] Yet Enron enhanced its position in a number of important ways. First, it brought in the financial participation of a variety of players with significant economic and political clout. In effect, this raised the costs to the MSEB and the Maharashtra state government of attempting to take advantage of Enron over the course of time since their actions were also likely to alienate powerful affected parties—including the U.S. government (via the Exim Bank), influential and resource-rich corporations (Bank of America, General Electric) as well as supporting Indian financial institutions. Similarly, Enron's linkage of the power project to the development of LNG sources not only increased its potential profit opportunities but also expanded the range of parties affected by the PPA to include Mideast natural gas producers.

Enron also bolstered its position by insisting on the inclusion of guarantees and strong enforcement mechanisms in the terms of its original contract entry bargain. Particularly important in this context were provisions for arbitration in London plus central and state guarantees for the obligations assigned to the MSEB in the PPA. The staging of investments into two separate phases strengthened Enron's hand in the short run since it gave the firm the ability to withhold the largest part of the planned investment if its bargain evolved in unfavorable ways. In a broader sense, the rapid pace of growth of Maharashtra's power demands and Enron's ability to marshal considerable resources to meet those needs over time tended to enhance the firm's bargaining power through the state's expected need for ongoing investment in the sector.

In the late 1990s one important challenge that Enron had yet to face was the reaction of electricity users to price increases that were likely to result as the DPC's production represented an increasing proportion of the total power generated in the state.[47] Although the MSEB might choose not to pass on to retail consumers the full impact of higher power costs, it is unlikely that the state would subsidize the full difference between current end-user prices and the cost of DPC power. The ultimate consequences of strong, perhaps violent, public protests to price increases were difficult to predict.

In a broad sense, Enron's most vulnerable spot remained its reputation, given its emphasis on leveraging the company's name and resources across a growing range of energy and other infrastructure businesses and geographic markets. Although the firm appeared to have "dodged the bullet" of bribery and corruption charges leveled after the SS-BJP electoral victory in Maharashtra, Human Rights Watch's criticism of Enron's human rights record at Dabhol had the potential to adversely affect its current and future bargains. Nevertheless, it appeared that despite some bumps in the road, Enron was well-positioned to take advantage of new entry opportunities in India and elsewhere at the start of the new millennium.

## CORRECTIONS CORPORATION OF AMERICA AND PRISON PRIVATIZATION

In contrast to large infrastructure projects such as toll roads and power plants, contract entry opportunities in the social services arena may seem much more modest in scale. Yet this need not be the case. For example, Nashville-based Corrections Corporation of America (CCA), the largest operator of private prisons in the world, had by 1997 become a half-billion-dollar-a-year corporation, with sixty-seven facilities in the United States, Puerto Rico, Australia, and Great Britain.[48] Yet, in the late 1990s, a series of controversies threatened to tarnish its reputation and, ultimately, its ability to maintain the double-digit growth rates it had posted throughout the decade.

CCA was founded in 1983 by Nashville lawyer Thomas Beasley, his West Point roommate Doctor Crants (a Vietnam veteran and graduate of Harvard Business School and Harvard Law School), and T. Don Hotto, a former state corrections commissioner. Although privately owned prisons were virtually unknown at the time, CCA's founders believed that chronic overcrowding in many of the nation's corrections facilities and the steady growth in the inmate population offered a significant business opportunity. Despite relatively modest growth in the 1980s, the firm took off in the early 1990s, spurred by a number of major contracts secured at that time. Throughout the firm's history, Crants had remained CEO, driving CCA to sustain its position as market leader.

In the mid-1990s CCA held a 52 percent share of private prison beds. Yet the private prison segment accounted for only 3 percent of total industry capacity. The U.S. market was by far the largest, its 1.8 million inmates accounting for half of all incarcerations worldwide.[49] Prison facilities differed by type of inmate and were typically classified as minimum security, medium security, or maximum security.

CCA entered into contracts with federal and state government agencies for the provision of incarceration services. The typical contract specified number and type of inmates and a per diem payment per inmate over the term of the contract.[50] Quality standards for prisoner amenities, security, and rehabilitation activities ordinarily were based on standards issued by the American Correctional Association (ACA), an independent accreditation body. Contracts generally included some subset of the 463 standards issued by the ACA. In general, standards tended to be process-oriented (for example, minimum requirements regarding experience and training of prison guards) as opposed to outcomes-oriented (for example, maximum number of violent incidents per prisoner per year). Individual standards could be quite detailed. For example, food-related standards included mandatory number of meals per day, minimum caloric intake, time between meals, food preparation and storage conditions, and "palatability" requirements. Contracts also specified a monitoring process, which might include the presence of one or more government employees on-site at the private prison.[51]

CCA has described its basic business strategy in the private prison market as follows. First, it prefers to control the design and construction of the facilities it operates, in contrast to many public prisons where these functions are carried out by separate parties. CCA maintains that this approach gives it a cost advantage, since its facilities are designed to allow superior monitoring of inmates, with fewer employees. Second, the firm relies on its size to take advantage of scale economies in its procurement activities. Third, CCA provides stock incentives to every employee to enhance motivation and productivity. Fourth, the firm works to keep its inmates busy with a wide variety of activities to reduce prisoner frustration and violence and, ultimately, to keep down costs. Fifth, CCA seeks to negotiate contracts at prices 10 percent to 15 percent below the daily per-prisoner rates of comparable public prisons and still earn a reasonable profit.[52]

Critics of CCA have charged that the firm's basic strategy is simply to staff its facilities with fewer workers at lower wages relative to public prisons, thus earning profits at the expense of service quality. CCA has also been accused of maintaining overly cozy relationships with politicians.[53] The firm's detractors have also pointed to a much-cited 1995 comparative study of prisons in Tennessee which found little difference between the operating costs of one of CCA's private prisons and two comparable public prisons.[54] A companion study found little difference in quality across the prisons, although it noted a greater number of reported incidents of violence in the CCA prison.[55] These criticisms, however, had little effect on CCA's rapid growth, fueled by persistent shortages of prison capacity in the United States.[56]

In June 1997 CCA came to Youngstown, Ohio, with an offer to build a new prison that would create 500 jobs for the city. The city readily agreed to CCA's construction of the Northeast Ohio Correctional Center, which was designed to accommodate 1,500 prisoners from the Washington, D.C., area. During the subsequent year, however, forty-four assaults and two fatal stabbings took place within the prison. Also, six inmates escaped from the facility, leading Youngstown residents to demand its closure. Youngstown mayor George McKelvy described the situation as "a nightmare," and the Ohio state attorney general initiated an investigation of the prison's operations. The Youngstown controversy came at a particularly delicate time for CCA, since the firm was in the midst of lobbying to win a federal contract to build a new 2,200-bed facility in southeast Washington.

CCA's contract with D.C. Corrections to hold prisoners in Youngstown was a one-year arrangement, renewable for up to five years, and valued at $182 million over the full term. Although the contract specified that only medium-security prisoners could be sent to the facility, over 100 maximum-security inmates arrived over time at the prison, many without complete case-history files. CCA maintained that it was not at fault for the error, which D.C. correction officials described as an "inadvertent mistake." An Ohio legislative committee, however, disagreed, arguing that CCA "knew that the District was not sending what any reasonable corrections professional would identify as a medium-security inmate."[57]

CCA was also criticized for initially denying that six inmates had escaped and for waiting a full hour before notifying local police.[58] In response to criticism from the legislative committee, CCA acknowledged that it had made mistakes, but assured officials that problems at the facility were being corrected.

In the midst of the controversy, Acting D.C. Corrections Director Edwards requested a sixty-day extension in the current one-year contract to renegotiate renewal terms so as to hold CCA more accountable for problems at the Youngstown facility. In particular, Edwards suggested that the new contract include provisions for substantial fines for various forms of noncompliance. At the same time, the state of Ohio began a review of its policies with respect to the operation of private prisons.

Meanwhile, in October 1998, a four-prisoner escape took place at another CCA-managed prison: the South Central Correctional Facility in Clinton, Tennessee. One week after the escape, longtime opponents of private prisons, including many unionized public sector corrections officers, staged a protest at the Tennessee state capitol and at CCA's nearby corporate headquarters. Chanting "public safety's not for sale" and "the governor's office is not for sale," protesters claimed that CCA was sacrificing security by "cutting corners." CCA's opponents also accused the firm of getting a free ride from the government, which organized escapee manhunts and financed medical payments for prisoners above CCA caps.[59] One item high on protesters' agenda was to stop the reintroduction of a bill in the Tennessee legislature that would permit the private management of 70 percent of the state's prison beds.

A CCA spokesperson dismissed the protests as publicity stunts and strongly defended the firm's safety record, noting that CCA's staffing and training levels ranked high in national statistics. She also noted that while unacceptable, prisoner violence and escapes occurred throughout the prison system, at both public and private facilities.

By 1999 it was unclear what the longer-term implications of the Youngstown and Clinton controversies would be for CCA. At a minimum, it appeared that the terms of its operation would come under closer scrutiny both for new contracts and renewals. Also, the future of the Youngstown facility and proposed southeast Washington project remained uncertain. In some ways, the firm was fortunate to be the market leader in such a fast-growing industry, where demand continued to outstrip supply. Yet at the same time, CCA's high visibility made it especially vulnerable to attacks by any and all opponents of prison privatization. These opponents included those who objected to private prisons on moral grounds, sometimes employing highly charged language, calling CCA's operation the "auctioning of humans for profit."[60] These sentiments, combined with public fear of nonsecure prison facilities, created a potentially volatile environment in which CCA's reputation could suffer if its problems reached a critical mass.

In June 1999 CCA named J. Michael Quinlan, a former director of the federal Bureau of Prisons, as president and chief operating officer. Quinlan quickly initiated a number of steps designed to stem recent criticism of the firm, including the release of data indicating that the escape rate from CCA facilities was less than half that of public sector prisons, and the adoption of a new corporate policy of reimbursing law enforcement agencies for expenses incurred in searching for CCA prison escapees. Quinlan also announced plans to establish community relations boards at all CCA facilities to improve local communications.[61] The long-term implications of these changes remained unclear in early 2000.

Some of the challenges CCA faced resemble those that Empresas ICA and Enron encountered in their contract entry opportunities. All three companies made large capital investments in assets with a long payback period. CCA's investments were somewhat less specialized than ICA's or the DPC's, however, since most of its prison facilities could be used to house inmates from a wide range of geographic locations. Therefore, CCA was less vulnerable to the possibility that its government clients would revise contract terms to the company's disadvantage over time. The continued shortages of prison beds also tended to reduce CCA's vulnerability in this respect. Nonetheless, the relatively short-term nature of its contracts, such as the one signed for the Youngstown facility, did leave it open to pressures at renewal time to make concessions in the face of public controversy.

Similar to ICA, CCA also confronted challenges related to monitoring. Detailed requirements involving standards—whether for highway design or prison conditions—placed extensive constraints on the firm's freedom of action and led it to incur substantial compliance and monitoring costs. Yet noneconomic objectives of the state and the broader society, including safety, security, and fairness, remained particularly strong in these sectors. Despite the sometimes significant potential for efficiency improvements and investment/production increases under contract entry reform bargains, the importance of achieving noneconomic objectives loomed large in determining the sustainability of these reforms over time.

Performance measurement often poses special challenges for the contracting out of social services, as we saw for CCA. The vast majority of standards it faced involved process- or input-related measures as opposed to outcomes. Yet the difficulty of measuring levels of "safety" and "security" in the prison sector—as well as "learning" in the education sector and "health" in the health care sector—has often created ambiguity and, at times, outright conflict in assessing the results of particular reform bargains. This is particularly true in the case of contract entry in the public school sector, as we will see below.

## EDUCATION ALTERNATIVES INC. AND URBAN PUBLIC SCHOOL MANAGEMENT

The challenges of contract entry do not always entail the construction of large greenfield facilities such as new highways, power plants, and prisons.[62] In some cases, the entry opportunity involves management of existing government-owned facilities under contract between a private firm and a public entity. We explore this form of contract entry by drawing on the experience of a private firm that contracted to manage public school districts in Baltimore, Maryland and Hartford, Connecticut. The notable failure of both of these entry efforts provides valuable lessons for assessing opportunity in the area of the privatization of social services.

Education Alternatives Inc. (EAI) was founded in 1986 by entrepreneur John Golle. Golle, who had sold his successful executive training business a year earlier, had a passion for improving childhood education based on the many problems encountered by his learning-disabled son in traditional schools. EAI's initial strategy was to open private schools that would employ a unique interactive and experiential learning curriculum called "Tesseract," adapted from proprietary materials acquired from the Control Data Corporation.[63]

EAI opened Tesseract schools in Eagan, Minnesota and Paradise Valley, Arizona in 1987 and within two years, students' test scores at the schools exceeded national averages by two grade levels. Golle, however, believed that EAI could make a far greater contribution to education reform by redirecting its efforts toward the public schools. In particular, Golle felt that EAI could leverage its limited financial resources much more effectively by entering into management contracts with existing public school systems as opposed to building more schools itself.

EAI's first public school contract entry opportunity appeared in 1990 when it won a competitive bid to manage South Pointe Elementary School, which was under construction in Miami—Dade County, Florida. EAI provided input into the formation of curriculum, hiring of personnel, and design of the facilities as part of its five-year management contract. EAI's contract gave it control over the school's budget, with the exception of overhead costs for local and state administrators. Although the firm could have tried to push through cost reductions to earn a profit on its contract, it decided instead to showcase its ability to improve student performance by raising additional resources for the school from foundations and other private sources, then breaking even on the overall contract.

In 1991 EAI enhanced its school management capabilities by forming an alliance with Johnson Controls and KPMG Peat Marwick. Under this arrangement, Johnson Controls would act as a subcontractor to provide or manage maintenance, food service, custodial, and other operations-related services, while KPMG Peat Marwick would provide financial management and other administrative services.[64] Based on EAI's results at South Pointe and the strength of its alliance, other public school systems around the nation began to show interest in securing a management contract with the firm.

In 1992 EAI won a five-year contract to manage nine of Baltimore's 179 schools with strong support from superintendent of schools Walter Amprey and Baltimore mayor Kurt Schmoke. At that time, students' standardized test scores were among the lowest in the state and the dropout rate of 14 percent was three times the state average. Under the terms of the contract, EAI received a budget of about $27 million per year based on average per-pupil spending levels for comparable schools in the Baltimore system. The contract also stipulated that administrative and teaching personnel would remain public employees under the terms of union agreements previously negotiated by the American Federation of Teachers (AFT). Although the contract did not specify any performance evaluation criteria, EAI and city officials were confident that student achievement would rise as a result of the company's innovative approaches to education.

A top priority in EAI's initial strategy in Baltimore was to invest $7.1 million in technology and building improvements, including four computer workstations in every classroom, a computer lab in every school, and high-quality telephones, fax machines, and copiers for faculty use. To pay for these improvements while still leaving room for profits, EAI targeted cost reductions in a number of areas. First EAI replaced "paraprofessionals," classroom assistants earning $12 an hour plus benefits, with "interns," recent college graduates earning $8 an hour with no benefits. Although many of the paraprofessionals did not have a college education, most had long-standing ties to the community and all were members of the AFT. These employees, as well as other unionized personnel not protected under EAI's contract with the school board,[65] complained to the union, parents, and the media about EAI's new labor practices. In response, EAI agreed to rehire all college-educated paraprofessionals.

EAI also reevaluated the status of "special needs" programs that segregated a growing number of students into smaller classes with a different curriculum. The firm concluded that the problems of some special needs students had been "overdiagnosed," and thus moved a number of these pupils back into regular classes ("mainstreaming"), where they would experience the same Tesseract-based learning curriculum as their classmates. While EAI argued that mainstreaming would actually improve the education and socialization of these students, the AFT and other critics accused the company of sacrificing the education of learning-disabled children in the name of higher profits.

In January 1994 the Baltimore City Public Schools' Department of Research and Evaluation issued its "Early Implementation" report assessing EAI's performance to date. Although the report praised the extensive improvements in school facilities, it criticized EAI for delays in implementing its computer-based instructional technology,[66] insufficient teacher training in the Tesseract method, and high turnover of interns. In May the AFT released its own report.[67] This harshly critical study found increases in absenteeism and declines in test scores at EAI schools in contrast to opposite trends at non-EAI schools in Baltimore. The report, which also questioned EAI's financial accounting practices and cutbacks in special education, found that EAI schools had actually received $500 more per student than average schools in the system. The AFT also requested that the U.S. Department of Education investigate EAI's special education program, which resulted in the award of compensatory hours to students moved out of the program in violation of official procedures. The AFT justified its vigorous and ongoing scrutiny of

EAI's activities by arguing that the firm was not accountable to anyone in its managerial and educational practices. EAI challenged the AFT's analysis of test scores and accused the union of subverting the real interests of teachers and students by defending outmoded work rules and bloated noninstructional payrolls.

In the midst of the controversy, the Baltimore Public School System commissioned University of Maryland researchers to assess EAI's performance during the first three years of its management contract with the school system. The report, released in September 1995, concluded that student test scores, although declining during the first year of EAI's contract, had risen during the subsequent two years, resulting in a modest net improvement. The report also found evidence of physical and curricular improvements at non-EAI schools, which may have been inspired by the demonstration effect of EAI's practices. The report concluded, however, that the expectations of dramatic change created by EAI's arrival had yet to be fulfilled, and that EAI's lack of financial accountability to the public was troubling.[68]

EAI attempted to put the best face on the University of Maryland's report and produced its own data showing that students remaining in EAI schools during all three years demonstrated strong test score gains. Yet public support for EAI was waning. Mayor Schmoke, in the midst of an election campaign and facing a large deficit in city finances, requested a renegotiation of EAI's contract to save the city $7 million. EAI refused, and the city canceled the contract. Although EAI threatened to remove capital equipment that it had installed in the schools, it decided to avoid further controversy and simply leave the city, recording a significant financial loss.

Unfortunately, EAI's woes were not confined to Baltimore. In 1994 EAI was actively courted by progressive members of the Hartford, Connecticut, School Board who were searching for a solution to the dismal performance of the city's school system. Although per-pupil spending of $10,000 was the highest in the state, student test scores were the lowest. In November the school board offered EAI a contract to manage the school system, with an annual budget of $170 million. Golle jumped at the opportunity, sensing strong benefits to having control over an entire school system as opposed to a small number of schools, as was the case in Baltimore and Miami. In addition, the high level of per-pupil spending—substantially above Baltimore's $5,900 level—appeared to offer tremendous potential for cost savings.

Despite strong support from the school board, the contract with EAI was opposed by the unions, the acting superintendent of schools, and some members of the Hartford City Council, based largely on negative publicity from the Baltimore experience. Golle, however, attempted to address the concerns of these groups by promising that no employees would be laid off and that major improvements to school facilities would be paid for out of savings generated through efficiency gains. Although the terms of EAI's contract with the school board gave it control rights over the school system budget, the precise mechanics of control were left unclear. Under the general process adopted, EAI would take responsibility for paying the school system's expenses (including payroll), submitting receipts at the end of every month for reimbursement. In effect, its profit would be determined by the amount of money remaining at the end of the year.

Soon after EAI's contract was signed, the school board notified the company of a $3.3 million shortfall in the school system budget. To avoid layoffs, the board, with EAI's assistance, negotiated a salary freeze, reduction in benefits, and a lengthening of the school day and school year with the teacher's union. Meanwhile EAI proceeded aggressively with expenditures on building improvements and installation of new computers. During this same period, EAI was shocked to find that the acting school superintendent, Eddie Davis, was continuing to make significant school-related purchases without EAI's approval. In addition, Davis submitted a budget for the 1995–1996 school year that did not include money for any of EAI's initiatives. EAI produced its own budget, which called for a radical decentralization of the school system to give greater power to local schools over curricular and financial decisions. EAI's plan also called for the reallocation of financial resources away from salaries and, instead, toward computers. In particular, EAI called for the elimination of 300 jobs made redundant by declining enrollments.

EAI's plan sparked outrage in Hartford much as had similar efforts in Baltimore. The teachers' union felt betrayed and school board members became increasingly uncomfortable with tensions between Davis and EAI. The situation escalated further when EAI submitted bills for reimbursement in May 1995 that included large expenditures for corporate travel, accommodations, and public relations activities. Reimbursement was delayed and in June, the school board approved a new budget that scaled back EAI's role to concentrate its work in six of the system's thirty-two schools.

Throughout the rest of the year, EAI pressed repeatedly for full reimbursement of its out-of-pocket expenditures, while striving to regain control over the budget. The school board, however, complained that the efficiency savings promised by EAI had not materialized, and that therefore it did not have sufficient funds for reimbursement.[69] By the end of the year, having received reimbursement of $343,000 for $12 million in expenditures, EAI made a final plea to the city for compensation. In January 1996 the school board canceled its contract with EAI, which filed suit against the city to recover its losses. In July 1996 Hartford and EAI reached an out-of-court settlement under which the city paid $6 million to end the litigation. By the time an agreement was reached, EAI's share price had fallen from a high of $50 in early 1995 to $3. After the Hartford debacle, EAI abandoned the public school contract management market altogether, returning to its roots as a builder and operator of private schools.

The experience of Education Alternatives Inc. provides variations on many of the challenges of contract entry seen earlier in this chapter. As in the cases of Empresas ICA and the Dabhol Power Corporation, EAI invested in a number of specialized assets that left it vulnerable to adverse changes in its bargains over time. In principle, EAI's up-front investments in building renovations and technology improvements could be recovered over the five-year term of its contracts. In practice, its largest contracts were terminated well ahead of schedule. Even the more mobile assets it purchased on behalf of school systems, such as computers and copiers, were virtually impossible to recover from school buildings once its contracts had been canceled.[70]

EAI might have avoided or at least reduced the extent of its losses had it paid more attention to issues of enforcement in the terms of its bargain. Recall, for example, that Enron was careful to build in clear provisions for arbitration in the terms of its contract as well as to secure guarantees from the state and central government regarding the obligations held by the Maharashtra SEB. In addition, Enron assembled a group of powerful equity partners and project lenders whose own interests would be adversely affected if the MSEB or other Indian government institutions attempted to make unilateral changes in the bargain unfavorable to Enron. In contrast, EAI assumed naïvely that its bargain would be enforced automatically, even in the case of Hartford, where some city councilors opposed the contract from the outset. Also, it does not appear that EAI used its strategic partners—Johnson Controls, KPMG Peat Marwick, and Computer Curriculum Corporation, a partner who joined in 1993—in any strategic manner to build bridges with affected parties in local communities or to exert leverage over key government officials. In fact, EAI seemed unable to manage its relationships with other actors through the use of either carrots (sharing gains) or sticks (posing credible threats).

As in the case of Corrections Corporation of America, performance measurement became a major source of contention under EAI's entry bargain. The dimensions of school quality are so numerous—test scores, dropout rates, absenteeism, condition of facilities, and so on—that it is difficult to provide a simple measure of performance at a point in time and over time. Also, as seen in the debate over test scores in Baltimore, alternative interpretations of the same statistics can lead to very different conclusions. EAI, however, made its predicament worse by ignoring measurement issues completely, in effect ceding this task to the school board and other affected parties. This is a particularly dangerous strategy in an industry in which the magnitude of inputs—for example, the number of teachers and the size of the budget—can be offered as proxies for quality in the absence of other measures. Ultimately, EAI failed to convince the public that cost-cutting and quality improvements were not mutually exclusive.

The importance of noneconomic objectives created challenges for EAI as well. The firing of paraprofessionals in Baltimore and the aggressive mainstreaming of former special needs students violated principles of fairness and due process that the public hold dear. In an overarching sense, parents' concern over the safety and well-being of their children made trust a critical component of any successful turnaround effort. Persistent questions regarding EAI's accountability, reliability, and ultimate motives—profits or education?—eroded the initial goodwill generated from the South Pointe experience and left EAI with few allies when it needed them the most.

Perhaps EAI's greatest failure was in its inability to manage expectations. The opening of markets formerly closed to private enterprises, whether in highway development, power production, incarceration services, school management, or other sectors, can be both exciting and threatening to the many parties affected by these reforms. EAI encouraged school boards, parents, and teachers alike to believe that significant improvements in school quality—vaguely defined—could be achieved quickly, while at the same time cutting costs in a relatively painless fashion. Although these expectations were useful in winning contracts, they proved disastrous for achieving a sustainable bargain over time. In the end, EAI lost touch with the realities of the education marketplace and the hidden boundaries they placed on entry opportunities offered by deregulation and privatization in the sector.

# 8 ✦ *The Empire Strikes Back: A Cautionary Tale*

$O$*n October 30, 1984*, the U.S. Congress passed the Cable Communications Act, ushering in the era of deregulation of the nation's cable television industry. After a two-year transition period, the vast majority of the nation's cable systems operators—virtually all locally franchised private monopolies—would be free to determine the prices and programming options offered to consumers. The act was designed to replace local government regulation of cable television pricing with the discipline of the "video marketplace."

The Cable Communications Act, which effectively established a nationwide reform bargain for the cable service market, was welcomed by cable system operators across the country, including Paragould Cablevision Inc. (PCI), which served the city of Paragould, Arkansas. Local municipalities, however, were wary of deregulation and the potential for significant price increases down the road as operators were freed to exercise their market power. This was particularly true in the case of Paragould, a city that owned and operated its own water, gas, and electric utilities and prided itself on offering high-quality service at low prices.

Over the course of the 1980s, tensions between PCI and the city mounted as the company raised cable prices significantly in the wake of deregulation. The Paragould city council, unable to attract a new entrant into the market, eventually constructed its own cable television system to compete with PCI. After seven years of brutal competition, PCI's parent company, New York–based Cablevision Systems, sold the private firm to the city at a considerable loss. Thus, by 1999 a deregulated private company had been superceded by a monopoly public enterprise. The story of how this happened in the era of the new market economy is a colorful yet cautionary tale for managers facing opportunity and risk under their own reform bargains. It also provides an ideal setup for the discussion of postreform strategy that comprises the book's final chapter.

## PARAGOULD, ARKANSAS

Paragould is a city of approximately 18,500 inhabitants located in the northeast corner of Arkansas.[1] Founded in 1883 at the intersection of railroads associated with the financiers J. W. Paramore and Jay Gould, the city's commerce a century later consisted of a mixture of agriculture and industry. The city also boasted the lowest electricity rates in the state of Arkansas and among the lowest in the nation. These low rates were attributed to the fact that electricity was provided exclusively by the municipally owned City Light and Water Commission. However, while some observers linked the low prices to the public interest objectives of the municipal system, others argued that rates remained low simply because of the city's ability to finance the utility through tax-exempt borrowing and the utility's exemption from income and property taxes.

In political terms, Paragould had a strong populist tradition. In fact, the city had established its municipal electric company in the 1930s at a time of heightened national scrutiny of the investor-owned utility sector. In a legal battle that extended to the U.S. Supreme Court, the judiciary affirmed Paragould's right to establish a municipally owned utility to compete against the existing privately owned electric utility monopoly, which served the city under a nonexclusive franchise. By 1953 the private utility had sold its assets to the city, leaving the City Light and Water Commission as the exclusive provider of electricity service to Paragould. In retrospect, it appears that PCI and its parent company would have benefited from a more thorough understanding of the city's historical experience in dealing with private monopolies.

During the post–World War II era, the citizens of Paragould remained overwhelmingly Democratic. Since 1978 the city's voters had repeatedly elected Democrat Charles Partlow to the post of mayor. Partlow remained Paragould's chief executive through the mid-1990s, supported by a loyal, unified city council.

## EARLY YEARS OF CABLE TELEVISION IN PARAGOULD

Cable television service first came to Paragould in September 1965 when Transwestern Video of Ardmore, Oklahoma, was granted a nonexclusive cable franchise covering all areas within the city limits. Paragould itself had no television station, and although households could receive over-the-air signals from several distant stations, reception was generally poor without the purchase of a large, unsightly antenna. However, the new cable system, incorporated as Paragould Cablevision Inc., offered clear reception of eight television stations, including signals from Jonesboro and Little Rock, Arkansas, Memphis, Tennessee, Cape Girardeau, Missouri, and Paducah, Kentucky.[2] To receive the service, subscribers paid a one-time $10 installation fee and a $5 monthly charge.

Within a few years PCI was acquired by Adams-Russell Co. Inc., based in Waltham, Massachusetts, which held ownership positions in several cable operations around the country. In the mid-1970s Paragould Cablevision added two channels to its basic package and increased the reach of its distribution lines, doubling the number of homes passed by the system. By 1978 advances in satellite technology enabled PCI to add Atlanta-based WTBS to its basic program schedule and to offer subscribers a premium movie channel, Home Box Office (HBO).[3]

In 1983, as PCI's original franchise was due to expire, the company negotiated a new ten-year franchise with the city, which included an option to extend the agreement for five additional years. Concerning fees for cable service, the franchise agreement obliged PCI to charge reasonable rates and provide sixty days' prior notice for proposed price changes. The agreement also obliged the operator to provide documentation supporting proposed rate increases if requested by the city. Historically, increases in PCI's cable charges had never been found to be unreasonable. In fact, the price of the firm's basic monthly service had risen at a slower rate than inflation during the period 1965–1983.

With respect to programming, the new franchise agreement was extraordinarily detailed, requiring that PCI

> provide subscribers in the City a basic program of not less than 11 channels, to include: the major networks; the nearest local station (Jonesboro); a station that broadcasts the Cardinal baseball games in St. Louis; one or more public TV stations; a religious station; an all sports network; one or more Little Rock stations including one that broadcasts Razorback [University of Arkansas]

*football and basketball games when they are televised; and one or more Memphis stations . . . and a channel for a pay TV program such as HBO, Cinemax, or Showtime which would not require a converter.*[4]

Other provisions of the franchise agreement included the requirement that PCI continue to pay an annual franchise fee to the city equal to 3 percent of gross revenues from cable services.

## Seeds of Controversy

In March 1984 Paragould Cablevision requested a rate increase of $1 per month for basic cable service. In response, the city's cable committee asked the company to provide justification for the rate increase. Adams-Russell's reply, received by the city five months after the initial request, did not satisfy the cable committee, which requested that the firm submit financial records for 1983 and 1984 so as to provide "a basis for forming an objective judgment of whether your requested increase is justified." This process of negotiation, however, was interrupted by the federal passage of the Cable Communications Act on October 30, 1984.

Under the terms of the act, local regulation of basic cable television rates would cease after December 31, 1986, except in a small number of communities where competition was deemed to be ineffective because of the lack of over-the-air broadcast signals.[5] The law also prohibited telephone companies from operating cable television systems.[6] The act permitted cable operators to raise rates up to 5 percent per year in 1984, 1985, and 1986 without first obtaining approval from the local franchise body. Paragould Cablevision responded to the law by raising its basic monthly cable rate $0.45 on December 31, 1984 (the day the pricing provisions took effect) and by increasing the rate an additional $0.47 on January 1, 1985.

During 1985 the city cable committee received a growing number of complaints from local cable subscribers regarding the recent price increases and the continued absence of certain mandated programming offerings—especially Razorback and Cardinals sporting events. However, Paragould Cablevision felt that its pricing and programming policies were fully consistent with the terms of the 1984 Cable Act.[7] Negotiations between the city and Paragould Cablevision failed to satisfy either party. As a result, some members of Paragould's city government began to explore alternative approaches for resolving the continuing cable controversy.

Initially, the city council wrote to East Arkansas Cablevision of Jonesboro, offering to grant the company a franchise to provide cable television service to Paragould in competition with PCI. The operator declined, which was not a surprising result given the natural monopoly character of cable television technology and the presence of a firmly established incumbent in the market. Following the rebuff by East Arkansas Cablevision, the city decided to take matters into its own hands.

## THE ROAD TO COMPETITION

In November 1985 the Paragould city council asked the City Light and Water Commission to pursue a feasibility study for the construction of a municipally owned cable television system. The report, completed by the Cable Television Information Center in early 1986, concluded that "at 40 percent of the market base, the city can offer a 'state-of-the-art' cable service at competitive rates." Specifically, the feasibility study determined that the city could construct a sixty-plus-channel cable system for $2.3 million and break even by charging $11 per subscriber for basic programming. The study also assumed that each month the average subscriber would pay $10 for premium services, $4.50 for an additional outlet (second TV hookup), and $3 for remote control rental. Such fees were typical in the industry at that time.[8]

Adams-Russell responded to the feasibility study in several ways. First, it promoted Paragould Cablevision's sales manager to local manager, a position that had been vacant for some time. Shortly thereafter, PCI committed to undertake a two-phase system-reconstruction project that would lead to (1) an expansion of channel offerings to include, for example, Razorback and St. Louis sporting events, and (2) a reduction in prices for premium channels. Furthermore, the company challenged the methodology, assumptions, and conclusions of the feasibility study, arguing that the proposed system could not break even without substantially higher market penetration and perhaps significant subsidization by the city.

Although pleased with the changes proposed by Paragould Cablevision, supporters of the municipal cable system argued that PCI's actions were simply a function of the threat of competition and that such responsiveness might quickly recede if plans for a city-owned system were withdrawn. In addition, a number of city officials were irritated by the tone adopted by the Adams-Russell representatives who traveled to Paragould in the spring of 1986. Specifically, some observers felt that the Massachusetts-based managers acted condescendingly toward elected officials—as if they were dealing with "a bunch of hicks."[9]

In April the city council, which unanimously favored the construction of a competing city-owned cable system, voted to hold a June referendum in which the citizens of Paragould would decide whether the municipality should proceed with the venture. After the referendum passed by a 4–1 margin, Paragould Cablevision introduced a "super tier" expanded basic service that included a total of eighteen channels for $15 per month.

As the city began to explore options for financing a municipally owned cable television system, it soon became aware of possible legal obstacles to the project. First, the Arkansas state constitution did not explicitly authorize municipalities to issue bonds for the purpose of constructing cable television systems. Furthermore, it was not clear whether Arkansas municipalities were allowed to operate a cable system once it was in place. Therefore, city officials worked with members of the Arkansas legislature, successfully securing the passage of legislation granting the necessary rights. In effect, Paragould's bargain with the state of Arkansas evolved. By the terms of the new law, bond issues for the financing of cable television systems required approval by voters via referendum.

During 1987 the Paragould city council authorized City Light and Water to establish and operate the proposed cable system. In December 1987 Adams-Russell was acquired by New York–based Cablevision Systems Corporation, a multisystem operator of cable systems serving almost 1 million subscribers in the eastern United States. The estimated purchase price for PCI was $16 million.[10] The new owner stated its commitment to continue expanding the channel capacity and enhancing the signal quality of the Paragould Cablevision system.

During early 1988 the change in ownership at Paragould Cable and the ongoing improvements to the PCI system appeared to reduce the city's incentives to move ahead with the proposed cable system. However, in April PCI announced an increase in the price of basic service by $2 per month and expanded basic by $1 per month. Although the company defended the changes as justified in light of extensive system improvements, complaints about the rate hikes helped to revive the momentum for a city-owned cable system.

In January 1989 the city council awarded a cable television franchise to City Light and Water, which, under the direction of manager Larry Watson, opened bids for engineering design work related to the construction of a city cable system. However, construction could not proceed unless and until voters approved a financing mechanism to fund the system. After extensive analysis of funding requirements, the city council proposed a twenty-five-year $3.22 million bond issue backed by a 6.5 mill suspended tax on all personal and real property in the city.[11] The referendum, held on October 31, 1989, was preceded by a publicity war between supporters and opponents of the city system. One advertisement by the ad hoc organization Citizens for Home-Owned Cable Systems was headlined "New York or Paragould" and closed with, "Let's keep the control and the revenue in Paragould."[12] The approval of the bonds by a vote of 1,549 to 1,102 came as somewhat of a surprise, given that the citizens of Paragould had defeated a bond issue for improvements to the local school system only a month before. Yet by this time, public anger and frustration with the private cable monopoly had acquired an unstoppable momentum.

## Legal Challenges to City Cable

On January 18, 1990, the firm Stephens Inc. of Little Rock, which had conducted considerable work for the city over the years, was on the verge of issuing Paragould's cable bonds when Paragould Cablevision filed a lawsuit in state court to block construction of the city cable system. The suit contended that (1) CLW was not authorized by state law to operate a cable television system; (2) the cable franchise agreement between the city and CLW was an unlawful delegation of legislative powers; and (3) the suspended 6.5 mill property tax, if activated to pay for city cable bonds, would violate the Arkansas constitution. Upon learning of the lawsuit, most of the investors with whom the bonds were to be placed backed out of the deal, leaving the issue temporarily in limbo.

On January 29, 1990 Paragould Cablevision filed a second lawsuit against the city, this time in federal court. In this complaint, the company charged Paragould with violating the Sherman Antitrust Act through an attempt to monopolize commerce and restrain trade in the city's cable television market. The suit also contended that construction of a city cable system would violate PCI's rights under the U.S. Constitution's First

Amendment (freedom of speech) and Fourteenth Amendment (depriva-
tion of property without due process).

The city of Paragould responded swiftly to these legal challenges,
requesting dismissal of all charges as groundless. Although dismissals
were granted quickly in both cases, Paragould Cablevision appealed the
decisions.[13] In June 1990 Stephens Inc. agreed to purchase the full issue
of the city's cable bonds itself, with the goal of remarketing the securities at a later date after all litigation had been resolved.[14] Thus, ironically, it was private capital that enabled the public entity to challenge
the private cable monopoly.

### City Cable Construction Phase

Paragould hired Jack Brinkley, former chief technician of Little Rock's cable
television to lead the construction and subsequent operation of City Cable.
The new system was to be a state-of-the-art sixty-six-channel capacity cable
television system, utilizing high-quality components in construction[15] and
"addressable" technology, which would allow for the turning on and off
of all basic and premium services from the system's central office.[16] The
system would also incorporate a local programming facility and a local
weather radar, neither of which were included in Paragould Cablevision's
current system. Five days after bids were awarded to begin construction on
the City Cable system, Paragould Cablevision announced the merging of
its nonpremium program tiers into a single basic package of forty channels,
priced at $14.50 per month. The firm unscrambled all nonpremium pro-
gramming signals, thus eliminating the need for subscribers with cable-
ready televisions to pay the existing $3/month converter box charge.[17]

Construction of the City Cable system proceeded throughout the fall
of 1990, with a target start-up date of March 1, 1991. In November the
company announced that it planned to offer basic cable service for
$12.50 per month; install up to two additional outlets in any home at no
extra charge; and provide converter boxes and remote control devices free
of charge for any subscribers lacking a cable-ready television. Paragould
Cablevision responded by lowering its basic rate to $11.50 and eliminat-
ing all additional outlet, converter, and remote control fees. In addition,
PCI announced that all households that had subscribed to its system for
at least one year would receive $1 off the monthly rate, while all that had
subscribed for at least two years would pay $2 less per month. In February

1991 City Cable announced its prices for a number of package deals, each including a different combination of basic and premium channels.[18] PCI in turn introduced comparable combination packages, each priced below City Cable's corresponding rate.[19] Both firms waived installation fees for basic and premium services. Clearly the original assumptions regarding service prices that were included in the city's initial feasibility survey were faulty. Essentially, the analysts failed to account for the dramatic impact competition would have not only on the level of programming fees but on the ability to charge for extras.

## CITY CABLE GOES ON-LINE

On March 1, 1991 City Cable connected its first subscriber to the system.[20] As the company's subscribership grew over the following months, City Cable's operations were supported by its own full-time employees as well as by the existing personnel of City Light and Water. The costs of shared personnel, facilities, and equipment utilized by City Cable were allocated to the division on a pro rata basis according to usage relative to other CLW divisions. City Cable believed that this arrangement allowed it to enjoy the benefits of certain economies of scope not available to a stand-alone cable operator.

City Cable aired its first live local broadcast on April 24. Throughout the spring, City Cable continued to expand its hours of live and prerecorded local programming as a means of differentiating itself from Paragould Cablevision. Yet while City Cable could boast of its local programming and weather radar, PCI could claim that it was the only system in town to offer The Nashville Network (TNN), St. Louis Cardinals baseball games, and ESPN *Sunday Night Football*. Although City Cable had sought to negotiate contracts to secure these program offerings, the vendors had been unwilling to deal with the municipally owned system. Because of the differences in program offerings, a small number of households subscribed to both systems, installing each to a separate television set. Both City Cable and PCI offered to switch subscribers from the other's system at no cost and typically responded to requests for installation and service calls on a same-day basis.

During the summer of 1991 City Cable initiated a subscriber promotional campaign under the slogan "3000 by 1992." The campaign included radio and print advertising as well as an employee incentive plan under which City Light and Water employees received rewards for bringing new subscribers to the system. These efforts supplemented ongoing promotional activities such as enclosing advertisements for City Cable in monthly CLW utility bills and encouraging new arrivals to Paragould to sign up for City Cable service at the time of initiating electric and water service.

Although City Cable's subscribership increased rapidly during the division's first year of operation, the system did not generate sufficient revenues to meet the coverage ratios and debt-service requirements specified in the bond covenants.[21] As a result, the city of Paragould was obliged to levy a tax of 2.786 mills on the total assessed value of real and personal property in order to raise the estimated $273,788 revenue shortfall. Based on the assessed value of the average Paragould home, CLW's controller estimated that the typical household would pay additional taxes of $33.43 to subsidize City Cable operations—far less than their annual savings on cable television service relative to prices charged in other U.S. markets.[22] Although subscribers to City Cable appeared to take the tax increase in stride, households subscribing to PCI as well as commercial property owners questioned the fairness of the levy. In response, Mayor Partlow maintained that not only did PCI subscribers themselves benefit financially as a result of competition from City Cable, but the city as a whole gained since profits previously flowing out of state to PCI's parent now remained in Paragould to the benefit of local commerce. PCI's manager noted in response that the firm's parent companies had actually made substantial investments in the community through recent system improvements.

During the spring of 1992 City Cable initiated a second major promotional campaign, this time with the goal of overtaking Paragould Cablevision in terms of total subscribership ("Number 1 by August 1"). However, PCI answered with a promotional campaign of its own, offering new (or returning) subscribers three months of basic service for $0.92, gift certificates for use in local businesses, and an opportunity to win a trip to Hawaii. Although the PCI program temporarily put a halt to City Cable's subscriber growth, the city resisted the temptation to respond with price cuts of its own. Instead, City Cable continued to promote itself as the superior provider of programming and customer service. During this period City Cable finally secured access to TNN and Cardinals Baseball, although PCI continued to retain an exclusive contract for ESPN *Sunday Night Football*. In addition, PCI began to offer a limited amount of local programming, albeit without the use of a dedicated production facility.

## Falcon/Capital Cable Offer

In May 1993 Falcon/Capital Cable, a St. Louis–based multisystem operator (MSO), made an unsolicited bid to purchase City Cable for $4 million.
CLW head Larry Watson dismissed the offer out of hand, noting that its
valuation at $1,100 per subscriber was far below the national average
acquisition price of $2,000 per subscriber. Ultimately, Watson believed
that the purchase of City Cable by Falcon or any other MSO would lead
to the end of cable competition in Paragould through a merger or buy-
out involving the acquired City Cable system and PCI. On May 10 the
Paragould city council rejected Falcon's offer by a vote of 8–0.

## The "Prisoner's Dilemma"

By the mid-1990s it was clear that City Cable and TCI were trapped in a
classic "prisoner's dilemma." Although each firm ran considerable financial losses,[23] neither would benefit from a price increase unless the other
adopted one as well. In fact, neither City Cable nor PCI had changed
basic or premium rates since competition began in early 1991, except for
PCI's short-term promotional offers. On the other hand, it did not appear
that either system was willing to abandon the market. Paragould had the
luxury of the property tax levy to cover its losses, and the public overall
was willing to incur these costs in exchange for perhaps the lowest cable
television rates in the nation. Cablevision Systems was presumably willing to subsidize PCI to avoid setting the precedent of "crying uncle" to a
competing municipal system. In particular, such a response might attract
similar competitive threats by other municipalities where it operated systems. As programming costs for existing cable networks continued to
escalate during the 1990s, and as new cable channels became available,
pressure on profitability mounted even further.

By 1997 a possible resolution had begun to appear. Cablevision Systems
announced a shift in its corporate strategy that involved concentrating its
cable holdings in a small number of clusters, so as to take better advantage
of certain scale and scope economies and position itself as a potential provider of telecommunications services in these areas. Since PCI was not
located near any of Cablevision Systems' other operations, it was a logical
candidate for sale. Given that the divestiture would be part of a larger cor-
porate-wide strategy under which a number of other systems would be sold
as well, the fear of setting a bad precedent no longer held much weight.

Yet who would be willing to buy a system trapped in a brutal competition with a municipally owned operator? In fact, the most logical bidder was the city of Paragould itself. In December 1997 Paragould acquired PCI for $2.25 million, or about $550 per subscriber. The two systems were integrated by City Cable and by the end of 1998 the municipal operator had earned its first surplus. The improved financial position was not due to price increases, but instead to the spreading of fixed costs over twice as many customers.[24] In December 1999, however, the Paragould city council approved rate increases of about 30 percent on City Cable's basic and premium services in response to cumulative increases in programming costs and other expenses over the course of the 1990s.[25] Yet even after these price increases, Paragould's cable rates remained well below those of comparable systems elsewhere in the United States.

## THE PERILS OF DISENGAGEMENT

The fate of PCI can serve as a warning to managers convinced that the steamroller of free markets and private ownership has swept away the relevance of government in the age of the new market economy. It is easy to sympathize with PCI and its owners, who undoubtedly questioned the appropriateness of government ownership in an industry that bears little resemblance to the classic public utility. Also, concerns regarding the fairness of the city's use of property taxes to support the operations of an entity competing directly with a private firm are legitimate.

Nevertheless, PCI's owners were woefully inattentive to the concept of the evolving bargain. Particularly as a "foreign-" ("Yankee-") owned corporation, the firm did surprisingly little to strengthen its relationship with the city government and, more broadly, the citizens of Paragould. The firm's apparent lack of knowledge of the city's historic conflicts in the electricity sector left it ill-prepared to assess the contextual environment of its bargain. Furthermore, its dismissive attitude toward city officials around the time of deregulation indicated a fundamental misreading of the deeper implications of reform. Later responses, including insensitive timing both for price increases and decreases and repeated attempts at litigation, only made a bad situation worse. In the end, City Cable was approved and constructed not primarily on economic grounds but on noneconomic ones: the desire to maintain local pride, control, and "sovereignty."

# 9 ✦ *Harnessing Opportunity in the New Market Economy*

*It is easy to be swept up* in the enthusiasm surrounding the dramatic changes in the role of governments and the growing scope of private enterprise that characterize the new market economy. The removal of long-standing restrictions on entry into many industry sectors and national markets has generated significant opportunities for entrepreneurs and established business concerns. The privatization of state-owned enterprises, and the removal of profitability restrictions in numerous sectors, has opened the way for private investors to transform the operations of established producers, creating and capturing economic value in the process.[1]

This book has explored these opportunities and their associated risks in a range of national and industry contexts. In this final chapter, we summarize a number of important lessons and their strategic implications for managers, starting at a general level, then shifting to the particular perspectives of incumbents, entrants, and concessionaires. The book closes with a look at the implications of neoregulation, especially with respect to the Internet, and the globalization of governmental institutions.

## GENERAL LESSONS AND IMPLICATIONS

Throughout this book we have seen that the new market economy does not represent a complete break with the past. One critical lesson is that government continues to play a significant role in shaping commercial opportunity and risk, even in sectors experiencing extensive deregulation and privatization. Reforms affecting the rules of entry and action within a market, as well as changes in the structure and ownership of individual players, alter the terms of the firm's bargain with the state, but the bargain remains in place and continues to evolve. Paradoxically, new obligations often accompany increased freedoms following reforms. New regulatory institutions and even ongoing government ownership stakes characterize many sectors supposedly liberated from state control.

A second lesson is that context matters in the design and evolution of an enterprise's bargain with the state and the broader society. In sectors in which the products or the production processes are seen as affecting the basic health and welfare of buyers and other parties—including goods and services viewed as integral to national security and cultural identity— firms tend to face more restrictive and often more volatile bargains. This tendency is accentuated when production involves significant, long-term investments in specialized assets. A nation's social, political, and economic context shapes the evolving bargain as well, affecting, for example, the specific rights and obligations of foreign-owned enterprises and private corporations following liberalization.

A third important lesson is that reform bargains create winners and losers as changes in market power and incentives alter market dynamics. "Losing" can be absolute or relative, full or partial, real or perceived. Residential electricity users in the United Kingdom, for example, regarded themselves as losers following power sector deregulation and privatization. Frustrated entrants in the New Zealand telecommunications sector were seen as losers following in the industry implementation of reforms. Losers typically strive to improve their position through efforts in the political arena, leveraging political power as a substitute for market power to shape the evolution of the reform bargain.

A final general lesson is that bargains, including reform bargains, inevitably evolve over time in response to market dynamics and political dynamics. While external events play a role in shaping these dynamics, the actions of affected parties in both the commercial and political arenas exert critical influence on the bargain's evolution. Given the newness of the terms of the reform bargain at the time of its adoption, one can expect the associated rights, obligations, and enforcement mechanisms to be tested, interpreted, and clarified over time. Depending on the relative political power of the losers, and the strength of the enforcement mechanisms, the terms of the reform bargain may undergo significant evolution. In some cases, such as that of Paragould Cablevision Inc., the reform bargain may evolve in ways highly unfavorable to the initial winners.

These general lessons have several important strategic implications. The first is that firms must recognize that the "devil is in the details" when it comes to evaluating business opportunities associated with reform bargains. Rather than simply equating deregulation with greater commercial freedoms, and privatization with reduced government ownership and control, firms should analyze the rights, obligations, and enforcement mechanisms associated with any reform bargain under which they conduct or plan to conduct business. A thorough assessment involves not only an evaluation of the firm's own enterprise bargain with the state, but also the web of interrelated bargains affected by the reforms. In addition, the analysis should pay close attention to the impact of contextual factors at the national and industry level on the firm's opportunities and risks under the reform bargain.

A second implication is that firms should not view reform bargains as fixed or predetermined, but instead should explore and take advantage of opportunities to shape the terms of the reform bargain before, during, and after its adoption. Firms should not restrict their vision of the means for shaping the bargain merely to traditional lobbying or public relations activities. Given the important linkages between market dynamics and political dynamics, firms should design their commercial strategy with conscious attention to the implications for the reform bargain and its subsequent evolution. This approach should be used proactively, to improve the terms of the reform bargain to the firm's advantage, as well as defensively, to protect the firm from adverse changes in the bargain.

In devising an appropriate strategy for shaping the terms and evolution of the reform bargain, the firm should work to identify the likely winners and losers from the reform process and assess their power to affect political dynamics. One option for reducing the negative impact of politically influential losers is for the firm to encourage the state to provide subsidies or other benefits to actual or potential losers following reform. The British government, for example, provided over £400 million to fund severance packages for workers laid off by National Power following privatization. As an alternative, the firm may find it beneficial to share with these parties some of the value it would ordinarily capture under the reform bargain. New England Electric System, for example, agreed to price cuts of 10 percent to Massachusetts residential electricity users to gain the support of this critical constituency for the terms of the Massachusetts Energy Act of 1998. Firms also should explore opportunities to cooperate in the political arena with reform bargain winners to preserve favorable aspects of the reforms and promote mutually beneficial changes over time.

Firms should also recognize the strategic importance of the expectations and perceptions of participants in the market and other parties affected by reforms. Unrealistically optimistic expectations at the time of the reform bargain tend to produce self-identified losers and generate backlash to the reforms. In effect, perceptions become reality. Overselling the short-term benefits of private management of public schools, for example, backfired on Education Alternatives Inc. In general, firms should strive to offset unrealistic expectations at the time of reform, while subsequently accentuating the benefits that flow to each of the affected parties.

Shaping the terms of reform is particularly important for firms whose business activities entail significant long-term investments in specialized assets. Since these firms are highly vulnerable to unfavorable changes in the bargain over time, they should pay close attention to shaping the formal and informal enforcement mechanisms upholding their rights and obligations in the marketplace. In addition, where feasible, they should stagger investments over time so as to reduce the prospect of being held hostage at a later date.

Finally, reform bargains pose strategic challenges in the creation and management of collaborative ventures, whether in the form of alliances, joint ventures, or consortia. As we have seen, multifirm ventures often provide a means for rapidly assembling diverse resources to purchase state-owned enterprises, enter deregulated markets, or bid on concessions. Yet the different objectives and constraints of the venture's participants tend to create tensions in the governance and stability of these organizations. These tensions are typically underestimated and are exacerbated by the rapidly evolving market and political dynamics normally associated with reform bargains.

## IMPLICATIONS FOR INCUMBENTS

The owners and managers of established firms undergoing a reform bargain tend to face extraordinary challenges in transforming their organizations into commercially oriented, market-driven enterprises. The wide-ranging nature of these changes takes place at the broad level of governance and strategy formulation, as well as at the operating level, as the firm reforms its internal systems and human resources and reshapes its relationships with suppliers and customers.

Given the significant demands imposed by commercial pressures and opportunities in the new market economy, it is understandable that incumbents would overlook, or at least underestimate, the ongoing importance of the role of the state following the reform bargain. But it is risky to ignore the evolving terms of the enterprise bargain as well as the web of interrelated bargains.

Ironically, dramatic short-term commercial successes by the incumbent often generate adverse political dynamics, which in turn may threaten long-term commercial performance. National Power, for example, enjoyed incumbent-on-top market dynamics in the initial years following reform, when it faced little effective competition and obtained significantly increased freedom of action in the commercial sphere. Over time, however, aspects of the firm's performance declined in the face of mandatory divestitures, a windfall profits tax, and restrictions on its freedom to engage in merger and acquisition activities.

Incumbents' challenges in the political arena are heightened by the increased expectations, visibility, and political participation that typically accompany deregulation and privatization. Consumers generally expect higher product quality and customer service, lower prices, and greater availability of goods and services provided by incumbents following a reform bargain. Particularly in sectors that involve goods and services affecting basic welfare and security, the general public tends to expect that incumbents' profits and executive compensation will be fair and reasonable—vague but nonetheless powerful concepts.

The gap between expectations and reality may be wide, since incumbents' incentives to exercise and expand market power and to reward managers for commercial successes are typically much stronger following reform. But differences in actual and expected performance are likely to be visible in the postreform context as incumbents face increased scrutiny by the financial markets, the media, and grassroots organizations. Also, privatized state-owned enterprises typically find their activities reviewed by newly created regulatory institutions, and all incumbents tend to experience greater scrutiny by antitrust authorities.

The heightened visibility of incumbents' performance, combined with the greater political access and participation that often accompany reform bargains, make it unwise for incumbents to ignore the impact of their commercial strategy on political dynamics and to neglect the development of a coherent governmental and public relations strategy following reforms. In the case of privatized SOEs, incumbents' vulnerability to unfavorable changes in political dynamics may be exacerbated by a shift in the allegiance of various government institutions from the firm to other affected parties in the market. Yorkshire Water, for example, found that in the midst of a drought-induced water crisis, local and regional government institutions that were its owners or close affiliates prior to privatization sided with angry consumers when reliability problems emerged following reform.

Incumbents should assess carefully the way in which their ownership structure is likely to affect both market dynamics and political dynamics. Although shareholdings by government institutions, unions, and politically influential private companies and individuals tend to place constraints on the incumbent's commercial strategy and overall governance, these shareholders typically provide critical support for the firm's efforts to manage its evolving bargain arrangement with the state. Rio Light's ability to weather the political fallout from electricity blackouts following privatization, for example, was bolstered significantly by the participation of the Brazilian steel giant Companhia Siderúrgica Nacional SA and various government shareholders in the firm's ownership structure. Incumbents also may be able to cultivate political support from government institutions or officials tied closely to the firm prior to the reform bargain. For example, Teléfonos de México, the former state-owned monopoly telecommunications company of Mexico, appears to have successfully leveraged its historical relationship with the nation's Secretariat of Communications and Transportation following privatization. Specifically, it secured a favorable evolution in its bargain with respect to interconnection fees charged to other carriers.[2]

A final critical challenge for incumbents is grappling with opportunities and risks in the area of corporate strategy that typically emerge following reforms. Incumbents often obtain the freedom to abandon activities they were obligated to perform prior to reforms as well as enter markets from which they were previously barred. In assessing options for divesting lines of business, outsourcing activities previously performed in-house, and curtailing social services traditionally provided for employees or local communities, incumbents should carefully analyze both the commercial and political implications of alternative strategies. In Australia, for example, Powercor's strategy for outsourcing meter reading and maintenance services to new firms created by former employees and industry unions provided a powerful combination of commercial and political benefits.

Incumbent's postreform options for vertical or horizontal expansion within an industry, or diversification into other product or geographic markets, should also be assessed carefully from both a commercial and political perspective. Intra-industry expansion may offer opportunities to achieve greater economies of scale or scope, while also increasing market power. Yet enhanced market power may trigger a strong political response from affected participants in the market. Product or geographic diversification may also provide incumbents with opportunities to exploit synergies with their existing activities, although the firm may lack the requisite skills and other resources—both commercial and political—to succeed in these other markets. National Power, for example, found by the end of the 1990s that its freedom under the initial reform bargain to expand beyond its core British power-generation activities appeared to be less a blessing and more a curse.

## IMPLICATIONS FOR ENTRANTS

One of the sobering lessons for entrants in the new market economy has been the extraordinary resilience of most incumbents following the adoption of reform bargains. Although scores of new carriers entered the U.S. airline industry following deregulation, virtually all of these entrants eventually went bankrupt or were acquired by incumbents. In the deregulated New Zealand telecommunications market, the privatized incumbent TCNZ became one of the world's most profitable telecommunication operators, while land-line entrant CCL and wireless entrant BellSouth New Zealand struggled to gain market share and achieve sustainable profitability.

It is critical for potential entrants to recognize that following a reform bargain, significant structural barriers to entry often remain in place despite the elimination of government-imposed restrictions on firms' freedom to participate in the market. In many instances, incumbents own or control access to critical infrastructure such as local telephone networks, airport gates, electricity transmission systems, or other assets that, for financial or logistical reasons, entrants cannot easily replicate or bypass. Although reform bargains typically include terms facilitating access to such gateway assets, the pricing, technical details, and enforcement mechanisms governing access may leave the entrant at a substantial disadvantage relative to the incumbent, as we saw, for example, in the case of CCL. Entrants often face additional structural barriers such as contractual arrangements between incumbents, suppliers, and buyers. Three-year contracts between incumbent British power producers and local distribution companies adopted at the time of the reform bargain effectively locked out potential entrants in the initial period following reforms.

From a strategic perspective, potential entrants should become involved as early as possible in the political process, shaping the design of the reform bargain, paying special attention to the ways in which the terms of the web of interrelated bargains affect structural barriers to entry. Entrants should also be prepared to devote resources to a government and public relations strategy that supports a favorable evolution of the terms of the bargain over time, including, in particular, the implementation of antitrust provisions. Entrants may find it useful to establish close commercial and political relationships with important supplier and customer groups. U.S. Baby Bells, for example, cultivated support from major telecommunications equipment suppliers in their efforts to obtain rights to enter long-distance markets. Firms looking to enter foreign markets following reforms often find that including a local partner in the venture's ownership structure can provide important benefits in shaping the terms and evolution of the reform bargain and securing access to critical resources. These potential benefits, however, must be weighed carefully against potential governance-related costs.

Even when firms are able to overcome barriers to entry, they should not be lulled into thinking that incumbents, often inefficient and/or unresponsive to customer needs at the time of reforms, are "sitting ducks." Privatization and deregulation significantly change the incentives facing incumbents, leading these firms to make dramatic changes in their business practices. As incumbents transform themselves into leaner, more responsive, and more innovative organizations, entrants often find that their competitive advantages at the time of deregulation and privatization are short-lived. Also, the larger size and deeper pockets of most incumbents relative to entrants typically enable the established firms to weather the adjustment period, then fight aggressively in both the commercial and political arenas against entrants attempting to capture any more than a minor share of the market. Entrants, therefore, must prospectively assess the market dynamics likely to flow from the reform bargain and evaluate the fit of their basic business model to these conditions. For example, does the reform bargain merely provide a short-term arbitrage opportunity as incumbents transform their business practices, or does the entrant possess particular resources and capabilities that enable it to offer superior value to at least some segment of the market over the longer run?

## IMPLICATIONS FOR CONCESSIONAIRES AND CONTRACTORS

As governments shift the provision of many services formerly performed by public sector institutions to the private sector, private firms face an increasing array of opportunities to negotiate or bid on concessions and other contracting arrangements with government institutions. It is tempting to view these opportunities as analogous to commercial contracts or private deals. But there are typically critical differences between these arrangements and traditional contracts, which lead to important strategic implications for concessionaires.

Many of these concession arrangements extend over long periods of time and are subject to enforcement mechanisms that are untested at the time of reform. The services covered by these bargains typically are regarded as affecting the basic health and welfare of buyers (or nonpaying users), which heightens the sensitivity of affected parties to both economic and noneconomic outcomes in the market. The very nature of these services often poses difficulties in the measurement and monitoring of performance, which complicates enforcement, as we saw, for example, in the cases of EAI and CCA.

Several strategic implications flow from the features of these concession arrangements. First, prospective concessionaires should carefully assess and, to whatever extent possible, shape the enforcement mechanisms associated with contract opportunities and the underlying performance measures on which enforcement will be based. Enron, for example, insisted that disputes between its Dabhol Power Corporation and the Indian government be subject to arbitration in London. In contrast, performance measures in EAI's public school management contracts were ill-defined, and these contracts left the firm with little recourse when the school systems failed to pay previously agreed upon compensation for services.

Concessionaires should also pay close attention to managing political dynamics, which often include a strong local component. Enron and CCA, for example, found that state politics had a critical impact on their evolving bargains, while EAI discovered that political dynamics at the city level were a major determinant of its performance. Managing the expectations of affected parties is particularly important, since losers are often able to organize more effectively at the local level. Also, it may be necessary to share some of the commercial benefits derived from private concessions with politically influential groups to secure their ongoing support, or at least dampen their opposition to the reform bargain. The failure of EAI to secure the support of teachers' unions, for example, proved highly damaging in its school management bargains.

Concessionaires, in particular, should also look for opportunities to stagger fixed investments over time, with additional expenditures contingent on favorable evolution of the reform bargain. Enron's two-phase structure of the Dabhol power project, plus the prospect of future investments in the Indian power sector, provided it with stronger bargaining leverage when political dynamics temporarily derailed the project during the construction phase. EAI, in contrast, made most of its expenditures on building improvements and installation of new computers early on in its management contract with the Hartford school system, leaving the firm particularly vulnerable to the subsequent unfavorable evolution of the bargain.

## THE THREAT OF NEOREGULATION

Much of this book has focused on sectors in which the role of government has been particularly strong during the twentieth century, including communications, transportation, utilities, energy, and the provision of social services. Although these sectors have been characterized by a considerable opening up of markets and infusion of private ownership, firms active in these markets have encountered limits to the retreat of the state. In some cases, public backlash has even led to a resurgence of the government's role, as seen vividly in the case of Paragould Cablevision, Inc.

Perhaps more surprising has been the emergence of pressures for more restrictive reform bargains in markets where the intensity of government intervention has been traditionally less pronounced. The case of the U.S. versus Microsoft is the most dramatic illustration of this phenomenon. Yet examples abound in other sectors as well, including calls for tighter restrictions on producers of genetically modified goods, providers of ATM financial services, and firms controlling access to Internet services.

Trends toward neoregulation in any given case are best understood as a consequence of one or both of two factors: (1) a shift in the perception of the products from nonessential to affecting basic health and welfare and (2) increasing market power of the industry producer(s). In Microsoft's case, not only has the personal computer (PC) operating system become increasingly regarded as an essential product, but the firm's success in capturing almost 90 percent of the market—and its leveraging of the operating system to establish dominance in other product markets—has made it increasingly subject to unfavorable shifts in political dynamics.[3]

An important implication of these trends is that firms should neither assume that the role of the state is diminishing uniformly across markets, nor that backlash leading toward more restrictive reform bargains can occur only in sectors traditionally characterized by high degrees of government intervention. In particular, firms active in high-tech sectors, including computer-related, biotech, and Internet products and services, should not be lulled into believing that society will gladly reward technological excellence for its own sake. These firms should incorporate a careful assessment of political dynamics into the design and implementation of both their commercial and political strategies. Ultimately, even in these industries, shaping expectations among affected parties, building political coalitions, and balancing value creation and value sharing may all be important elements to sustaining success in the new market economy.

The role of the Internet sector is intriguing with respect to neoregulation and the evolving bargain. Although the Internet holds much promise for reducing barriers to entry and increasing competition in a wide range of markets, the growing dominance of particular firms in various Internet submarkets—for example, America Online, Amazon.com, Yahoo!, and eBay—raises the vulnerability of companies to more restrictive bargains as they continue to take advantage of scale, scope, and network economies. At the same time, the Internet serves as a means for reducing the organizing costs of affected parties across markets in general, which tends in turn to enhance their market power—for example, via boycotts, creation of buying networks, and so on—and their political power. Thus in developing strategies for the new market economy, firms should incorporate an explicit assessment of the ways in which the Internet will affect both market dynamics and political dynamics, and the evolution of the firm's web of interrelated bargains.

## THE GLOBALIZATION OF GOVERNMENT INSTITUTIONS

Deregulation and privatization have unleashed a tremendous amount of economic activity transcending the borders of individual nations. These increasing flows of goods and services, labor, and capital—including rapid growth in cross-border mergers and acquisitions—have not only attracted the attention of regulators at the national level but have also come increasingly under the regulatory auspices of transnational government institutions.

In fact, national governments have ceded considerable authority for designing and enforcing critical terms of enterprise bargains to regional bodies such as institutions of the European Union, NAFTA, and Mercosur, as well as international institutions such as the World Trade Organization (WTO), the International Monetary Fund (IMF), and the International Court of Justice. At the same time, the legitimacy of these institutions has come under attack from a wide range of parties, including nationalists, local producers of goods and services, environmentalists, labor organizations, and even anarchists. Witness the violent protests against the WTO at its conference in Seattle in late 1999.

The strategic implications of these trends are twofold. First, firms should recognize the increasing role played by transnational government institutions in shaping and enforcing their evolving bargains and should take into account the objectives and constraints of these organizations when devising their commercial and political strategies. American Airlines and British Airways, for example, appear to have seriously misjudged the importance of the European Union's competition commissioner in their failed effort to consummate an alliance in the late 1990s.

A second implication is the need to assess, shape, and respond to the power of affected parties not only with respect to political dynamics at the national and local level, but also at the regional and international level. In some instances, affected parties themselves are able to enhance their market and political power by developing alliances with similarly interested parties in other political jurisdictions. Producers of genetically engineered goods, for example, have found themselves increasingly under attack by international coalitions of opponents, which have organized transnational economic boycotts, public relations campaigns, and lobbying efforts.

In the final analysis, it is critical to recognize that bargains will continue to evolve following the liberalizing reforms of the late twentieth and early twenty-first century. In this environment, firms can best position themselves to make the most of their internal resources and capabilities and their external context by designing and implementing strategies that anticipate and shape market dynamics and political dynamics over time. As these enterprises navigate between opportunity and risk in the new market economy, the only true constant will be change.

# *Notes*

## Preface

1. These scholars include a number of colleagues at Harvard University who have been particularly influential in the development of my thinking in these areas—namely James Austin, John Donahue, Alexander Dyck, José Gómez-Ibáñez, Yasheng Huang, George Lodge, Thomas McCraw, John Meyer, Forest Reinhardt, Richard H. K. Vietor, Raymond Vernon, and Louis Wells.
2. These scholars also include a number of Harvard colleagues, specifically Adam Brandenburger, Richard Caves, Pankaj Ghemawat, Robert Kennedy, Anita McGahan, Cynthia Montgomery, Michael Porter, David Yoffie, and Michael Yoshino.

## Introduction

1. Susan Strange, *The Retreat of the State: The Diffusion of Power in the World Economy* (Cambridge: Cambridge University Press, 1996); Robert Kuttner, *Everything for Sale: The Virtues and Limits of Markets* (New York: Knopf, 1997); Lowell Bryan and Diana Farrell, *Market Unbound: Unleashing Global Capitalism* (New York: Wiley, 1996); William Greider, *One World, Ready or Not: The Manic Logic of Global Capitalism* (New York: Simon and Schuster, 1998).
2. Cartoon by Robert Mankoff, *The New Yorker,* 25 May 1998.

## Chapter 1

1. These terms are typically set by a variety of government institutions at the national, state or provincial, and local level. Thus in referring to "the government" or "the state," it is important to keep in mind the complexity and in some cases, internal conflicts, that characterize this bargaining agent for society.
2. This notion of property is quite broad. It includes tangible property—such as land, buildings, and equipment—as well as intangible property, such as patents, copyrights, trademarks, and licenses. Intangible property also includes the firm's contracts with suppliers, customers, and other organizations.

3. Philip Rosenzweig, "Mercedes-Benz," Case No. 9-394-084 (Boston: Harvard Business School, 1993), 4.

4. Physical infrastructure assets—such as a rail system—cannot be shifted for use in other markets in a cost-effective manner. In contrast, assets such as basic equipment and commercial vehicles often can be redeployed within the firm or sold in the market at (depreciated) book value. The challenges associated with "asset-specificity" are examined in detail by Oliver Williamson in *The Economic Institutions of Capitalism* (New York: The Free Press, 1985).

5. Technology characteristics that favor the emergence of a "natural monopoly," or a very small number of producers in an industry, include significant economies of scale and scope, and network externalities. Network externalities represent benefits that individual consumers obtain when other consumers utilize the same network—for example, a telecommunications system or a computer operating system. See Alfred Kahn, *The Economics of Regulation*, Volume 2 (Cambridge, MA: MIT Press, 1988), 113–126, and Carl Shapiro and Hal Varian, *Information Rules* (Boston: Harvard Business School Press, 1999), 173–225.

6. The basic intuition in this context is that prior to making the investment, the firm has greater bargaining power, but after the investment has been completed, and is virtually impossible to remove, bargaining power shifts to the state. Raymond Vernon, *Sovereignty at Bay: The Multinational Spread of U.S. Enterprises* (New York: Basic Books, 1971), chapter 2.

7. David Baron provides an alternative framework for analyzing political dynamics that distinguishes a firm's "market strategy" from its "nonmarket strategy." David Baron, "Integrated Strategy: Market and Nonmarket Components," *California Management Review* 37, no. 2 (Winter 1995): 47–65.

### Chapter 2

1. This early history of the U.S. airline industry draws extensively on Francis A. Spencer, *Air Mail Payment and the Government* (Brookings Institution, 1941) and J. Howard Hamstra, "Two Decades—Federal Aero-Regulation in Perspective," *The Journal of Air Law and Commerce* 12, no. 2 (1941): 105–147.

2. U.S. Constitution, Article I, Section 8.

3. The act fixed air mail rates at a minimum of ten cents per ounce for transport up to 1,000 miles; fifteen cents up to 1,500 miles; and twenty cents for more than 1,500 miles. Spencer, *Air Mail Payment*, 32.

4. Henry L. Smith, *Airways: The History of Commercial Aviation in the United States* (New York: Alfred A. Knopf, 1942), 106.

5. Until 1933, the majority of airline industry revenues came from mail transport, not passenger transport.

6. Hamstra, *Two Decades*, 131.

7. Media pressure also played a role in shaping the political dynamics through a series of investigative stories on air mail contracting by a Hearst newspaper reporter. Hamstra, *Two Decades*, 121, footnote 40.

8. Spencer, *Air Mail Payment and the Government*, 60.

9. Richard E. Caves, *Air Transport and Its Regulators* (Cambridge, MA: Harvard University Press, 1962), 133–136. The most attractive markets for intrastate carriers were California and Texas.

10. Carriers were also required to obtain approval to abandon service on an existing route. Such requests rarely occurred, however, given positive trends in market growth and the CAB's favorable approaches to pricing and entry issues (see below).

11. Civil Aeronautics Act, Section 1002(e).

12. Richard H. K. Vietor, *Contrived Competition* (Cambridge, MA: Belknap Press, 1994), 42–43.

13. These trends for the 1950s and 1960s are analyzed in detail in William E. Fruhan, Jr., *The Fight for Competitive Advantage* (Boston: Harvard Business School Division of Research, 1972).

14. Calculated from Thomas McCraw, *Prophets of Regulation* (Cambridge, MA: Belknap Press, 1984), 267.

15. Vietor, *Contrived Competition,* 51–52.

16. The critical role played by Kahn with respect to U.S. airline industry deregulation is analyzed in McCraw, *Prophets of Regulation,* 259–296. Note that Kahn's predecessor, Ford-appointee John Robson, had introduced some liberalizing experiments prior to Kahn's arrival.

17. Quoted in Vietor, *Contrived Competition,* 57.

18. Although Delta and Eastern had effectively created hubs prior to deregulation, American pushed the concept to an even greater extent. By the early 1980s, almost three-quarters of its flights were connected to its Dallas/Fort Worth hub.

19. American Airlines's strategic adjustments to industry deregulation are examined in detail in Vietor, *Contrived Competition,* 61–77.

20. As noted above, safety regulation under the Federal Aviation Administration remained unchanged following deregulation.

21. The terms of U.S. antitrust policy are defined primarily in the Sherman Act (1888), the Clayton Act (1914), and the Robinson-Patman Act (1936). The Robinson-Patman Act also prohibits most forms of price discrimination.

22. Outside the United States, antitrust policy is often referred to as "competition policy."

23. Quoted in "Doesn't Anyone Give a D—-?" *Business Week,* 5 August 1985, 92.

24. "Airlines and Congress," *Journal of Commerce,* 13 August 1992, 8A.

25. "Court OKs Discount Coupons to Settle Airline Suit," *The Phoenix Gazette,* 1 December 1994, A17. The conditions governing the use of the discounts, however, were quite restrictive from the consumer perspective.

26. Martin Tolchin, "Six Airlines Settle Suit by Government on Fares," *New York Times,* 18 March 1994, D2.

27. "Airlines and Antitrust," *Journal of Commerce,* 1 April 1993, 8A.

28. Bruce Ingersoll, "Air Carriers Face 'Dumping' Enforcement," *Wall Street Journal,* 13 March 1998, A3.

29. The Railway Labor Act, a law originally passed in 1926, was amended in 1936 to cover important aspects of airline industry labor relations. Under the terms of the act, the president could suspend an airline strike for 60 days and appoint a Presidential Emergency Board to help mediate the dispute. *Railway Labor Act,* Section 10.

30. Thomas Petzinger, Jr., *Hard Landing* (New York: Times Business/Random House, 1995), 333.

31. See, for example, John T. McQuiston, "Air Traffic Controllers Testify About Old, Failing Equipment," *New York Times*, 27 August 1998, A24.
32. This restriction applied, for example, to New York's LaGuardia Airport.
33. Scott McCartney, "American Airlines Adds Continental to Love Field Suit," *Wall Street Journal*, 20 May 1998, A8.
34. For example, Delta Airlines not only was unwilling to sell LaGuardia slots to start-up ValuJet in 1995, but gained control of ten slots that ValuJet had been close to leasing from TWA. Martha Brannigan, "Why It Costs So Much to Fly into LaGuardia," *Wall Street Journal*, 30 November 1995, B1.
35. Bruce Ingersoll, "America West, Five Smaller Airlines Get O'Hare, LaGuardia Landing Rights," *Wall Street Journal*, 22 April 1998, A4.
36. From 1995–1998, thirty additional open skies agreements were signed between the United States and foreign governments. Data provided by the U.S. Department of Transportation.
37. The British government maintained that the slots could only be transferred to a "corporate successor" of TWA, as opposed to being sold separately to another carrier. Thomas Petzinger, Jr., *Hard Landing*, 379.
38. Thomas Petzinger, Jr., *Hard Landing*, 389.
39. In 1986 the European Court of Justice determined that air transport was subject to EU competition rules (antitrust policy). Throughout the 1990s, the EU gradually adopted policies promoting an increasingly competitive common market for air transport among member nations. Mark W. Zacher, *Governing Global Networks* (New York: Cambridge University Press, 1996), 118–119.
40. Of the total, 230–240 were to be relinquished at Heathrow, and the remainder at London's less capacity-constrained Gatwick Airport. The number of slots was sufficient to allow nineteen daily round trips between the U.S. and London. Carole Shifrin and Pierre Sparaco, "American, BA Move Closer to Partnership," *Aviation Week and Space Technology*, 13 July 1998, 24.
41. Bruce Barnard, "BA Windfall Rests on Britain Defying EU on Landing Slots," *Journal of Commerce*, 12 August 1998, 12A.
42. "Slot Market," *Financial Times*, 12 August 1998, 13.
43. Data from Air Transport Association, cited in Richard Tomkins, "When Fares Aren't Fair," *Financial Times*, 10 February 1998, 21.
44. Calculated from Air Transport Association of America, *Air Transport 1978* (Washington, D.C.: Air Transport Association of America, 1978) and Air Transport of America, *Annual Report 1999* (Washington, D.C.: Air Transport Association of America, 1999).

## Chapter 3

1. Coverage was highly skewed toward the major cities, leaving rural areas with telephone density of about 2 per 100 inhabitants.
2. The Organization for Economic Cooperation and Development (OECD) included at that time the United States, Japan, Korea, Mexico, New Zealand, and the nations of Western Europe.
3. Ben Petrazzini, "Telephone Privatization in a Hurry," in *Privatizing Monopolies*, ed. Ravi Ramamurti (Baltimore: Johns Hopkins University Press, 1996), 112, 115, 116.

4. In 1904 the Argentine president issued a decree requiring all private operators to report their activities to the executive, and in 1907 a second decree was issued, authorizing the federal government to set telephone service rates. See Alice Hill and Manuel Angel Abdala, "Regulation, Institutions, and Commitment: Privatization and Regulation in the Argentine Telecommunications Sector" (World Bank Research Department, 1993), 8–9. In practice, however, it does not appear that these decrees were enforced.

5. The term *laissez-faire*—French for "let them do as they wish"—is often used to describe the role of the state in an idealized capitalist economy: nonintervention in the affairs of firms, organizations, and individuals. We will use the term to refer to a bargain that entitles the firm to property rights protection while obligating it to respect the property rights of other actors. Additional obligations and entitlements are minimal under this type of bargain.

6. The largest of these was the Compañía Argentina de Teléfonos (CAT), which eventually came under the control of its principal supplier, the Swedish telecommunications equipment manufacturer Ericsson. The remaining firms were typically stand-alone cooperatives.

7. This is particularly true for local telephone service, but less so for long-distance service, where a much smaller investment in fixed costs is required.

8. "Distribution" in this context includes both long-distance and local transmission.

9. The geographic and product scope of the natural monopoly in any particular case, however, would depend on demographic and topographical features, in addition to technological considerations. For example, water distribution systems tend to be localized, leading to the emergence of multiple nonoverlapping water monopolies across a nation.

10. Fairness in this sense goes beyond the economic issues of how to "divide the pie."

11. Petrazzini, "Telephone Privatization in a Hurry," 111.

12. This topic is given excellent treatment in Daniel Yergin and Joseph Stanislaw, *The Commanding Heights* (New York: Simon and Schuster, 1998), chapters 1–3.

13. The principal sectors included railways, ports, power, and telecommunications.

14. In addition to international telecommunications, railways, and utilities, the British government also nationalized the coal and iron and steel industries. Unlike the situation in Argentina, however, the firms nationalized in Britain were owned by domestic, as opposed to foreign, investors. Yergin and Stanislaw, *The Commanding Heights*, 25–26.

15. Hill and Abdala, "Regulation, Institutions, and Commitment," 9.

16. Petrazzini, "Telephone Privatization in a Hurry," 139, footnote 6.

17. Recall the discussion of the "obsolescing bargain" in chapter 1.

18. In the early 1970s, the Chilean government under President Salvador Allende nationalized assets of firms, including ITT, with little or no compensation. In response, the U.S. government, through the Central Intelligence Agency, intervened to destabilize Chile's government, helping pave the way for the eventual coup by General Augusto Pinochet.

19. Ericsson, the owner of the rural Argentine telephone company, CAT, wanted to sell out to the Argentine government on terms comparable to those obtained by UTRP/ITT. The deal, however, was never completed—primarily due to the decline in Argentina's foreign exchange reserves.

20. Initially the firm was called the Dirección Nacional de Teléfonos del Estado (DNTE) but was renamed ENTel in 1956. During the years following national-ization, DNTE/ENTel acquired a number of small, previously independent telephone companies serving mostly rural provinces. Hill and Abdala, "Regu-lation, Institutions, and Commitment," 9.

21. Swedish-owned CAT, however, remained independent.

22. Hill and Abdala, "Regulation, Institutions, and Commitment," 10; *Statistical Abstract of Latin America for 1957* (Committee on Latin American Studies, UCLA), 5.

23. Most of Argentina's presidents during this period came to office through mil-itary coup.

24. This law was part of a broader strategy of import substitution designed to reduce national dependence on foreign sources of goods and services. Many developing countries adopted import substitution policies during this period. In addition to national procurement rules, governments typically promoted import substitution through a combination of "carrots" (for example, pro-ducer or consumer subsidies) and "sticks" (for example, high tariffs or quotas on imports of substitutable foreign goods.)

25. Alcatel was an affiliate of France Telecom and Telettra an affiliate of the Italian firm STET. The parent companies eventually became winning bidders in the privatized northern portion of ENTel. Equitel was a subsidiary of ITT, the for-mer owner of UTRP.

26. For example, a joint venture of the Japanese manufacturer NEC and local Argentine conglomerate Pérez Companc (Pecom-NEC) sold digital equipment to ENTel in the 1980s at 300 percent over international prices. Walter Molano, *The Logic of Privatization* (Westport, CT: Greenwood Press, 1997), 88.

27. Petrazzini, "Telephone Privatization in a Hurry," 114.

28. Customers did enjoy real price declines during the period of high inflation in the 1980s. Yet the value captured was offset to a large extent by lower quality of service.

29. Since the enterprise was publicly owned, the ultimate losers were Argentine taxpayers.

30. In 1982, the Argentine military government declared war on Great Britain in a challenge over the sovereignty of a group of small islands off the coast of Argentina. At that time, the Falkland Islands—referred to as Las Malvinas by Argentina—was inhabited by several thousand British citizens.

31. The monopoly would cover all wired telephone and cable television service, but not cellular and telegraph services. The deal included the option for the firm to extend the lease for ten years. Molano, *The Logic of Privatization*, 80.

32. President Alfonsín was a member of the Radical Party, whose name belied its centrist political philosophy.

33. World Bank, *World Development Report 1990* (New York: Oxford University Press), 178.

34. Under the terms of Argentina's constitution at that time, the Argentine presi-dent was not permitted to run for a second term. Thus the Radical Party's can-didate was not Alfonsín but Angeloz.

35. Since Chile was located directly next to Argentina, the nations often viewed each other as rivals of sorts. Chile's dramatic economic reforms in the 1970s and 1980s, and vigorous economic growth in the mid-1980s,

served as both an example and a challenge to Argentina to undertake comparable reforms.

36. See Yergin and Stanislaw, *The Commanding Heights,* for in-depth description and analysis of these changes.

37. Buenos Aires was split between the two companies, with the majority of the capital city falling under the control of the southern company.

38. Argentine sovereign debt—loans made to the Argentine government by foreign banks—traded on the secondary markets at prices between 10 percent and 15 percent of face value in 1990. Although the government was not permitted to repurchase its debt at a discount, by accepting payment for ENTel's equity in the form of its own sovereign debt, it would indirectly enjoy the opportunity to retire debt at the lower market price. In other words, Menem's sales approach represented an arbitrage opportunity for the Argentine government with respect to its own external debt.

39. Indirect competition could take the form of yardstick or benchmark competition through which the prices, efficiency, and service quality of the providers could be compared even if they did not compete directly in each other's markets.

40. They were not entitled, however, to monopoly rights for Startel's services.

41. A number of these targets were specified by province, including the number of new lines and pay phones.

42. Recall that real prices for telecommunications services had declined significantly in the 1980s due to a combination of price controls and hyperinflation.

43. Cross-subsidization also shifted the distribution of value creation toward residential households, an important political constituency of the Peronist government.

44. Other elements of the reform bargain included the removal of a 30 percent service tax imposed on telecommunications services supporting the national pension system and the addition of a guarantee that the privatized firms would be subject to the same tax levels applicable to the Argentine corporate sector in general.

45. Telefónica de España's largest shareholder was the Spanish federal government (40 percent).

46. The winning bid consisted of $114 million in cash, plus $2.72 billion in Argentine sovereign debt.

47. The northern company was first awarded to a consortium led by Bell Atlantic, which proved unable to raise sufficient sovereign debt to close the deal. The winning consortium was required to pay the amount offered by the Telefónica group for the northern company: $100 million in cash, plus $2.308 billion in Argentine sovereign debt.

48. The effective returns earned by the initial consortium members have been substantially higher than those suggested by accounting data since the consortium purchased its equity stake primarily with highly discounted Argentine sovereign debt (see note 38 above).

### Chapter 4

1. For an excellent treatment of the broad challenges facing firms in turnaround situations, see Rosabeth Moss Kanter, *When Giants Learn to Dance* (New York: Simon and Schuster, 1989).

2. Understanding these challenges is also relevant to government policymakers and regulators, who may have an inadequate awareness of the trade-offs faced by incumbents in the transformation process.

3. The acronym PLC stands for "public limited company"—that is, the company's shares are publicly traded and its shareholders are subject to limited liability. In the text, we will refer to National Power PLC simply as National Power.

4. This approach follows in the tradition of James Austin's *Managing in Developing Countries: Strategic Analysis and Operating Techniques* (New York: Free Press, 1990), which provides a framework for assessing broader strategic and organizational issues as well as decisions at the operating level.

5. The industry was composed of both private and municipally owned firms operating under a number of different technical standards. Note that the analysis of National Power PLC and the British electricity industry in chapters 4 and 5 draw heavily on Willis Emmons and Edward Simnett, "National Power and the Privatization of the British Power Generation Industry," Case No. 9-796-066 (Boston: Harvard Business School, 1996).

6. In 1995 the area boards spun off the National Grid into an independent, publicly listed company.

7. The basic form of regulation employed by OFFER was that of the price cap. Essentially, the REC monopolies were allowed to increase the price for distribution by the percentage change in the retail price index (RPI)—the previous year's rate of inflation—adjusted by a percentage $X$ set in advance by OFFER. The adjustment factor might allow for additional price increases, if anticipated investment needs were high, or require price decreases to reflect anticipated productivity gains. The cost of power generation and transmission were passed through—that is, simply added to the price of distribution in arriving at a final price for the end customer. This form of regulation provided a strong incentive for the RECs to reduce costs so as to increase profitability under the price cap.

8. Privatization revenues from the area board offerings totaled £8 billion ($14.2 billion) while the partial sales of National Power and PowerGen generated slightly more than £2 billion. The government announced prior to the privatizations that it would sell its remaining shares in National Power and Power-Gen by March 1995.

9. The British government combined the assets of Nuclear Electric Ltd. with Scottish Nuclear Ltd., and sold the new firm, named British Energy, in a July 1996 IPO for £1.4 billion.

10. During 1990, National Power accounted for 46 percent of England's power generation, PowerGen 28 percent, Nuclear Electric 18 percent, and others (including Scottish and French interconnectors), 8 percent. Monopolies and Mergers Commission, *National Power PLC and Southern Electric PLC: A Report on the Proposed Merger* (London: Her Majesty's Stationary Office, April 1996), 64.

11. At the time of privatization, 72 percent of National Power's generating capacity was coal-fired.

12. In Great Britain, a board of directors officially represents the interests of a corporation's shareholders. Alternative governance models exist for private corporations in other countries. For example, in Germany, firms are required to

maintain a supervisory board, with members selected by shareholders (50 percent) and unions (50 percent), in addition to a management board composed of the firm's top executives.

13. Executive directors serve as full-time managers in the corporation in addition to serving on the board of directors.

14. For an excellent discussion of the impact of changes in governance and product market competition on the performance of British state-owned enterprises see M. I. Cragg and I. J. A. Dyck, "Management Control and Privatization in the United Kingdom" *RAND Journal of Economics* 30, no. 3 (Autumn 1999): 475–497.

15. In contrast to Britain's reform bargain for the nation's electric utility industry, Malaysia's approach did not include a prior restructuring of the industry into separate generating, transmission, and distribution entities.

16. See Ian Duncan and Alan Bollard, *Corporatization and Privatization: Lessons from New Zealand* (Auckland: Oxford University Press, 1992).

17. See, for example, Armen Alchian, "Some Economics of Property Rights," *Economic Forces at Work* (Indianapolis: Liberty Press, 1977), 127–149.

18. Peter Shirtcliffe, chairman, Telecom Corporation of New Zealand, interview by author, Wellington, New Zealand, 4 March 1997.

19. Some state-level regulations also restricted commercial banks from opening branches outside the city in which the bank was based.

20. In some cases, the SOE's bargain with the home government obligates the firm to confine its operations to the domestic market. In other cases, the restriction on expansion abroad derives from the unwillingness of the relevant foreign government(s) to engage in a bargain with the SOE.

21. Within the core business itself, the incumbent, in principle, might adopt one of three approaches to competitive positioning. (These are developed in Michael Porter, *Competitive Strategy* [New York: The Free Press, 1980].) One alternative would be a low-cost strategy vis-à-vis competitors in which the incumbent would draw on extensive scale and scope economies in conjunction with an aggressive cost-reduction program. A second approach would be a differentiation strategy that emphasizes full-service provision and/or reputation for reliability—assuming that such a reputation could be solidified early under the reform bargain. Alternatively, the incumbent might choose to become more of a niche player over time, focusing on certain attractive market segments while abandoning others altogether. The incumbent, however, may be subject to restrictions under the terms of the reform bargain that limit its ability to adopt one or more of these approaches. For example, the incumbent may face universal service requirements that make it impossible to pursue a niche strategy, and may also limit the feasibility of adopting a low-cost strategy.

22. For a broad treatment of issues related to resources, capabilities, and corporate strategy, see David Collis and Cynthia Montgomery, *Corporate Strategy: Resources and the Scope of the Firm* (Chicago: Irwin, 1997).

23. This discussion of American Airlines's strategy draws heavily on chapter 2 of Vietor, *Contrived Competition*.

24. This discussion of YPF's strategy draws heavily on Michael Yoshino, "Argentina's YPF Sociedad Anonima (A)," Case 9-396-023 (Boston: Harvard Business School, 1996).

25. Heinz Dürr, chairman, Deutsche Bahn, interview by author, Frankfurt, Germany, 11 December 1996.
26. RailTrack was eventually sold through an initial public offering. The ROSCOs were sold through competitive bidding. The remaining elements were auctioned in the form of seven-year franchises to provide the relevant services along specific routes. Edward Bucham, managing director, Close Brothers Corp. Finance, interview by author, London, UK, 4 December 1996.
27. This section draws on Richard H. K. Vietor, "CSX," Case 9-386-156 (Boston: Harvard Business School, 1986).
28. Daniel Machalaba, "Back on Track: CSX Is Returning to Its Basic Business," *Wall Street Journal*, 28 December 1989, A1.
29. For an excellent treatment of the challenges of strategy design and implementation for multinational corporations in general see Christopher Bartlett and Sumantra Ghoshal, *Managing Across Borders: The Transnational Solution*, 2d ed. (Boston: Harvard Business School Press, 1998).
30. David Wighton, "U.S. Projects Force £25 Million Provisions on Thames," *The Daily Telegraph London,* 27 October 1993, 25, and Martin Waller, "Corporate Profile: Thames Water," *The Times of London*, 3 August 1998, F41.
31. The Spanish government owned a controlling share of TdE's equity from 1945 until 1996. In 1998, the privatized firm was renamed Telefónica SA.
32. Craig Karmin, "Telefónica Tender Offer for Four Major Telecoms Ignites Frenzy on Latin American Markets," *Wall Street Journal*, 14 January 2000, C12.
33. Nisha Gopalan, "Interview: National Grid CEO Sees Early Energis Sale," *Dow Jones Newswires*, 14 April 2000.
34. Kyle Pope, "For Sale: Airport Privatization Begins to Take Off, Led by Britain's BAA," *Wall Street Journal*, 24 September 1996, A1. BAA's strategy, however, was adversely affected by the abolition of duty-free shopping in the European Union beginning in mid-1999.
35. John Goulter, chief executive, Auckland Airport Authority, interview by author, Auckland, New Zealand, 6 March 1996.
36. National Power built goodwill as well with the Labor government by consenting to the continuing purchase of coal from RJB Mining (the successor company to British Coal), thus helping indirectly to support jobs in the shrinking coal mining sector.
37. Andrew Taylor, "Affair Ends in Tears and Recrimination," *Financial Times*, 30 April 2000, 23.
38. To be precise, the Electricity Act of 1989 empowers the head of OFFER, the Director General of Electricity Supply (DGES), to carry out this function. The DGES's authority over National Grid and the RECs was even greater, including responsibility for setting annual price caps on a company-by-company basis for electricity transmission and distribution.
39. Littlechild had been a professor at Birmingham University and had assisted in the design of the reform bargain for the British electricity sector.
40. A major exception involved accusations of anticompetitive behavior by the CEGB following the Energy Act of 1983, which ostensibly opened the power market to competition by mandating open access to the national grid. Potential competitors alleged that the CEGB discouraged entry by raising transmission prices and lowering (its own) generation prices to the extent that competition would not be viable.

41. Unless otherwise specified, "Yorkshire Water" will refer to "Yorkshire Water Services Ltd.," a monopoly water utility with service territory broadly in Yorkshire and part of Humberside, England. The firm is a wholly owned subsidiary of Yorkshire Water PLC, which, following privatization, established additional, much smaller subsidiaries engaged in international activities and other "nonregulated" business.

42. Toward the end of the ten years, Ofwat would establish price caps for the next ten-year period. Ofwat tailored the price cap applicable to each water company under its jurisdiction based on its assessment of necessary capital investments and expected productivity gains. Under certain conditions, Ofwat was authorized to make interim adjustments in price cap levels or move forward its timetable for a ten-year prospective review. *The Water Share Offers Prospectus* (Offers for Sale by Schroders on behalf of The Secretary of State for the Environment and The Secretary of State for Wales) (London: Burrup Mathieson & Co. Ltd., 1989), 38–41.

43. Meteorologists subsequently estimated that the severity was a once-in-500-years phenomenon.

44. David Wilkinson, director of the Bradford Chamber of Commerce, quoted in Tim King, "Short of Water? Give Staff a Holiday Firms are Told," *Daily Telegraph London*, 30 August 1995, 1.

45. Trevor Newton, managing director, Yorkshire Water Services Ltd., quoted in "Yorkshire's Outpourings While a Crisis Ran and Ran," *The Independent (London)*, 18 May 1996, 6.

46. This level of leakage was not unusual for a water system of Yorkshire's vintage, given the age of the pipes and expense of locating and repairing leaks, particularly in urban locations. Nevertheless, the public was largely uninterested in these trade-offs and was unmoved by the fact that Yorkshire's leakage rate was comparable to that of other British water companies. Clive Stones, deputy managing director, Yorkshire Water Services Ltd., interview by author, York, England, 2 December 1996.

47. See, for example, Brian Cathcart, "Fat Cataclysm," *The Independent (London)*, 25 February 1996, 10–12; Chris Barrie, "Ofwat Canes Three Water Companies," *The Guardian*, 14 December 1994, 16; and "Yorkshire's Board Rigid," *Financial Times*, 16 September 1994, 18.

48. Brian Cathcart, "Fat Cataclysm." For purposes of comparison, Yorkshire Water PLC's operating profits for the fiscal year ending March 1995 were £200 million.

49. Specifically, Kevin Bond was named managing director and chairman of Yorkshire Water Services Ltd.

50. *Water Supply in Yorkshire: Report of the Independent Commission of Inquiry*, Chairman Professor John Uff QC, May 1996 (Produced by Scope Communications).

51. Martin Wainwright, "Damning Verdict on Yorkshire Drought," *The Guardian*, 18 May 1996, 5.

52. Clive Stones, deputy managing director, Yorkshire Water Services Ltd., interview by author, Boston, MA, 5 February 1997.

53. Quoted in Cathcart, "Fat Cataclysm."

54. Light's ownership structure was complex. The Brazilian National Development Bank (BNDB) participated as a passive investor in the consortium's 51 percent controlling stake. The remainder of the shares were controlled by Brazilian government entities and Light's employees. See José Gómez-Ibáñez,

"Privatization of Light-Servicos de Eletricidade, SA," Case 1540.0 (Cambridge, MA: John F. Kennedy School of Government, Harvard University, 1999) and Ben Blackwell, "AES, EDF Set to Divide Up Brazil's Two Major Electricity Markets," *Dow Jones International News*, 27 January 2000.

55. Matt Moffett, "In Brazil, a Utility Dims Public's Enthusiasm for Privatizations," *Wall Street Journal*, 27 April 1998, A1.

56. Recall that OFFER had the explicit authority to set price caps for electricity transmission and distribution services, but not for wholesale power. Nevertheless, the DGES's mandate to "promote competition in the generation and supply of electricity" appeared to provide it with the flexibility to take action in cases where insufficient competition had adverse effects on wholesale power prices.

57. This price was commonly referred to as the "strike price."

58. Although National Power and PowerGen owned only about 75 percent of total industry generating capacity during the early 1990s, they controlled almost 90 percent of nonbaseload capacity. Since baseload capacity, such as nuclear power, was operated twenty-four hours a day, its cost had no impact on pool prices. Instead, the cost and availability of nonbaseload capacity—also referred to as mid-merit or peak capacity—in effect determined the level of pool prices at any given point in time. Thus the potential impact of National Power's and PowerGen's behavior on pool prices was substantial.

59. Power plants were not always available to generate power, due to maintenance and repair needs.

60. The sale was structured to encourage Eastern to use the plants as a marginal bidder into the pool as opposed to a baseline power producer that produced power around the clock. But since the sales contract required Eastern to make royalty payments to National Power for sales into the pool, it had the incentive to engage in practices that kept pool prices high.

61. In 1996, Southern Electric participated in IPPs with aggregate capacity of 1,911 MW. Its investment share represented a prorated 591 MW. *National Power PLC and Southern Electric PLC*, 74.

62. PowerGen's effort to acquire Midlands Electricity paralleled that of National Power's acquisition attempt. It was also provisionally approved by the MMC, but rejected by the government.

63. See, for example, "Short Circuit," *The Economist*, 13 April 1996, 47.

64. Ironically, share prices in these firms *increased* when the tax assessments were announced, since the amounts were generally lower than expected. National Power's assessment was £266 million, or 8.2 percent of the firm's cumulative after-tax profits from 1991 to 1997.

65. Although based in Massachusetts, NEES also owned utilities operating in New Hampshire.

66. The U.S. Congress passed the Energy Act of 1992, which reformed enterprise bargains in interstate power transactions by requiring utilities to grant access to their transmission systems for transporting ("wheeling") wholesale power sold in transactions between generators and distributors. The price and terms of access to transmission lines—typically monopoly gateway assets—was subject to review by the U.S. Federal Energy Regulatory Commission. The act left it to the individual state governments to develop and implement policies for

creating open access to local distribution systems for transporting electricity to end customers (referred to as "retail wheeling").

67. Environmentalists feared that deregulation would lead to losses in environmental quality by increasing sales of lower-cost power generated with cheap high-sulfur coal over power generated through more environmentally friendly, but higher-cost processes.

68. "NU, NEES Pose Transition Scenarios to State Regulators," *Electricity Journal* 8, no. 4 (May 1995), 7–9.

69. Gains from generation assets sold at a premium to book value would be used to reduce the level of these surcharges.

70. These groups argued that the benefits expected to flow from the reform bargain would be gained disproportionately by the incumbents. They maintained that the mandatory retail price reductions were too small and that the allowed recovery of all stranded costs would leave consumers burdened with the legacy of incumbent's past mistakes for years into the future. In contrast, incumbents argued that attempts to renegotiate the reform bargain could delay benefits for all parties. Furthermore, these firms asserted that they had made their investments under the full supervision of the DPU with the implicit assumption that they would be permitted to earn a fair return on the investments. Incumbents were prepared to challenge in court any reform bargain that did not include full recovery of prior investments.

71. Under the administrations of Republican governors William Weld and A. Paul Celluci, appointees to the DPU were generally evenhanded, from incumbents' perspective, in their interpretation and enforcement of the terms of the prereform bargain under their jurisdiction.

## Chapter 5

1. Mark Duyck, executive vice president, Brussels Airport Authority, interview with author, Boston, MA, 6 November 1996.

2. *Main Prospectus for Offers for Sale of Shares in National Power and PowerGen* (Offers for sale by Kleinwort Benson Limited on behalf of the Secretary of State for Energy) (London: Williams Lea, 1991), 87.

3. Peter Windsor, manager of western hemisphere international operations, National Power, interview by author, Boston, MA, 15 April 1997.

4. One study has documented net long-term employment gains among a sample of incumbents consisting of SOEs privatized through public share offerings. See William L. Megginson, Robert C. Nash, and Matthias van Randenborgh, "The Financial and Operating Performance of Newly Privatized Firms: An International Empirical Analysis," 49, no. 2 *Journal of Finance* (June 1994).

5. Air Transport Association, annual reports (Washington, D.C.: Air Transport Association, various years) and Eno Transportation Foundation, *Transportation in America* (Washington, D.C.: Eno Publications, 1998).

6. Due to extensive merger and acquisition activity in the industry, however, employment has increased within the remaining railroads simply through absorption.

7. Yoshino, "Argentina's YPF."

8. Michael Pittman, vice president of human resources, PacifiCorp, interview by author, Boston, MA, 1 November 1996.

9. The operations director, however, had been employed by the CEGB prior to his tenure at China Light and Power.

10. The firm did have a group responsible for government and public relations, although below the director level.

11. In exploring opportunities for the firm abroad, National Power had initially drawn on the skills of employees in the former CEGB subsidiary, British International Enterprise (BIE), which National Power had inherited in the privatization process. The extent of the subsidiary's experience, however, was insufficient on its own to support National Power's aggressive international expansion efforts.

12. Patrick Hernandez, manager of staffing and development, Public Service of Colorado, interview by author, Boston, MA, 19 November 1996.

13. Paul Anthony, managing director, Contact Energy, interview by author, Wellington, New Zealand, 7 March 1997.

14. Following U.S. railroad deregulation in 1980, a number of short feeder lines were divested by the major railroads and subsequently operated independently or through short rail holding companies such as Central Wisconsin Railway and RailTex.

15. Francis Small, managing director, Tranz Rail, interview by author, Wellington, New Zealand, 3 March 1997.

16. Because of lags and other imperfections in the regulatory process, firms were sometimes able to earn profits in excess of allowable returns. However, the ability of these firms to influence profitability in a significant way was limited.

17. Emmons and Simnett, "National Power and the Privatization of the British Power Generation Industry," 11.

18. Vietor, *Contrived Competition*, 75–76.

19. Quantitative analysis in this section is computed from data in National Power PLC Annual Reports and Datastream market returns data.

20. These expenses do not include severance payments.

21. Of course, cultural or regulatory constraints may exist with respect to the types of incentives that can be offered or the likely effectiveness of the incentives.

22. Malaysia's population consists of three principal ethnic groups: indigenous Malay peoples or the *bumiputra* (58%), ethnic Chinese (26%), and ethnic Indians and other (16%). In 1969 groups of *bumiputra* rioted in opposition to the growing financial and political power of the country's ethnic Chinese population. In response to this violence, the Malaysian government adopted an extensive system of affirmative action for the *bumiputra*—the New Economic Policy—that included job quotas and ownership quotas in private firms. Employment in state-owned enterprises was almost exclusively held by *bumiputra*. Although the rigid quota system was relaxed in 1991 with the adoption of the National Development Policy, the government continued to be wary of the potential for ethnic violence. Forest Reinhardt, "Malaysia in the 1990s (A)," Case 9-797-074 (Boston: Harvard Business School, 1997), 4–5.

23. Dato' Ahmad Tajuddin Ali, chief executive, Tenaga Nasional Berhad, interview by author, Kuala Lumpur, Malaysia, 13 March 1997.

24. Paul Anthony, interview.
25. Ing. Carlos Bacher, vice president, Ferrocarriles Pampeano, interview by author, Buenos Aires, 22 April 1997.
26. Under cost-plus or rate-of-return regulation, incumbents often favored more technologically sophisticated equipment or components than required in order to enhance the internal satisfaction of the workforce and external prestige for the organization. "Gold-plating" of power plants or telephone systems, for example, represented a form of overinvestment in quality. The distortion may involve not only excessive total capacity, but a bias toward capital versus labor in production. This phenomenon is referred to as the Averch Johnson effect by economists. See H. Averch and L. Johnson, "Behavior of the Firm Under Regulator Constraint," *American Economic Review* 52, no. 5 (December 1962): 1052–1069.
27. One gigawatt equals one billion watts. Each watt of generating capacity operated for one hour produces one watt-hour of energy.
28. The potential benefits of plant closures to the CEGB would have been muted by the difficulty of laying off workers in these plants.
29. Jonathan Friedland and Benjamin Holden, "Utility Deregulation in Argentina Presages Possible U.S. Upheaval," *Wall Street Journal*, 19 June 1996, A1.
30. The time horizon covered by these contracts, however, was shorter than the expected life of the generating assets. Therefore, National Power continued to face risk at the time of contract renegotiation.
31. Similar to the case of National Power, however, the payback period for these new investments generally extended beyond the period of protection. Also, the bargains of Telefónica and Telecom placed limits on the maximum prices that could be charged for services during the period of market exclusivity.
32. Guy Canavy, director general, Aguas Argentinas, interview by author, Buenos Aires, 22 April 1997.
33. In fact, during the 1990s, Telefónica and Telecom did implement reductions in long-distance rates, but in conjunction with price increases for local and other charges. Collectively this rate rebalancing was revenue-neutral for the firms.
34. Emmons and Simnett, "National Power," 14.
35. Heinz Dürr, chairman, Deutsche Bahn, interview by author, Frankfurt, Germany, 11 December 1996.
36. Anonymous utility industry executive, interview by author, Buenos Aires, 21 April 1997.
37. RJB Mining purchased virtually all of state-owned British Coal's assets in a 1995 privatization.
38. PowerGen supported the deal as well and also agreed to continue purchasing substantial volumes of coal from British Coal.
39. In rare cases, average prices charged by an SOE are set at levels high enough to generate profits exceeding the cost of capital. This approach, employed at times in bargains of state-owned purveyors of luxury goods such as liquor, allows the government to generate additional revenues in a form other than a tax.
40. Although most of National Power's output was pre-committed through contracts with the RECs, the firm was permitted to sell up to 15 percent of its power directly to large users and could sell any remaining production at spot prices through the pool.

41. Price sensitivity in this context is commonly referred to by economists as "price elasticity of demand."

42. Power generation at off-peak times relies on base load capacity characterized by relatively low operating costs. In contrast, peak load generation typically draws on seldom used capacity with relatively high operating costs.

43. Ultimately, rebalancing involves changes in relative prices. Therefore, in some cases, the incumbent may actually increase all prices under the reform bargain, although raising prices for some products and customers more than others. Conversely, other incumbents may lower all prices following reforms, but lower some more than others.

44. The terms of Telecom Corporation of New Zealand's bargain are even more explicit in this area. Beginning in 1989, this incumbent has been prohibited from charging more than NZ$29.70 per month (adjusted annually for inflation) for residential, unlimited local calling service. Willis Emmons and Martin Calles, "Clear Communications Ltd. vs. Telecom Corporation of New Zealand (A)," Case 9–798–085 (Boston: Harvard Business School, 1998), 6.

45. "Deutsche Telekom's Bumpy Ride," *Euronomey* (August 1999), p. 26.

46. Ricardo Zenaruzza, manufacturing director, Siderar SA, interview by author, Boston, MA, 6 November 1996.

47. Anonymous international telecommunications executive, interview by author, 6 January 1997.

48. Nigel Lawson, *The View from No. 11: Memoirs of a Tory Radical* (London: Bantam Press, 1992), 199.

49. Some incumbents that plan to expand significantly outside their traditional geographic or product market(s) adopt more radical name changes. For example, many U.S. natural gas and electric utilities whose operations historically covered a single energy product and a narrow geographic market have adopted names designed to invoke the image of a boundaryless energy corporation—for example, Louisiana Gas & Electric Corporation's shift to "Entergy Corp" and San Diego Gas and Electric's shift to "Enova Corp."

50. Prior to deregulation, for example, most U.S. commercial banks did not impose fees on many individual transactions such as check clearing and visits to teller windows. When incumbents began to levy such fees after deregulation, particularly on depositors who maintained low average account balances, these customers and a number of consumer advocacy groups complained about these actions and, in some instances, called for legislation designed to restrict such practices.

51. Recall that assets of privatized British water companies are "ring-fenced" within a corporate structure that typically includes a parent holding company and several other businesses outside the British water sector.

52. Constraints on the government's willingness or ability to increase its borrowings or raise taxes leaves some state enterprises starved for external investment funds. Price controls on the SOEs' goods and services often exacerbates the need for such external funding. Worse yet, governments sometimes siphon off internal cash flow of SOEs with substantial investment requirements to fund other state programs.

53. See, for example, Michael Jensen, "The Modern Industrial Revolution, Exit, and the Failure of Internal Control Systems," *Journal of Finance* 48, no. 3 (July 1993): 831–880.

54. When these large payouts take the form of earnings repatriated to foreign shareholders, pressures for changes in the bargain's terms or enforcement may be even stronger.

55. For example, the British price cap approach for regulating prices of monopoly enterprises typically involves the setting of allowable annual price changes five years into the future. In 1998 a major British water company appeared to delay the payment of any special dividends to shareholders until Ofwat, the water industry regulatory body, had completed its 1999 review of company operations and finances and set price caps for the years 2000–2004.

56. Maxus's production was focused primarily in Indonesia, although it also held production rights in the United States and several additional markets. Yoshino, "Argentina's YPF."

57. The indexes are adjusted for dividend payouts and share splits, and thus reflect overall gains in market value.

58. Large industrial buyers, however, were able to use their right to buy directly from the generators—and in some cases, their ability to switch fuel sources or invest in cogeneration facilities—to secure more favorable prices from generators.

59. National Power's fiscal year ends in March.

## Chapter 6

1. The British government privatized British Energy, a holding company for the former SOEs Nuclear Electric and Scottish Nuclear, in two stages in 1996. The sale raised a total of £1.5 billion in revenues.

2. The ownership rights associated with these concessions may be complex. For example, the government may retain ownership of land associated with a concession but not the plant and equipment. In some cases, all assets associated with a concession convert to government ownership at the end of the concession period.

3. For an overview of entry barriers see Porter, *Competitive Strategy*, 7–17; for strategy related to entry into new businesses, see 339–357.

4. Superior price/quality combinations obviously would include products identical to the incumbents' but offered at a lower price, and products of higher quality offered at the price charged by incumbents. In some cases, however, the consumer may be willing to pay higher prices to obtain higher quality or be willing to accept lower quality at a lower price.

5. The term *third-party access* (TPA) is often used to describe the right of a competing entrant to this type of access.

6. Although the Telecommunications Act of 1987 provided for entry deregulation in the market, this provision did not take effect until 1989. Essentially, the New Zealand government wanted to provide a period of transition to allow the corporatized TCNZ to implement a transformation strategy prior to facing competition.

7. New Zealand initiated sweeping economic policy reforms following a severe foreign exchange crisis in 1984. These reforms were wide ranging, and involved changes in macroeconomic policy (e.g., fiscal, monetary, trade, exchange rates) as well as microeconomic policy (e.g., industrial, labor). Within less than a decade, New Zealand was transformed from being one of the least to one of

the most market-oriented nations in the OECD. See Lewis Evans, Arthur Grimes, David Tecce, and Bryce Wilkinson, "Economic Reform in New Zealand 1984–95," *Journal of Economic Literature* 34, no. 4 (December 1996): 1856–1902.

8. Recall from chapter 4 that reform of government enterprise in New Zealand began with the 1986 State Enterprises Act, which required SOEs to adopt a corporate organizational form and focus primarily on commercial objectives.

9. In order to serve a particular local market, CCL planned to construct a partial local network of its own that would, at a minimum, provide access to the city's central commercial district. As in the case of long-distance service, however, CCL would depend on TCNZ for connections to and from callers not directly linked to the CCL network.

10. Even if an incumbent's owners decide to sell their stake in the enterprise, the business itself remains a going concern. Depending on the terms of the reform bargain, the incumbent may or may not have the right to exit various geographic or customer segments of the market.

11. As we have seen, reform bargains are often adopted concurrently with macroeconomic reforms in fiscal, monetary, and trade/exchange rate policy. These changes, as in the case of Argentina, for example, may lead to significant changes in national income.

12. For issues critical in general to international partnering arrangements see Michael Yoshino and Srinivasa Rangan, *Strategic Alliances: An Entrepreneurial Approach to Globalization* (Boston: Harvard Business School Press, 1995), Benjamin Gomes-Casseras, *The Alliance Revolution* (Cambridge, MA: Harvard University Press, 1996), and Yves Doz and Gary Hamel, *Alliance Advantage* (Boston: Harvard Business School Press, 1998).

13. The four participating RECs are Midlands Electricity, Northern Electric, South-Western Electricity, and South Wales Electricity. The largest equity share in the Teesside IPP, 42.5 percent, is held by Enron. Monopolies and Mergers Commission, *National Power PLC and Southern Electric PLC*, 91.

14. Similar governance problems are often present as well in the case of joint venture owners of incumbents and contract entry concessionaires. See discussions in chapters 4 and 7.

15. The statement made in 1988 was cited in the 1992 High Court decision on interconnection.

16. A nation's judicial system often represents the final authority for interpreting and enforcing the terms of the bargain. Thus entrants tend to be wary of courts that are not independent of influence from other parts of the government—particularly if the incumbent continues to have "friends in high places" under the reform bargain.

17. These included, for example, investments in paging services and satellite communications. The subsidiary was originally named RWE Unitel.

18. Mannesmann's other lines of business in the early 1990s included machinery, plant construction, automotive technology, electrical and electronic engineering, tubes and pipes, and trading. The firm's cellular operations grew out of its winning bid for Germany's second digital mobile telephone license in 1992 through Mannesmann Mobilfunk, a joint venture with U.S.-based Pacific Bell/Airtouch Communications, which owned 35% of the venture.

19. CNI was limited to competing in the value-added services market until 1998, when the entire market would be opened to competition.

20. "RWE Goes Solo in Germany," APT Data Services Network Briefing, 3 November 1995.
21. RWE was also rumored to be unhappy that Mannesmann was unwilling to give up part of its 50 percent stake to allow a more balanced ownership structure (from newsweekly *Focus*, cited by Reuters Financial Service, 13 August 1995, BC cycle). AT&T and its partner in the international telecommunications venture Unisource (based in the Netherlands) took over RWE's former stake in CNI.
22. VEBA, like RWE, was based in the German state of North Rhine Westphalia.
23. Their cellular service became known as E-Plus.
24. VEBA held 10 percent of the shares in Iridium, an international satellite telephone venture led by Motorola. The firm also owned 100 percent of Germany's second largest cable television operator, Tele Columbus.
25. By that time, both RWE and VEBA had applied for and received licenses to provide fixed-wire telephone service on a national basis.
26. The German government sold 25 percent of DT's shares in the initial public offering.
27. Other major entrants with substantial investments in telecommunications infrastructure included VIAG Interkom and WorldCom. Several additional entrants grew quickly in 1998 as resellers of wholesale capacity purchased from Deutsche Telekom. The most successful of these firms was MobilCom, whose rapid growth demonstrated that under the new regulatory regime, firms with minimal fixed investment in telecommunications infrastructure could be quite profitable. Ralph Atkins, "Rivalry Transforms Market," *Financial Times*, 10 November 1998, 10.
28. O.tel.o's public voice services were not available until mid-March 1998. In addition, consumers were required to register to use o.tel.o's services, although they could use other alternative long-distance providers by simply dialing a special five-digit code before placing the call.
29. "O.tel.o Heads for Big Losses After Sales Miss Target," IAC Newsletter Database, 29 October 1998.
30. Teletalk editor Olaf Strawe observed that "o.tel.o was mired in reorganization from the beginning. They never had a rational strategy and everything they did was marred by in-house fighting between VEBA and RWE." Quoted in "Small Telecom Players Make Mark in Germany," *DM News*, 21 September 1998, 10.
31. By the fall of 1999, these firms had refocused their strategy on the core electricity business as VEBA announced a merger with VIAG and RWE a merger with VEW, a major Dortmund-based utility.
32. The Cable and Broadcasting Act of 1984 created a framework for the licensing of cable television franchises under The Cable Authority. The Cable and Broadcasting Act of 1990 provided more attractive terms by removing ownership restrictions, reducing the number of must-carry channels, and freeing the operators from previous requirements to provide most of their own programming. From 1984 to 1990, competition within the telecommunications market was restricted to British Telecom and the new entrant, Mercury. This transitional phase in the sector's evolving bargain was designed in part to provide temporary protection for Mercury as it developed into a more vigorous competitor to the privatized incumbent. From 1991 on, cable operators were

free to offer both television and telephone service, which could be provided by installing joint coaxial/fiber optic transmission lines.

33. Although the franchises were issued on a nonexclusive basis, it was almost never economically attractive to invest in a second system once the initial entrant had wired the franchise area.

34. U.S. West's cable television investments were made through its MediaOne subsidiary.

35. Anonymous British cable television executive, interview with author, London, UK, 3 December 1996.

36. The offering raised £414 million. The following year, Telewest raised an additional £734 million through a bond offering.

37. Each firm received about a 12 percent equity stake in Telewest.

38. Vivendi's stake was approximately 8.5 percent of Telewest's total equity.

39. The BT-MCI joint venture was established in the fall of 1993 and began operations in early 1994.

40. By early 2000 the consolidation of the British cable television market had reduced the industry to two major players: Telewest, with a one-third share of the market, and NTL, with a two-thirds share, pending British government approval of its acquisition of Cable and Wireless Communications PLC's residential business. David Benady, "CWC Boss Poised for Top NTL Job," *Marketing Week*, 16 March 2000, 5.

41. Andrew Makin, chief executive, Clear Communications, interview by author, Auckland, New Zealand, 5 March 1997.

42. In the legal system employed by British Commonwealth countries, the High Court was the first venue for corporate litigation. Its authority was comparable to that of a Federal Court in the United States.

43. See, for example, "New Zealand: Network Ruling Welcomed by Williamson," *New Zealand Herald*, 9 February 1995.

44. Emmons and Calles, "Clear Communications (A)," 13.

45. New Zealand Commerce Act, Clause 53.

46. By 1994 TCNZ's ROE had risen to 24 percent and its cumulative market returns since 1991 had exceeded those of the New Zealand all-share index by over 200 percent. Emmons and Calles, "Clear Communications (A)," 22–23.

47. Since the New Zealand government had never exercised its right to impose price controls, it was reluctant to set a precedent in this situation. Furthermore, the imposition of price controls appeared to conflict with the spirit of light-handed regulation that underlay the terms of the reform bargain in the telecommunications sector.

48. "Snapping at Goliath's Heels," *The Christchurch Press*, 11 November 1998, 6.

49. Richard Pamatatau, "Hands-Off Policy Unfair, Say Telecom Rivals," *NZ Infotech Weekly*, 30 November 1998.

50. Ian Muir, human resources manager, Mercury Communications, and Nigel Parnell, manager of corporate customer service, Mercury Communications, interview by author, Woking, England, 4 December 1996.

51. Although the parent organization(s) that hold stakes in a wholly owned or joint venture entrant may have publicly listed shares, returns on these shares reflect the performance of the entire firm. In some cases, the parent organization(s) will eventually spin off the entrant, thus providing a focused indicator of the mar-

ket's assessment of the firm's performance. Recall that National Grid, the privatized British electricity transmission company, sold 25 percent of Energis, its wholly owned telecommunications subsidiary, in a 1997 initial public offering.

52. A. Bianchi, "Tech's Free Agents," *Forbes,* 5 October 1998, 73.

53. Friedland and Holden, "Utility Deregulation in the Argentina Presages Possible U.S. Upheaval."

54. Miguel Ortiz, CEO, Central Costanera SA, interview by author, Buenos Aires, Argentina, 24 April 1997. Most of these contracts were for terms of eight years. Thus incumbents would not be able to expect indefinite protection from rapid increases in industry-wide capacity. At the same time, growth in power demand was so rapid in Argentina following Menem's reforms—over 10 percent per year—that the initial excess capacity was not likely to continue past the contract expiration period.

55. Small, high-tech cell phones are increasingly viewed by some customers as status symbols or fashion accessories. S. Mehta, "When They Build a Better Cell Phone, Less is Usually More," *Wall Street Journal,* 8 August 1998, A1.

56. It appeared that the MSOs, which almost never entered each other's markets, often supported each other's efforts to block entry through limiting access to programming.

57. In effect, the courts determined that internal wiring, whether or not paid for through an explicit installation fee, became property of the homeowner once installed.

58. Leslie Canley, "Rivals Hung Up on Baby Bells' Control over Local Markets," *Wall Street Journal,* 24 October 1995, A1.

59. Enron signed up only 30,000 of California's 10 million electricity customers before abandoning its effort. Rick Burnham, "Enron Dumps Plan to Woo California Residents," *Press-Enterprise,* 23 April 1998, and Kathryn Kranhold, "Enron Scales Back California Power Sales," *Wall Street Journal,* 22 April 1998, A2.

60. The analysis presented in this paragraph may hold even if the entrant is only partially owned by a foreign entity.

61. Philip Amend, general manager, WorldCom Telecommunication Service GmbH, interview with author, Frankfurt, Germany, 11 December 1996.

62. CCL attempted a similar strategy in its effort to secure a contract to provide local and long-distance service to the Justice Department's new courts buildings in Wellington in 1991. However, CCL's inability to secure a local interconnection agreement with TCNZ prevented CCL from fulfilling the contract and led the entrant to file suit against TCNZ for abuse of its dominant position in the market.

63. Mark Simonian, director, Diamond Cable Communications, interview by author, London, 3 December 1996.

64. Following deregulation German customers could choose to formally switch to a new default carrier, although to do so, they were required to pay a one-time fee of DM 26.8 ($14.80). This fee, however, was typically absorbed by the new carrier so as to minimize the customer's switching costs. O.tel.o's initial strategy was to acquire new default customers, as opposed to offering service through access codes. As noted above, however, this strategy was not very successful, apparently due to risk aversion on the part of customers faced with severing their relationship with Deutsche Telekom.

65. Although the use of a preapproved list may create first-mover advantages among entrants, the balloting procedure does not preclude customer switching among firms on the original list or to new entrants in the future.

66. These costs typically entail changes in software code used for call-routing, as opposed to hardware changes.

67. Willis Emmons and Martín Calles, "Clear Communications Ltd. vs. Telecom Corporation of New Zealand (B)," Case 9-798-091 (Boston: Harvard Business School, 1998), 1.

68. In some cases, maximum prices are controlled indirectly—for example through the rate-of-return regulation historically employed in the U.S. utility sector and reasonable-investment-return criteria employed in the U.S. airline industry under the prereform bargain.

69. Three utilities, each with a geographically separate monopoly franchise, had provided most of the state's electricity prior to deregulation. The incumbents included Narragansett Electric Co., Blackstone Valley Electric Co., and Newport Electric Co.

70. See Jeffrey Krasner, "For Real Competition in the Energy Market, the Price Isn't Right," *Wall Street Journal*, 31 December 1997, NE3, and Sonia Ellis, "Services Firms Unbundle," *Chemical Week*, 28 October 1998, 30.

71. These statistics represent the price associated with a typical call from Auckland to Wellington (New Zealand's two largest cities) and New York and Boston, which were located approximately the same distance apart.

72. Under this scenario, the incumbent earns lower margins on the access-dependent product through bundling to end users, yet cripples the competitive position of the entrant by leaving the price of access unchanged. In some cases, of course, the production of multiple goods and services may allow the incumbent to reduce its costs through scale and scope economies. In these instances, bundling may allow the incumbent to improve its competitive position relative to the entrant's without sacrificing profitability.

73. Although Frontier was willing to sell credit information on individual customers to entrants, competitors complained that the incumbent was profiting unfairly from information obtained under a state-enforced monopoly. "Local Dial Tone Competition—Nine Months of Reality in Rochester," Opening Session of 23rd Annual Telecommunications Policy Research Conference, September 30, 1995.

74. Anonymous British cable television executive, interview by author, London, UK, 3 December 1996.

75. Calculated from TCNZ and CCL annual reports.

### Chapter 7

1. The ownership rights associated with these concessions may be quite complicated. For example, the government may retain ownership of land associated with a concession but not the plant and equipment. In some cases, the ownership of all assets associated with a concession converts to government ownership at the end of the concession period.

2. More precisely, private ownership tends to lead to the minimization of cost for any given level of quality.

3. In some cases, these roads are free roads, in other cases, toll roads.

4. In the case of services, the "production facility" may consist of a collection of assets used to provide the service. For example, a private garbage hauler typically owns the trucks required for pickup and disposal.

5. Much of the background for this section is drawn from Willis Emmons and Monica Brand, "Empresas ICA and the Mexican Road Privatization Program," Case 9-793-028 (Boston: Harvard Business School) and Willis Emmons, "The Mexican Toll Roads Program," in Ravi Ramamurti, ed., *Privatizing Monopolies: Lessons from the Telecommunications and Transport Sectors in Latin America* (Baltimore: Johns Hopkins University Press, 1996).

6. All concessionaires were required to hold a minimum equity stake equal to 25 percent of the concession's total investment costs, while the remaining capital typically took the form of loans from financial institutions. The concessionaire's equity stake did not have to be contributed up front, but would accumulate over time in the form of "sweat equity." Specifically, a portion of the billings for highway construction costs invoiced to the concessionaire by its parent construction firm would be deducted and credited instead to the firm's equity stake in the concession.

7. The terms of the concession established the initial maximum toll level by vehicle type. Compensation for the effects of inflation would be provided to the concessionaire in one of two forms—toll increases or extensions in the length of the concession period.

8. The additional compensation could take the form of government subsidies, toll increases, or extensions of the length of concession period. The SCT had the right to determine the form of compensation in any given case of traffic shortfall.

9. Bidders were required to submit a statement of technical qualifications and a detailed financial and operating plan as part of their bid. If the SCT determined, based on this evidence, that the bidder was not qualified to carry out the project, its bid would be rejected, regardless of the length of concession period offered.

10. In the case of some large toll highways, the concessionaire was a joint venture consortium owned by two or more construction companies.

11. Ironically, all major Mexican financial institutions were still government-owned at the start of the toll highway program, a legacy of the nationalization of the banking system during the 1982 external debt and peso crisis. Most of the Mexican banking sector was privatized in the early 1990s.

12. Recall, however, that a portion of the construction billings, typically 25 percent, was converted into the parent company's sweat equity stake in the concessionaire.

13. The equity itself would have no terminal value, since the highway reverted to the state, without compensation, at the end of the concession period.

14. Government restrictions on foreign investment in large infrastructure projects discouraged foreign participation in toll road concessions. However, even in the absence of these restrictions, foreign firms would have been reluctant to take part due to exposure to foreign exchange risk and the broader uncertainties associated with the actual implementation of this new concession program.

15. The Mexican government's high levels of foreign and domestic debt left it in a poor position to raise additional capital for infrastructure development or

even maintenance purposes. In fact, during the 1980s, the de la Madrid administration even diverted internal resources generated by the highway sector—revenues from government-owned toll roads—for use in social programs deemed more critical for the nation.

16. The free roads were generally of much lower size (in terms of number of lanes) and poorer quality.

17. These costs also included costs related to delays caused by the specification changes/inaccuracies. Officially, compensation was due only if the cost overruns exceeded 15 percent of projected costs.

18. These "equity" contributions were effectively subsidies, since they were nondividend earning. The contributors included CAPUFE, the state-owned toll road operator, PEMEX, the national petroleum company, and the state government of Guerrero, though which the highway passed.

19. Shorter concession periods were arguably consistent with the noneconomic goal of restoring direct control over critical infrastructure to the public sector as soon as possible. In fact, at the beginning of the toll roads program, Mexican law allowed for only a twenty-year maximum concession period. By 1992, however, the government extended the maximum length to thirty years as a means of reducing tolls, adopting this legislative change in June.

20. Empresas ICA Sociedad Controladora, SA de CV, Prospectus, 8 April 1992.

21. ICA's shares were traded in the form of ADR's (American Depository Receipts) on the New York Stock Exchange.

22. During the early 1990s, financial instruments with terms as long as five years became available to some concessionaires. In addition, a few concessionaires had succeeded in cashing out of their equity through international bond offerings secured by toll revenues of highways in operation. Nevertheless, most concessionaires remained dependent on financing on much shorter terms than the length of the concession.

23. The present value of these future toll revenues was estimated at roughly 40 billion pesos. Eduardo Garcia, "Mexico Plans Bailout of Toll Road System," *San Diego Union-Tribune,* 23 August 1997, C1.

24. "Crash Leaves the Way Ahead Clear," *Financial Times,* 29 August 1997, 20.

25. This section draws on background information provided by V. K. Rangan, K. G. Palepu, and L. Wells, "Enron Development Corporation: The Dabhol Power Project in Maharashtra India (A), (B), (C)," Cases 9-797-085, -086, -087 (Boston: Harvard Business School, 1997).

26. Enron Corporation's roots were in the U.S. natural gas sector. The company thrived in the aftermath of deregulation and by the early 1990s was organized into five major business units: Enron Operations Corporation (development and operation of gas transportation systems and related facilities in developed markets worldwide), Enron Capital and Trade Resources (natural gas risk management and trading services), Enron Oil & Gas (oil and gas exploration and production), Enron Global Power and Pipelines (builder of natural gas pipelines and power plants in emerging market economies), and Enron Development Corporation (see text for details).

27. According to the Indian constitution, infrastructure development is the responsibility of state governments, not the central government.

28. Plant load factor is a measure of capacity utilization. A plant load factor of 68.5 percent was considered efficient for coal-fired generating plants, the technology most commonly used in Indian power generation. By operating at a higher plant load factor, firms would earn a rate of return higher than 16 percent under the reform bargain. Enron's natural-gas-fired generating plants typically operated at an 85 percent to 90 percent load factor.

29. Both GE and Bechtel would be major suppliers to the project.

30. The "Exim" Bank is a promotional financial institution owned by the U.S. government.

31. OPIC provides political risk insurance in addition to loans.

32. The IDBI is owned by the Indian central government.

33. To transport natural gas by ship, as opposed to pipeline, the gas must first be compressed into liquid form, then regassified upon delivery for most applications.

34. Enron planned to develop these natural gas supplies through another of its affiliate companies.

35. A megawatt (MW) is a unit of power generating capacity. One MW operated for one hour produces one million watt-hours of electricity.

36. The phase 1 generating facility would initially rely on a petroleum-based fuel known as distillate. The plant would be converted to use natural gas when LNG supplies became available in phase 2 of the project.

37. The Shiv Sena (SS) Party was strongly provincialist and nationalist in character and drew much of its support from the poorest members of the electorate. The Bharatiya Janata Party (BJP) was a more moderate, national party and a traditional competitor to the Congress Party. Although generally supportive of private enterprise, the BJP was less favorably inclined toward foreign investment than was the Congress Party.

38. Allegations of corruption and outright bribery of officials in the former government to win support for the project were vigorously denied by Enron.

39. In support of its findings, the committee cited a December 1992 World Bank consulting study for the Indian government—highly criticized by Enron—which concluded that the Dabhol project was an expensive alternative to traditional coal-fired plants and that it would create a situation of serious overcapacity in the market.

40. Marcus Brauchli, "Enron Power Project Is Scrapped by India State," *Wall Street Journal*, 4 August 1995, A3, cited in "Enron Development Corp (B)," 4.

41. Sunil Jain and Hardev Sanotra, "The Power Fallout," *India Today*, 31 August 1995, 41, cited in "Enron Development Corp (B)," 2.

42. K.S. Nayar and Milind Palnitkar, "Enron Decision Shock Waves," *India Abroad*, 11 August 1995, 1, cited in "Enron Development Corp (B)," 2.

43. Inflation-related escalation clauses would be activated at the completion of phase 2. The MSEB continued to bear all foreign exchange risk.

44. Important sources of cost savings included (1) the fall in costs and rise in efficiency of gas turbine generating equipment available on international markets, (2) a switch to the use of domestically available naptha as the fuel for the phase 1 facility as opposed to imported LNG, (3) the removal of the regassification facility from the capital costs of the phase 2 project, and (4) the expansion of the total capacity installed from 2,105 MW to 2,450 MW, thus allowing the realization of greater economies of scale.

45. "India: Enron Violating Human Rights," *FT Asia Intelligence Wire*, 25 January 1999.
46. This situation recalls the notion of the "obsolescing bargain," discussed in chapter 1. The concept's relevance has been reemphasized in the context of deregulation by Louis Wells and Eric Gleason in "Is Foreign Infrastructure Investment Still Risky?" *Harvard Business Review* 73, no. 5 (September–October 1995): 44–55.
47. The DPC's facilities were projected to add capacity of 2,450 MW to the state's preexisting baseload capacity of 9,500 MW. Given the high projected efficiency of DPC's plants, its share of the state's total power generation was likely to exceed its share of capacity.
48. Principal sources for this section include Bonna de la Cruz, "CCA Prisons Under Fire," *The Tennesseean*, 17 October 1998, 1A; John Donahue, *The Privatization Decision* (New York: Basic Books, 1989); J. P. Donlon, "The P&G of Prisons: Interview with Doctor Crants, CEO of Corrections Corp. of America," *Chief Executive*, May 1998, 26; Michael Erskine, "Executive Says Private Prisons Receive Undue Criticism," *The Commercial Appeal* (Memphis), 16 August 1999; Oliver Hart, Andrei Shleifer, and Robert Vishny, "The Proper Scope of Government: Theory and Application to Prisons," *Quarterly Journal of Economics* 112, no. 4 (November 1997): 1127–1161; Cheryl Thompson, "Ohio Sours on Prison Managed by Private Firm," *Washington Post*, 19 October 1998, B1; U.S. GAO, "Private and Public Prisons: Studies Comparing Operational Costs and/or Service Quality," GAO/GGD-96-158.
49. Donlon, "The P&G of Prisons."
50. Some contracts also included a fixed construction fee.
51. Hart, Shleifer, and Vishny, "The Proper Scope of Government," 1149.
52. Donlon, "The P&G of Prisons."
53. Crants was revealed to be the largest contributor to Tennessee legislative candidates in 1996 and 1997. Crants and other CCA board members and affiliates made their largest contributions to the House Speaker, whose wife was employed as a CCA lobbyist. Sheila Wissner, "CCA-Linked Cash Aiding Office Holders," *The Tennesseean*, 1 March 1998, A1.
54. Tennessee Legislature Fiscal Review Committee, *Cost Comparison of Correctional Centers* (Nashville, 1995).
55. Tennessee Legislature Select Oversight Committee on Corrections, *Comparative Evaluation of Privately Managed CCA Prison and State-Managed Prototypical Prison* (Nashville, 1995).
56. In some instances, shortages were exacerbated by the poor condition of older public prisons, many of which were forced to close for renovations or were removed entirely from the system.
57. Thompson, "Ohio Sours on Prison Managed by Private Firm."
58. The escapees were eventually recaptured, with no harm to any local citizens.
59. de la Cruz, "CCA Prisons Under Fire."
60. Eric Bates, "Crime Pays," *Sacramento Bee*, 18 January 1998, F1.
61. Erskine, "Executive Says Private Prisons Receive Undue Criticism" and "Limits Urged on Private Prison," *Chattanooga Times*, 10 July 1999, B8.
62. Principal sources for this section include Carole Asher, Norm Fruchter, and Robert Berne, *Hard Lessons: Public Schools and Privatization* (New York: Twen-

tieth Century Fund, 1996); Greg Dees and Jaan Elias, "Education Alternatives, Inc.," Case 9-395-106 (Boston: Harvard Business School, 1995); Alexander Dyck and Danielle Melito, "Private Management and Public Schools (A)," Case 9-797-113 (Boston: Harvard Business School, 1997); Robert Frahm and Rick Green, "Hard Lessons in Hartford," *Hartford Courant*, 20 May 1996, A1; and Amy Virshup, "Schools and Capitalism 101," *Washington Post*, 7 April 1996, W11.

63. The Tesseract method emphasized the use of computers, the involvement of parents, and the design of an individualized learning program for each student.

64. In 1993 the Computer Curriculum Corporation (CCC) joined the alliance to provide technology-related support for both instructional and administrative needs.

65. For example, custodians, who were also union members, saw their salaries reduced by about 20 percent on average. The activities of some stand-alone, nonteaching employees such as counselors, librarians, and nurses, were consolidated into a fewer number of positions in some schools.

66. This "SuccessMaker" technology was developed with EAI's alliance partner, the Computer Curriculum Corporation.

67. The report was entitled "The Private Management of Public Schools: An Analysis of the EAI Experience in Baltimore."

68. Unlike public school boards, EAI—a private corporation—was not required to open its (financial) books to the public.

69. The school board's funding was appropriated by the city council, as was the case in Baltimore as well.

70. In some cases, the city threatened to impose a restraining order on EAI to foreclose its access to school buildings.

## Chapter 8

1. This chapter draws heavily on Willis Emmons, "Paragould City Cable," Case 9-794-030 (Boston: Harvard Business School, 1996).

2. The system also provided a ninth channel that included text (e.g., time and weather reports) and FM music.

3. Subscribers paid an additional $20 installation fee and $8 monthly fee to receive HBO.

4. Clause 5.1 of the 1983 PCI franchise agreement.

5. In particular, the FCC determined that only in communities receiving fewer than three over-the-air broadcast signals could the local municipality continue to regulate basic cable rates.

6. This prohibition was designed to prevent telephone companies from extending their local monopoly power into the local cable service market.

7. In terms of nonprice-related franchise provisions, the Cable Act allowed for the renegotiation of "commercially impracticable" requirements imposed on the cable operator. PCI maintained that channel capacity constraints and other factors presented obstacles for satisfying all of the programming provisions included in its 1983 franchise agreement.

8. CTIC Associates, *Municipal Ownership of a Cable Television System in Paragould, Arkansas: A Feasibility Study,* 21 February 1986.

9. Larry Watson, manager, Paragould City Light and Water Commission, interview by author, Paragould, AR, 23 August 1993.

10. Kenneth Heard, "Cable TV in Paragould Makes Profit," *The Arkansas Democrat-Gazette*, 1 July 1998, B3.

11. In other words, a tax of up to $0.0065 per $1 of assessed property value could be imposed annually on Paragould property owners if revenues from the cable system proved inadequate to service the bonds.

12. Emmons, "Paragould City Cable," 15.

13. Final appeals of the lawsuits were not resolved in the city's favor until mid-1991.

14. The bonds were of maturities ranging from twenty-two to twenty-five years and carried coupon rates of 6.2 percent to 7.5 percent.

15. For example, Brinkley planned to construct a reinforced concrete building to house the system's head-end reception and transmission facility and intended to specify high-grade sheathed cable for use throughout the system. A backup battery system capable of maintaining 100 percent service for up to two hours was to be included as well as part of the design.

16. The addressability feature would allow subscribers to order pay-per-view events with the use of a remote control device and would enable City Cable to add or disconnect specific channels without having to modify equipment at the subscriber's residence. In addition, by making the system addressable, subscribers with cable-ready televisions would not be required to rent a special converter box (with accompanying remote control device) in order to unscramble satellite channels as was the case with Paragould Cablevision's nonaddressable system.

17. Cable operators often scrambled (distorted) these signals to discourage the theft of the service by nonsubscribers.

18. A surcharge of 3 percent would be added to all City Cable service prices to cover its required franchise fee to the city of Paragould. In contrast, PCI's prices incorporated all franchise fees.

19. For example, basic cable plus HBO, Showtime, The Movie Channel, and the Disney Channel were offered for $36 per month by City Cable and $32.50 by PCI.

20. On March 12, Paragould Cablevision filed suit against City Cable to prevent it from disconnecting PCI's wires in subscriber homes. City Cable argued that PCI's suit was groundless since (1) recent U.S. Supreme Court decisions had established that once installed, wiring became the property of the homeowner, and (2) the subscriber contract signed between City Cable and the household contained a limited-power-of-attorney clause permitting City Cable to disconnect existing wiring as needed to install the new cable television service. The lawsuit was eventually dismissed in September 1991.

21. According to the terms of the bond agreement, revenue adequacy was estimated in July of each year for the following twelve-month period. The suspended tax would be levied in the following calendar year only if a shortfall was projected.

22. The average price for basic cable television service in the United States in 1991 was $18.10 per month. Emmons, "Paragould City Cable," 14.

23. The city of Paragould continued to levy additional property taxes of over $200,000 per year to conform to the terms of its bond covenants. Although

PCI's financial statements were not publicly available, its financial losses may have been even greater than City Cable's due to its lower prices.

24. Prices for former PCI subscribers, however, were raised to City Cable price levels.

25. Stan Gray, "City Cable in Paragould to Hike Its Rates," *The Jonesboro Sun*, 14 December 1999, 1A.

## Chapter 9

1. These changes have also created a host of opportunities for advisers and inter-mediaries, including consultants, investment bankers, accountants, and lawyers.

2. Julia Preston, "Competitors of Telmex Say It Still Acts Like a Monopoly," *New York Times*, 4 April 2000, C4.

3. Steve Lohr, "Microsoft Resisted Government Control of the Features Windows Could Get," *New York Times*, 4 April 2000, C13.

# Selected Bibliography

Alchian, Armen A. *Economic Forces at Work*. Indianapolis: Liberty Press, 1977.

Anderson, Terry L., and Peter J. Hill, eds. *The Privatization Process: A Worldwide Perspective*. Oxford: Rowman and Littlefield, 1996.

Armstrong, Mark, Simon Cowan, and John Vickers. *Regulatory Reform: Economic Analysis and British Experience*. Cambridge: MIT Press, 1994.

Austin, James E. *Managing in Developing Countries: Strategic Analysis and Operation Techniques*. New York: Free Press, 1990.

Averch, Harvey, and Leland Johnson. "Behavior of the Firm Under Regulatory Constraint." *American Economic Review* 52, no. 5 (December 1962): 1052–1069.

Bailey, Elizabeth, and William Baumol. "Deregulation and the Theory of Contestable Markets." *Yale Journal on Regulation* 1, no. 2 (1984): 111–137.

Baron, David. "Integrated Strategy: Market and Nonmarket Components." *California Management Review* 37, no. 2 (Winter 1995): 47–65.

Bartlett, Christopher, and Sumantra Ghoshal. *Managing Across Borders: The Transnational Solution*. 2d ed. Boston: Harvard Business School Press, 1998.

Baumol, William, John C. Panzar, and Robert D. Willig. *Contestable Markets and the Theory of Industry Structure*. New York: Harcourt Brace Jovanovich, 1982.

Becker, Gary. "A Theory of Competition Among Pressure Groups for Political Influence." *Quarterly Journal of Economics* 98, no. 4 (1983): 371–400.

Berle, Adolph, and Gardiner Means. *The Modern Corporation and Private Property*. New York: Macmillan, 1933.

Berne, Robert. *Hard Lessons: Public Schools and Privatization*. New York: Twentieth Century Fund, 1996.

Bishop, Matthew, John Kay, and Colin Mayer. *The Regulatory Challenge*. London: Oxford University Press, 1995.

Boardman, Anthony, and Aidan Vining. "Ownership and Performance in Competitive Environments: A Comparison of the Performance of Private, Mixed, and State-Owned Enterprises." *Journal of Law and Economics* 32, no.1 (April 1989): 1–33.

Bork, Robert H. *The Antitrust Paradox: A Policy At War with Itself*. New York: Basic Books, 1978.

Boycko, Maxim, Andrei Shleifer, and Robert W. Vishny. "A Theory of Privatization." *Economic Journal* 106, no. 435 (March 1996): 309–319.

Breyer, Stephen. *Regulation and Its Reform*. Cambridge, MA: Harvard University Press, 1982.

Bryan, Lowell, and Diana Farrell. *Market Unbound: Unleashing Global Capitalism*. New York: John Wiley, 1996.

Clarke, Thomas, and Christos Pitelis, eds. *The Political Economy of Privatization*. London: Routledge, 1993.

Collis, David J., and Cynthia A. Montgomery. *Corporate Strategy: Resources and the Scope of the Firm*. Chicago: Irwin, 1997.

Cragg, Michael I., and Dyck, I. J. A. "Management Control and Privatization in the United Kingdom." *RAND Journal of Economics* 30, no. 3 (August 1999): 475–497.

Crew, Michael, ed. *Pricing and Regulatory Innovations under Increasing Competition*. Boston: Kluwer, 1996.

Demsetz, Harold. "Why Regulate Utilities?" *Journal of Law and Economics* 11, no. 1 (April 1968): 55–66.

Derthick, Martha, and Paul Quirk. *The Politics of Deregulation*. Washington, D.C.: Brookings Institution, 1985.

Donahue, John. *The Privatization Decision*. New York: Basic Books, 1989.

Downs, Anthony. *An Economic Theory of Democracy*. New York: Harper and Row, 1957.

Doz, Yves L., and Gary Hamel. *Alliance Advantage: The Art of Creating Value through Partnering*. Boston: Harvard Business School Press, 1998.

Duncan, Ian, and Alan Bollard. *Corporatization and Privatization: Lessons from New Zealand*. Auckland: Oxford University Press, 1992.

Dyck, I. J. Alexander. "Privatization in Eastern Germany: Management Selection and Economic Transition." *American Economic Review* 87, no. 4 (September 1997): 565–597.

Encarnation, Dennis, and S. Vachani. "Foreign Ownership: When Hosts Change the Rules," *Harvard Business Review* 63, no. 5 (September–October 1985): 152–160.

Evans, Lewis, Athur Grimes, Bryce Wilkinson, and David Teece, "Economic Reform in New Zealand 1984–95: The Pursuit of Efficiency." *Journal of Economic Literature* 34, no. 4 (December 1996): 1856–1902.

Gabel, David, and David F. Weiman, eds. *Opening Networks to Competition: The Regulation and Pricing of Access*. Boston: Kluwer, 1998.

Galal, A., et al. *The Welfare Consequences of Selling Public Enterprises*. New York: Oxford University Press, 1994.

Ghemawat, Pankaj. *Commitment: The Dynamic of Strategy*. New York: Free Press, 1991.

Gomes-Casseras, Benjamin. *The Alliance Revolution*. Cambridge, MA: Harvard University Press, 1996.

Gómez-Ibáñez, José, and John Meyer. *Going Private: The International Experience with Transport Privatization*. Washington, D.C.: Brookings Institution, 1993.

Goodman, John, and Gary Loveman. "Does Privatization Serve the Public Interest?" *Harvard Business Review* 69, no. 6 (November–December 1991): 26–38.

Greider, William. *One World, Ready or Not: The Manic Logic of Global Capitalism*. New York: Simon and Schuster, 1998.

Grossman, Sanford, and Oliver Hart. "The Costs and Benefits of Ownership: A Theory of Vertical and Lateral Integration." *Journal of Political Economy* 94, no. 4 (August 1986): 691–719.

Guislain, Pierre. *The Privatization Challenge: A Strategic, Legal, and Institutional Analysis of International Experience.* Washington, D.C.: World Bank, 1997.

Hakim, Simon, Paul Seidenstat, and Gary W. Bowman, eds. *Privatizing Transportation Systems.* Westport, CT: Praeger, 1996.

Hart, Oliver, Andrei Shleifer, and Robert Vishny. "The Proper Scope of Government: Theory and an Application to Prisons." *Quarterly Journal of Economics* 112, no. 4 (November 1997): 1127–1161.

Horwitz, Robert Britt. *The Irony of Regulatory Reform: The Deregulation of American Telecommunications.* Oxford: Oxford University Press, 1989.

Jensen, Michael. "The Modern Industrial Revolution, Exit, and the Failure of Internal Control Systems." *Journal of Finance* 48, no. 3 (July 1993): 831–880.

Jomo, K. S. *Privatizing Malaysia: Rents, Rhetoric, and Realities.* Boulder, CO: Westview Press, 1995.

Joskow, Paul. "Asset Specificity and the Structure of Vertical Relationships: Empirical Evidence." *Journal of Law, Economics, and Organization* 4, no. 1 (1988): 95–117.

Joskow, Paul, and Nancy Rose. "The Effects of Economic Regulation." In *The Handbook of Industrial Organization,* ed. Richard Schmalensee and Robert Willig. New York: North Holland, 1992.

Joskow, Paul, and Richard Schmalensee. *Markets for Power: An Analysis of Electricity Industry Deregulation.* Cambridge, MA: MIT Press, 1983.

Kahn, Alfred. *The Economics of Regulation: Principles and Institutions.* Vols.1–2. New York: John Wiley, 1970.

Kanter, Rosabeth Moss. *When Giants Learn to Dance.* New York: Simon and Schuster, 1989.

Kaserman, David, and John Mayo. *Government and Business: The Economics of Antitrust and Regulation.* Fort Worth, TX: Dryden Press, 1995.

Krueger, Anne. "The Political Economy of the Rent-Seeking Society." *American Economic Review* 64, no. 3 (June 1974): 291–303.

Kuttner, Robert. *Everything for Sale: The Virtues and Limits of Markets.* New York: Alfred A. Knopf, 1997.

La Porta, Rafael, Florencio Lopez-de-Salines, and Andrei Shleifer. "Corporate Ownership Around the World." *Journal of Finance* 54, no. 2 (April 1999): 471–517.

La Porta, Rafael, Florencio Lopez-de-Salines, Andrei Shleifer, and Robert Vishny. "The Quality of Government." *Journal of Law, Economics, and Organization* 15, no. 1 (April 1999): 222–279.

Lodge, George C. *Managing Globalization in the Age of Interdependence.* San Diego: Pfeiffer, 1995.

Lopez-de-Silanes, Florencio. "The Determinants of Privatization Prices." *Quarterly Journal of Economics* 112, no. 4 (November 1997): 965–1025.

Lopez-de-Silanes, Florencio, Andrei Shleifer, and Robert Vishny. "Privatization in the United States." *RAND Journal of Economics* 28, no. 3 (Autumn 1997): 447–471.

MacAvoy, Paul W. *The Failure of Antitrust and Regulation to Establish Competition in Long-Distance Telephone Service.* Washington, D.C.: AEI Press, 1996.

Majone, Giandomenico, ed. *Deregulation or Re-regulation? Regulatory Reform in Europe and the United States.* New York: St. Martin's Press, 1990.

Marcus, Alfred et al. *Business Strategy and Public Policy.* New York: Quorum Books, 1987.

Mathews, Jessica. "Power Shift." *Foreign Affairs* 76, no.1 (January–February 1997): 50–66.

Megginson, Nash, and Van Randenborough. "The Financial and Operating Performance of Newly Privatized Firms: An International Empirical Analysis." *Journal of Finance* 49, no. 2 (June 1994): 403–452.

Noll, Roger, and Bruce Owen. *The Political Economy of Deregulation: Interest Groups in the Regulatory Process.* Washington, D.C.: American Enterprise Institute, 1983.

North, Douglass. *Institutions, Institutional Change, and Economic Performance.* New York: Cambridge University Press, 1990.

Olson, Mancur. *The Logic of Collective Action: Public Goods and the Theory of Groups.* Cambridge, MA: Harvard University Press, 1971.

Peltzman, Sam. "Towards a More General Theory of Regulation." *Journal of Law and Economics* 19, no. 2 (1976): 211–240.

Perotti, Enrico. "Credible Privatization." *American Economic Review* 85, no. 2 (September 1995): 847–859.

Porter, Michael E. *Competitive Strategy: Techniques for Analyzing Industries and Competitors.* New York: Free Press, 1980.

———. *Competitive Advantage: Creating and Sustaining Superior Performance.* New York: Free Press, 1985.

———. *The Competitive Advantage of Nations.* New York: Free Press, 1990.

Ramamurti, Ravi, ed. *Privatizing Monopolies: Lessons from the Telecommunications and Transport Sectors in Latin America.* Baltimore: Johns Hopkins University Press, 1996.

Ramamurti, Ravi, and Ray Vernon, eds. *Privatization and Control of State-Owned Enterprises.* Washington, D.C.: World Bank, 1991.

Rodrik, Dani. "Why Do More Open Economies Have Bigger Governments?" *Journal of Political Economy* 106, no. 5 (October 1998): 997–1032.

Ryan, Daniel J., ed. *Privatization and Competition in Telecommunications: International Developments.* Westport, CT: Praeger, 1997.

Sappington, David, and Joseph Stiglitz. "Privatization, Information and Incentives." *Journal of Policy Analysis and Management* 6, no. 4 (1987): 567–582.

Savas, Emanuel. *Privatizing the Public Sector.* Chatham, NJ: Chatham House, 1982.

Schelling, Thomas C. *The Strategy of Conflict.* Oxford: Oxford University Press, 1960.

Shapiro, Carl, and Hal Varian. *Information Rules: A Strategic Guide to the Network Economy.* Boston: Harvard Business School Press, 1999.

Shleifer, Andrei, and Robert Vishny. "Politicians and Firms," *Quarterly Journal of Economics* 109, no. 4 (November 1993): 599–618.

Sidak, J. Gregory, and Daniel F. Spulber. *Deregulatory Takings and the Regulatory Contract.* New York: Cambridge University Press, 1997.

Spiller, Pablo T., and Carlo G. Cardilli. "The Frontier of Telecommunications Deregulation: Small Countries Leading the Pack." *Journal of Economic Perspectives* 11, no. 4 (Fall 1997): 127–138.

Spulber, Nicolas. *Redefining the State: Privatization and Welfare Reform in Industrial and Transitional Economies.* New York: Cambridge University Press, 1997.

Stigler, George. "The Theory of Economic Regulation." *Bell Journal of Economics* 2, no. 1 (Spring 1971): 3–21.

Strange, Susan. *The Retreat of the State: The Diffusion of Power in the World Economy.* New York: Cambridge University Press, 1996.

Train, Kenneth E. *Optimal Regulation: An Economic Theory of Natural Monopoly.* Cambridge, MA: MIT Press, 1991.

United Nations Conference on Trade and Development. *Comparative Experiences with Privatization.* New York: United Nations, 1995.

Vernon, Raymond. *Sovereignty at Bay: The Multinational Spread of U.S. Enterprises.* New York: Basic Books, 1971.

———. *Storm over the Multinationals: The Real Issues.* Cambridge, MA: Harvard University Press, 1977.

———. *In the Hurricane's Eye: The Troubled Prospects of Multinational Enterprises.* Cambridge, MA: Harvard University Press, 1998.

Vickers, John, and George Yarrow. *Privatization: An Economic Analysis.* Cambridge, MA: MIT Press, 1988.

———. "Economic Perspectives on Privatization." *Journal of Economic Perspectives* 5, no. 2 (spring 1991): 111–132.

Vietor, Richard. *Contrived Competition: Regulation and Deregulation in America.* Cambridge, MA: Belknap Press, 1994.

Viscusi, W. Kip, John Vernon, and Joseph Harrington. *Economics of Regulation and Antitrust.* Lexington, MA: D.C. Heath, 1992.

Vogel, Steven K. *Freer Markets, More Rules: Regulatory Reform in Advanced Industrial Countries.* Ithaca, NY: Cornell University Press, 1996.

Wells, Louis, and Eric Gleason. "Is Foreign Infrastructure Investment Still Risky?" *Harvard Business Review* 73, no. 5 (September–October 1995): 44–53.

Williamson, Oliver. *The Economic Institutions of Capitalism: Firms, Markets, Relational Contracting.* New York: Free Press, 1985.

———. "Franchise Bidding for Natural Monopolies—In General and with Respect to CATV," *Bell Journal of Economics* 7, no. 1 (Spring 1976): 73–104.

Winston, Clifford, "U.S. Industry Adjustment to Economic Deregulation," *Journal of Economic Perspectives* 12, no. 3 (Summer 1998): 89–110.

———. "Economic Deregulation: Days of Reckoning for Microeconomists." *Journal of Economic Literature* 31, no. 3 (September 1993): 1263–1289.

Wolf, Charles. *Markets or Governments.* Cambridge, MA: MIT Press, 1988.

World Bank. *Bureaucrats in Business: The Economics and Politics of Government Ownership.* New York: Oxford University Press, 1995.

Yergin, Daniel, and Joseph Stanislaw. *The Commanding Heights: The Battle Between Government and the Marketplace That Is Remaking the Modern World.* New York: Simon and Schuster, 1998.

Yoffie, David. "The Politics of Business: How an Industry Builds Political Advantage." *Harvard Business Review* 66, no. 3 (May–June 1988): 82–89.

Yoshino, Michael, and U. Srinivasa Rangan. *Strategic Alliances: An Entrepreneurial Approach to Globalization.* Boston: Harvard Business School Press, 1995.

Zacher, Mark, and Brent A. Sutton. *Governing Networks: International Regimes for Transportation and Communications.* New York: Cambridge University Press, 1996.

Zajak, Edward E. *The Political Economy of Fairness.* Cambridge, MA: MIT Press, 1995.

# Index

# About the Author

**William (Willis) M. Emmons III** is an Associate Professor at Georgetown University's McDonough School of Business in the areas of strategy, public policy, and ethics. His research focuses on the interaction between government policy, industry dynamics, company strategy, and performance. Previously, Professor Emmons spent ten years on the faculty of Harvard Business School in the areas of business, government, and international economy. He teaches in corporate executive development programs and consults extensively with corporations and governments on domestic and international issues relating to business strategy and government policy. He has conducted field research in Argentina, Germany, Malaysia, Mexico, New Zealand, Norway, Russia, Ukraine, the United Kingdom, and the United States. Professor Emmons has published in the *RAND Journal of Economics, Review of Economics and Statistics,* and *Journal of Economic History* and is the author of over thirty Harvard Business School case studies and conceptual notes. He received a Ph.D. in Business Economics, an M.B.A. with high distinction, and a B.A. in Government, *Phi Beta Kappa,* all from Harvard University.